BUDDHA BRATS

a modern tale of enlightenment

by Adamas

ß

www.buddhabrats.com

Some names and identities have been changed to protect
the privacy of the individuals involved.

ISBN 978-1469940755
ISBN 1469940752

Typeset in Plantin Volume 1 by Pierpont

Edited by Anri Wyma
Introduction, Glossary, Interior Layout & Cover Design by Anri Wyma
Cover image Copyright ©Anri Wyma

Prepared for print by Anne Höfinghoff

www.buddhabrats.com

To the diamond warriors of the new age.

Content

Content

Author's Preface

I wrote this book to share my vision with the world, my vision of the beauty inherent in every moment if one just stops to pay attention to the detail and synchronicity of the reflection. At the same time I was so bored with things I was seriously considering driving my shiny new motorbike over a cliff and into the ocean. Two seemingly incompatible views and yet there I was thinking that if I was going to end it all I should at least tell my story as an epitaph, and tell it in its entirety. There is nothing like the looming spectre of death to put things into perspective. When you have nothing to lose and are contemplating the end, things get very clear. The writing of the book re-inspired me with some of the original vision which is why you are even reading this now.

I always heed the words "do not sell your therapy as art" and this applies doubly when writing autobiographically about your memories fused into a storyline. This is always the case when writing – who is ones target audience and adhering to a view without indulging that too much yet making it as interesting as possible to hook as many along the way as one can.

A good friend mentioned that this was in fact two books, yet the challenge for me has been in uniting the story and the mind technology into a fluid whole. The story without the tech would have been fun but just someone else's story and the tech without the story would have just been a manual which one definitely wants to avoid. I have endeavored to fuse the two aspects into a tapestry of what is to come, a vision of a life lived and a view held that may appeal to some and seem inconceivable to others. The story carries the message and the message supports the story, left and right hand acting together as one. If this had been two books they both would have been lacking and so combining them into one has been a labour of timing and love.

When you cut yourself you bleed and yet the mind bleeding out onto paper is a more controlled and deliberate act with all sorts of strange consequences that I am still savoring and appreciating. To not have included the teachings in the book would be like destroying a newborn world – a crime against existence itself and it is in this mood that I offer it to you, still pink and steaming, freshly ripped from my mind.

The vision has moved on, as all visions do however the core remains eternal – the rock from which new waterfalls spring and it is in the skillful dealing with the mutability of things that true art is born. This is my offering to the world squeezed from my blood and ground from my bones as a final testament to a better world with all the tech to bring it about. Of course all of this is meaningless unless it is applied but that is the job and the challenge to you the reader, to pick up the gauntlet or to walk on by. No one forces anyone else to do anything, we choose and then we act and this book is all about action springing from the mood and leading off to a promised land of ones own creation.

For the enjoyment and benefit for everyone who has the good fortune to pick it up, a rare and beautiful gem torn from the centre of the earth for mankind's pleasure.

Many thanks to all the characters in the book, some of whose names have been changed. And extra special thanks to Anri, whose priceless contributions run like a lattice of life-giving arteries through every page of this book. She has my heartfelt and everlasting gratitude.

Live long and prosper.

Adamas
January, 2012

Editor's Preface

"Fearlessly we enter the void"
– Adamas

Three years ago when Adamas handed me the first draft of his book I would never have dreamed that events would turn out as they did.

Fresh out of film school and with some pretty good contacts I was set to start the journey of becoming a cinematographer. At that time film making was experiencing a lull though and with every new opportunity to 'get in there' my plans would suddenly come crashing down as big budget films were cancelled one after the other. In the meantime between looking for new offers I would steal a few moments to read the manuscript of what would become such an all-consuming project that would not only leave me utterly unemployable as a rat race zombie, it would also test my commitment, resolve and faith to the deepest core.

I was always avidly interested in literature, something I had forgotten while travelling the globe and later studying film, so editing came naturally to me. Of course what the book needed wasn't just an editor; it was a surgeon with the determination of a desert camel and the grace of an angel but I did not realize it yet.

What started out as a few pencil scribblings correcting some sentence structure here and there soon turned into a full-scale reworking of what at the time was a 250+ page A4 document. Undaunted by the prospect of such a hefty piece of writing, it literally thudded onto a table when you put it down, I acquired something ridiculous like a fifty odd set of coloured pens and proceeded to meticulously organize the content of this very niche subject.

Perhaps, when I think of it in retrospect, the manuscript somehow voodoo-ed me into a state of enchantment – a case of it chose me and not the other way around. I was jinxed. I can only describe the feverish need with 'getting it right' as a state akin to that of a trance medium channeling some extra-terrestrial or archaic ancestral being of sorts as time faded away completely and I fell totally under the spell of the book. Either that or it was a case of inexplicable and inescapable obsessive compulsive neuroticism, whichever explanation you like.

I can't even remember how many times I read and re-read it – definitely over fifty for sure, and that's only speaking of in its entirety. Strangely enough I never got sick of it. Driven by this burning need to ensure that it represented the teachings as closely as to how I experienced them, it took on the role of something between a frightening sage, a stubborn child and a very good friend. It wasn't long before the outside world faded into nothing more than background noise while I became so ensconced in its bubble landscape that we became utterly inseparable, me and my infernal little friend.

Believing that it held what can easily be described as the most effective techniques for liberating the mind ever, bar none (and if you don't believe me research the sheer historical evidence of fully realized beings which has been meticulously recorded and compare it to any other system) I knew that come what may I had committed myself to one of the greatest causes any human being could be fortunate enough to be a part of. If I could manage to do it some small measure of justice, even if only one person in the world read it, that I had done my bit to create an opportunity for the eventual and total enlightenment of the human race. Anything and everything else paled in comparison as I made it not only the single most important priority in my life, I also saw it as my own personal process of liberation, playing out right here in real-time. Mostly during this process there was just enough resources to get by and keep going and little else and yet few people have the opportunity to spend their time solely focused on their passion projects. When creating the world of our dreams it is important to recognize the blessings on the way, the Wish Fulfilling Gem shines brightest when polished with gratitude.

It was certainly not a process free from pain and sorrow, doubt and despair. At times the banshees of doubt screeched in my ears. Was I being too pedantic? Was I slacking? Why do I have to spend hours finding the ever elusive *Ekajati* Mantra to put on the cover of the book? What is the point of adding another chapter that talks about visions and why does everything have to be so meticulously demonstrated and explained? Besides for the editing I mostly went in blind, with nothing but my stubborn commitment to quality, my endless curiosity, raw gut instincts and devotion to the Teachings to guide me. When it got hairy, which it often did, my devotion to the Teachings was the only thing left.

Film studies prepared me a little for designing but I had not the vaguest idea about how to structure a website or a book, let alone the subtle but powerful effect of for example fonts both on the cover and inside. Endless details, tiny things, woven like tantras that would either draw someone in, or push them away. It was imperative that the style of design was as neutral as possible, lest the message comes out wrong. Let the message speak for itself, and any dodgy interpretations be the result of the junk in people's own heads. Make it a mirror, crystal clear and unstained. This was the goal that I would get back to over and over again. I also got an excellent education to boot, which stands for a lot in my books.

Gritting my teeth I succeeded for the most part in convincing everyone, including myself that I like fussing over the details. Turned out not to be true. However there was simply no one else to do it, and so, for the sake of the Teachings and because I will do what needs to be done, I continued. I was taught that a good film maker serves the story above all else. I'd like to think that is exactly what I did because if ever there was a message worth serving – this was it. When you dance in the fire the ashes are soft under your feet, and anything done in the name of self-liberation reveals beauty eventually. The sound of ones victory is not announced with the pompous blaring of trumpets but a fierce and soul-shattering howl. Look, can you see the pattern, if you stand just so you will see that I danced us a mandala, with each step forging our phoenix world. See those dark drops scattered everywhere, that's how you know it's not just wishful thinking – I have paid for it in blood.

That said, enlightenment techniques at its best are a hard sell as it is, especially when focused on people doing it for themselves where there is no one to obey or blame. Of course it doesn't help that the book is based on such obscure and secret teachings traditionally considered so advanced that they are said to be energetically sealed from being understood by those not ready to receive them. Not only that but Adamas' take on it is completely fresh and totally radical, so he does not even have the orthodoxy to officially back him up with public endorsements to ensure a definite market segment to be tapped into. In fact, for the most part the sheer novelty of the content is like sending a brick-sized container into space hoping, but certainly not counting on, someone, somewhere, one day able to open it and marvel at the impact of its meaning. Nevertheless and despite the myriad obstacles encountered, reality conspired to weave together a set of specific events to ensure its eventual exposure.

As to its reception, well that is anyone's guess. I expect that some people will take exception to the visionary content. Others, especially the more scientific types will dismiss Homoeopathy as a farce – no surprise there. A few others, those who want complicated rituals and rules of behavior will balk at the simplicity of it. And those who have been following more traditional paths will get all tied up in knots about the fact that he dares to make these teachings personal by taking it and running with it. And the rest, well most people would have to admit that even taken at the most mundane level it makes for a fun read.

I know that there are Diamond Warriors who have been waiting for just these teachings. The loners, the rebels, those fearless beings who refuse to bow down to any system, least of all systematic ignorance imposed by themselves onto themselves. The aim here, therefore, is not to encourage slavish devotion to a system – quite the opposite in fact. To really benefit from the techniques spoken of in the book is to use them as methods for liberation, nothing more, nothing less. Each teaching precept is backed up with personal story line which is intended to serve as inspiration for people to put the teachings to use according to their personal predilection and to express their realization in ways that are uniquely and totally aligned with their own natures. This serves to make Buddha Brats inclusive, rather than exclusive provided that each individual is prepared to surrender the Self unequivocally. Total freedom demands total commitment to ones own awareness where no concept, person, object and experience is too precious to be sacrificed on the altar of Liberation.

As the final tweaks to the book finally come to an end, this voodoo child fed and burped, I let it out into the world to grow wings (and claws and fangs) as it heralds the dawn of the New Age. For my part I have done as much as I could to ensure that it is safely cocooned in my love as it flies in the face of convention. This book is more of a magical artifact than a simple manuscript and more than one person have commented on its energetic affects. Truth be told, it is specifically designed to take apart and dissolve mental constructs and I believe it is only a matter of time before it takes full effect.

Regarding the Apocalypse and when and how it will take place, I have enough experience with visions to know that it will happen in a way that is not only inconceivable but also perfect. Until then, I will continue to dance through the web of reality, unearthing gems, expressing my love of these incredible teachings and building a network of likeminded people who are ready to make the shift. As more and more veils are being lifted to reveal the immensity of our existence I stand confident and committed to the ideal that nothing is impossible. It is for this reason that I believe this document chose me as its midwife – a message from the universe reminding me of the truth that I have felt since childhood and at the same time testing my resolve as Rider of the Apocalypse. As the wave comes ever closer the challenge and the pleasure, even in the midst of blinding despair as the shackles of ignorance are torn from our beings, is to ride the storm to the not-so-distant shores of our dreams.

It is with sincere love and excited expectation that I fervently hope to see you, dear reader, on the other side.

For the privilege of receiving these Teachings, I dedicate every fiber of my being to the liberation of mankind from the prisons of their minds. May all beings find happiness and freedom from suffering in this very lifetime!

Anri Wyma
Januaray, 2012

Ps. My sincere gratitude to Nicky Newman who is a torrent of artistic inspiration, a subtle and honest mentor in the ways of engaging this sometimes alien world, and a very dear friend without whose encouragement I might very well have given up. Very special thanks to Anne Hoefinghoff who finalized the document with me and prepared it for print and whose support, attention to detail, professionalism and patience meant the world to me, especially during those final and most difficult days. To both these women, I wish that you may be blessed with long lives in which all of your brightest personal dreams come true.

Notes on Formatting

There are a few small details to note for ease of reading.

Regarding words in *italics*:
In a few instances these are words from other languages, most notably the Latin names of medicines and other French or Spanish phrases as for example *Corvus Corax* (indicating a remedy made from raven's blood) or *"raison d'etre"*. Italic is also used in the case of particular Dzogchen tenets, like *play of the mind* or *abiding in ones nature.*

Regarding Capitalized words:
It either indicates the English name for a homeopathic remedy, for example a remedy made from rattlesnake venom will appear as Rattlesnake; Chinese astrological names such as Dragon, Monkey etc. to indicate the year in which someone was born and especially words that are elevated above their ordinary use such as Emptiness, Awareness, Dance of Reality and so forth.

Regarding words that appear in a different font:
We have endeavored to present the concepts in this book in such a way as to make it accessible to readers with no background of Buddhism. However, there is a rich and profound tradition represented here so for those readers who are interested in further elucidation on concepts the **Glossary** at the back should be consulted. More than just a standard definition of the terms, many of the explanations include the very specific Buddha Brats take on it.

Most of the concepts are revealed over the course of this book so we would recommend that you read the Glossary right at the end, skimming through it for juicy bits of information (that's what we do).

Some of the most notable terms in the Glossary include:
Body Of Light, Buddha,
Chakravatin, Cosmic Soup,
Dakini, Demons, Dzogchen,
Effortlessness, Ego, Emptiness, Enlightenment,
Five Lights,
Natural State, Non-Dual View,
Samsara, Self-Secret, Siddhi, Spontaneous Accomplishment,
Thigle, Thogal,
Vajra Chains, Vajra Pride,
Wheel Of Conditioned Existence,
Yidam.

We hope you enjoy.
The BUDDHA BRATS.

Introduction

This is a modern tale of enlightenment, the story of one man's journey to Liberation and the techniques with which he attained it while having a fabulous time.

Adamas insists that enlightenment is an immediate possibility, not just a pie in the sky with the chanting of monks as background music. On the contrary, it can be a highly enjoyable experience with the bustling of a modern city as backdrop.

Buddha Brats represents the culmination of a wide range of mythologies, skillfully brought to a startling climax. The essence of this book is about Eastern ideas with a distinctly Western taste and is without doubt the only document of its kind.

Without being draped in laborious language and complicated initiation rites, it engages complex ideologies in a way that the ordinary man can understand. Through the fascinating and provocative fusion of Homoeopathy, Buddhism, sex, drugs and rock 'n roll it makes for a wildly entertaining read – in true Buddha Brat style it is spiritual but with attitude.

Adamas is a doomsday prophet with a wicked smile on his lips, the rebel at the school of enlightenment, shunning conventional methodologies and structures. He dares us to grab enlightenment by the horns and milk it for everything it is worth. One moment you're appalled and pissed off and the next you are compelled to mimic his rebellious attitude and do it yourself. He teases and aggravates you to the point where you decide that you're going to try for the biggest goal in existence – Liberation.

At the same time the threads are woven from compassion and the sincere desire to provide people with a real chance at freedom from Samsara. The characters whose stories add color to the narrative have suffered greatly themselves, and the overcoming of their adversities becomes a beacon of hope for anyone reading it.

This book is a labour of love, offering a way out for all humanity if they choose to take it. It is brutally honest about the sacrifices entailed but there is always a luminous thread running through, prodding us playfully and unashamedly toward the fulfillment of our wildest dreams.

"After all" to quote Adamas, *"if someone else can do it, so can you"*.

An Apocalypse doesn't just organise itself.

ONE

The **Grand Plan**

I have seen myself riding The Storm.

When people are turning french wine into ethanol it is surely the final trumpet call to re-boot the show and start again with a new virus-free paradigm.

Recruiting the services of Thor, my self-destructive Dragon, we borrowed a friend's car and snuck into the city's main water supply. I poured the entire contents of my Weapon of Mass Liberation into the water to be pumped through the city.

I had anticipated generalized mass hysteria and total meltdown in the streets. Soon people would start going into religious ecstasies, desperately battling the demons in their heads or simply exploding into light as they spontaneously combusted from the pressure of instant Enlightenment. Anything was possible, brain fragments exploding from people's skulls, waves of rainbow lights in the sky or people incapacitated by involuntary convulsions. It would quite simply be, in a nutshell – pandemonium. Fortunately it wouldn't last very long, despite its intensity, and would shortly give way to transcendence and mass liberation, sweeping across the planet once critical mass had been reached.

The effect on me was instantaneous, every cell in my body started vibrating and raising its frequency, it was glorious. Returning home I wrote out my will, leaving my various bits and pieces to the relevant parties and then settled down on my couch, ready to come apart at the seams in comfort. I put on my favourite music, disconnected my phones and waited as the process began to accelerate...

To understand me, one has to understand that the Apocalypse has one way or another, in vision and mood coloured most of my life, mostly for the better but then sometimes for the worse. Throughout my life I have created and taken part in a range of scenarios to accelerate the process in order to bring it about. I consider this a kind of duty as a Rider of the Apocalypse.

My good friend Luc even made me a t-shirt with *"Adam Warlock - Apocalypse Herald"* on it which I initially wore with some trepidation, but shortly came to realize that the scope of what I was planning was so outlandish that it was safe from interference due to its raw inconceivability, 'hidden in plain sight' as it were. My main task was finding the other Riders or letting them find me and then put into action a series of events that would bring about the end of the world as we know it to make way for a new and more beautiful paradigm.

Apocalypse comes from the Greek meaning *"lifting of the veils"* or *"revelation"*. It usually indicates a body of knowledge normally unknown or hidden to the general masses because of its ability to grant deep insight into the true nature of the universe. It is often used in the context of mystical revelation on any level in an individual's life, but is more often used in prophetic terms as a future event that will reverse the state of ignorance and suffering of humanity, resulting in Enlightenment.

My standard toast used to be a hearty *"to the Apocalypse"* with a wildly inspired and slightly deranged smile. Toasting to it always filled me with an exultation of what is to come and that has been enough to sustain me through my own valley of shadows with all its attendant critters, as I dipped into the pits of doubt and despair. Later on I understood that it was just a transition phase so I added, *"and beyond"* which had the effect of mollifying some of the more lukewarm folk I interacted with. It is good for morale – always throw them a few carrots when waving the stick of doom in their face.

I had wanted out since I was a child due to my distaste for the degenerate state of the world and nothing ever really made sense to me except total freedom. I was and always have been driven to find a way out. I remember swearing to myself as an eight year old that I would escape this thing even if it killed me. Not to be at the mercy of my moods, which changed every day, seemed to be a righteous pursuit for my existence, and the only thing that ever really made any sense.

The whole white picket fence thing had left me rather cold and one of the most horrible things my mother inadvertently said to me as a child was that I was just an ordinary middle class boy. How could she not have seen the magnitude of what I represented? It was an attempt on her part to put an end to my grandiose scheming yet it ended up pushing me further along the path and I love her for it. I just had to show her instead and I have since aspired for the greatest achievement available to man – Enlightenment.

I was not deterred from this goal as I grew up, those that had the same drive became my kin, and the rest of humanity seemed like a different species. Any mundane suffering I went through at the hands of the world actually spurred me on and now seems like a memory that never happened. The personal satisfaction, bliss, and peace I gathered from my journey paid me back a hundred times. The truth be told, nothing else has ever really held any attraction for me which is why I had such a hard time choosing a career. Liberation from Suffering is truly the highest goal one could wish for because then wherever you are and whatever you are doing will be pure pleasure. I succeeded and now plan to take everyone with me if they wish to come.

The Apocalypse, Dzogchen and Homoeopathy are the triad of principles upon which my world view is based. By using Dzogchen (the highest Buddhist view) in conjunction with Homoeopathy (the art and science of treating like with like) I have largely managed to free myself from residual patterning that binds me into conditioned behavior.

Having observed my own ongoing process of treatment and the results I had personally achieved with the remedies, I decided to use my skills to find a way to dose the entire city I lived in, in one grand strike. The key to this whole plan was to release everyone at the same time, as they were making their morning cups of tea and bathing in the water. I believed that if I put the appropriate remedies in the main water supply for the city it would release a massive amount of bound up energy that people were using to play out their dysfunctional patterns. Imagine if every person in the city all of a sudden stopped playing out their petty control dramas, had all their resentments, angers, fears, guilt, and self-doubts removed in one fell swoop. Things would definitely change for the better.

What I anticipated was that if the energetic release was sufficient, the whole city would be going through their entire lifetimes of memories in a matter of minutes or at most conservative a matter of hours – an acceleration of the death process while people were still alive. This would, I theorized, result in a wave of energy which would snowball and send the whole city into Enlightenment en masse. There would be enough human energy released to fire off the rest of the planet in a kind of knock-on effect and the whole planet would go Body of Light. In the end people would be infinitely happier and thank me for it.

Having observed the city where I lived for a while I decided upon the Homoeopathic remedies that would best suit the majority of people who lived there. I put about 15 different remedies into the bottle which is something one normally never does. Homoeopathic remedies are diluted well beyond the point where any physical traces of the original substance is left while retaining their pure frequencies, so anything can be safely used. I included remedies made from Ganges water, anti-matter, hydrogen, nitrogen, and Stonehenge, plus the specifics for the people of the city based on environmental exposure. This included granite, which makes up a large part of Table Mountain, salt, silica and a fluoride or two. I also included Monatomic Gold, Platinum, Rainbow (which is made from passing light through a prism and into water), some potentized Buddhist *Dhutsi* (blessed substance) and the Chalice Well. The

6

Chalice Well is a remedy made from the water of the well where Joseph of Arimathea is said to have hidden the Chalice of The Last Supper. Miracles and cures have been reported from drinking the water of this well. The only problem was the dilution factor, which I compensated for by super potentizing my little energetic offering to the world.

I even took the combination remedy for a ride on my friend's 15ft gyroscope, which was designed according to the Golden Mean. The gyroscope was spray-painted gold with seven interlocking metallic rings. It weighed more than a ton and was welded from steel, titanium and tungsten and once strapped in allowed movement through any conceivable position possible for the human body. This reportedly had the added benefit of unlocking inherent genetic memory stored in the body through accessing unusual combinations of rotation and extension. I reasoned that this would add an extra degree of juice and perfection to my already potent Weapon of Mass Liberation.

The various flashes and dreams I have had of riding the energetic wave as it sweeps across the world are things I have actually seen in waking life, real time visions which are hard to argue with. Above and beyond it all I believed and still believe in it, as the connection to it sings in my blood. It is a part of my hard-wiring, the only thing that really makes sense to me and denying it would be like denying myself. When you go to war with yourself you always lose.

Those that were too attached to their memories when the wave hit would be reduced to a happy energetic soup. I had even told some of the stragglers not to resist if they felt me pulling at them as everything amped up and went haywire. To process ones entire life's memory in a matter of hours is a challenge that most people won't even dare to fantasize about, let alone consciously attempt, yet this is what would occur.

On the other hand, those who had a more diffuse view of their own personalities would surf the final wave and ride the whirlwind to form the seeds that made up the blueprint for a new reality. Of course my crew would be prepared to ride out the energetic effects of the communal raising of frequency, keeping those special nuances that made them Riders of the Apocalypse.

I had gathered a range of people who carried certain cultural lineages. Sumerian, Egyptian, Greek, Norse, Celtic, Hindu etc. Nothing would be lost in the process and all the beauty, creativity, art, technology and innovation from all spheres would be taken with. All the useless nastiness of reality that permeates our world would be deleted. The New World would be based on those who were suitably advanced in their paradigms and understanding. Having sufficiently broken their attachment to 'self' they would come through the meltdown unscathed. In other words, they would get to bring their personalities with them.

Once I returned home after dosing the water I started getting further and further away from reality and dissolving more and more, my visual field turned into an array of spinning coloured spirals that were slowly enlarging and intensifying. The Tibetan word for these is *thigle* which is considered to be the core fabric from which reality is woven, the ground substance as it were.

At this point my friend Athena refused to leave me alone and kept calling me back into reality by engaging me. Every time I had to listen or speak to her I was forced to establish a personality in order to communicate. She would not relent, perhaps resenting the fact that I might leave before her. We had always been quite competitive especially when it came to awareness, and the thought of me leaving first probably prompted her to throw a spanner in the works - she refused to let me dissolve in peace.

Little did I know that poor Thor, who was on a photographic shoot at the time had started dissolving as well, and was also forcibly being drawn back into reality by the demands of the world. The way he described it to me later on was that he started seeing through things including other people and even his own hands, literally watching himself becoming ethereal.

Needless to say, the rest of the city was unaffected otherwise you would not be reading this book. Why it happened to us, and why the rest of the city was unaffected could have been because sunlight destroys the efficacy of the remedies and it was in an open water source. What was equally likely was that the dilution of the little bottle into say 100 million litres was not nearly strong enough. The other possibility was that the chemicals they were introducing to the water functioned as an antidote to the remedies. Either way, I was given a taste of the experience of the Body of Light and that alone made it worthwhile.

One can only push up the apocalyptic timeline to a certain point and if it were solely up to me, it would have happened yesterday. Despite this I trust that the Wave of Dissolution will happen exactly when it is meant to, and I have no doubts about the fact that it is coming soon. Had the whole planet become enlightened from the remedies, it would have been too easy, as Liberation is something people should and can only do for themselves.

I came to realise that since the Dissolution of the World is just around the corner, the only compassionate thing to do would be to spread the Teachings on the Nature of the Mind as far and wide as possible. I have no illusions about how many people will take it and run with it, enlightenment is after all *"not for everybody"*, but everyone deserves to at least be given a chance at it.

Such is the nature of the game. We are thrown in the ring with bulls and only the blessed, the brave or the crazy make it out in one piece. Not my rules, but at least everyone has a chance and if they choose not to take it then what can one do?

They will not suffer when the energetic wave hits.

TWO

The **Path** & **Goal**

It doesn't matter how you get there,
as long as you get there
and stay there.

The word Buddha literally means 'awake', awake to ones Natural State. When the Buddha woke up to his natural condition, the first person he met was a holy man to whom he proclaimed that he was Buddha (awake). The holy man, mistaking it for his name, called him Buddha and the rest is history.

Traditionally the Buddha is pictured standing next to the Wheel of Conditioned Existence and pointing away from it, showing sentient beings what they need to do – free themselves from the cycle of entrapment by their desires and aversions. The Dalai Lama said that *"Buddhism is not a religion it is a science of the mind"* as according to the Buddhist view, it is our own minds that cause suffering. The amusing thing is that the mind is technically already *"awake"*, it is just our wrong perceptions that delude us into thinking differently, which brings a whole process of unnecessary suffering into play.

Another translation for sentient beings is *bewildered beings* which I often find more appropriate, as people are not aware of their own potential and are hopelessly entrained by their passions, constantly playing out the same repetitive patterns of behaviour. This causes endless suffering and I maintain that the only real evil that exists is Ignorance of the Nature of the Mind, which is definitely curable.

All human suffering has been to get people to a point where we are willing to risk crossing the river to the Island of Jewels. When the torment of life on this side outweighs the fear of the currents and the crocodiles, people begin to dive into the water and it is happening, albeit slowly. Everything is accelerating and it is precisely this chaos which provides the energetic springboard for us to launch deep into the river and give us a head start. The crocodiles are savage but we have a fighting chance, which is better than no chance at all.

Every cyclone, every earthquake, every plague, every war, and every terrifying news headline brings us closer to being willing to dive in. When one has nothing to lose one is more likely to risk the flood than if one is busy driving sports cars around and sipping champagne on the balcony of ones beach house. Although it is quite possible to reach Enlightenment on the French Riviera, it is often the combination of unpleasant events that fuel the flames and push us deeper into the process.

Everyone suffers until they find a way out, the rich just suffer in more comfort. There is no escaping the dark nights of the soul, and we all have to cling to whatever we have to get through them. The best defence against despair is Knowledge of the Nature of ones Mind and its intricate workings. This is the only real comfort that will keep you warm at night when things start to get really heavy as the world around us begins to fall apart.

Suffering gives us the spur to get out of it in the first place. If we are too comfortable we will not have a reason to change anything for the better. Without suffering this book would not have been written, or would have been on the dental features of the albino rat.

To free yourself from the chains of your mind is going to hurt in ways you can't even begin to think of and yet pain is just a fleeting sensation whereas suffering is eternal. So the means definitely justify the end. There is only the question of how much pain you can handle at once and that is largely personal. If it goes too far you might just start looking expectantly down the barrel of your .357 seeking obliteration.

Suicide is no way out either as it just ensures that you re-enter the Wheel of Conditioned Existence in some form or another, fated to deal with the same unresolved issues you tried to escape from before. You have to respect someone that can take their own life though, in the same manner as someone who shoots nail polish remover into their veins, more than a bit tweaked but still worthy of respect – at least they do not lack guts or commitment. If people only used this same motivation for their own Liberation, they would surely be there already.

Suicide has not been a stranger in my life, and it assails me when I am weakest, or lacking a juicy mission to get my claws into. This said, one dusts oneself off and forges on and sooner or later everything that you need is already waiting for you. The more one pushes the boundaries of what is possible the more reality comes up to meet you. Every moment of my suffering has been perfect. It pushed me to the point where I refuse to suffer, disallowing such eventualities from ever occurring again. This is not denial, it is the resolve not to go back down the same road that has hurt so much before.

I categorically and absolutely refuse to suffer any more. I have been there and will never go there again. I do empathize with the suffering of others but realize that the only thing I can really do to help them is to spread the Teachings on the Nature of the Mind. This is the only true solace at the end of the day. No matter how much food-aid we throw at the Third World, if we do not give them the gift of *"Liberation from Suffering"* it is at best just tokenism.

What I was effectively doing by dosing the water supply was a 20th century accelerated combat version of the Buddha's journey to enlightenment – same objective but harder, faster, and as epic as possible. It was not as if I was the principal orchestrator of reality, but for some reason it had fallen to me to gather the troops, help the stragglers, and get everyone fighting fit for when the wave eventually did hit. This said and done, I love my job and my hardwiring.

My motto has always been *"do it right this time"*, remake a world you actually want to live in and would be happy to bring children into. The Apocalypse for me represents a place beyond the horror where things work properly and people are able to express what they want, when they want, and how they want. From my view it will fulfill all our dreams and a whole lot more we can barely begin to conceive of at this point

Being enlightened is no guarantee of painlessness though, but each time one sheds another layer one comes that much closer to complete Liberation. This for me has always been the end point, the highest goal there is, and the price quite simply is everything you have. All your ideals, often your sanity, and the willingness to surrender your life if that is what it takes, which often it is.

What people don't realise about this process is that all your Holy Cows will show up to be slaughtered along the way which is never a pleasant experience.

Attachment is a curly friend, it wheedles its way in and gets its hooks into your flesh and to disentangle it often requires a fair amount of pain, the deeper the hooks the greater the pain. The breaking of attachments, especially the nice ones, hurt like birth. Things will often be taken away from you when you are too attached to them.

When my attachment to friendship, love, trust and integrity, but more importantly the 'preciousness of the awareness space' where all broken simultaneously by my girlfriend Cat, it almost tore me apart.

Since the forces arrayed against us breaking out of the cage of our own minds are so powerful to begin with, we need to use anything and everything on this path. The Buddhist word Sadhana translates as *"means to enlightenment"* and describes the range of strategic tools with which one removes binding obscurations. One uses ones personal toolkit of techniques to shift the mind from its bewildered state back to its natural state, where it actually wants to be.

Dzogchen says that you can use anything and everything to

propel you forward and if you are truly committed you can use the increased energy of the world gone mad to fuel your process. Better hold on tight though because it's going to be a bumpy ride. The challenge should spur us on even further, because if we succumb to doubt or despair we end up as a chip fryer or with a bullet in the brain, and if I had to choose, I would probably go for the bullet.

I would argue that our sadhana is surely up to our own likes and tendencies and varies from person to person, from yoga, to sitting meditation and visionary work, exercise or listening to music. Using whatever, which in my case included Dzogchen and a range of wild and ancient Tibetan practices, Homoeopathy, amphetamines, mescaline, heartbreak and betrayal, to name but a few. Whatever we can get our hands on, but to make them truly our own by using them in the service of our own Enlightenment.

The heartbreak and betrayal I would not willingly have chosen since it was me that was heartbroken and betrayed. In retrospect though, I see the divine wisdom and perfection in both of these as they destroyed huge fields of holy cows that I was holding up as part of my cherished illusion.

I have always been driven to cross to the Island of Jewels in spite of the cost to myself. Would I have jumped in if I had known what was to come? Hard to say, probably yes. To arrive at the Island of Jewels has been something I have wanted since I was a child. Would I have spared myself some of the suffering? Probably not, it was all perfect. When the heart is wide open one can sense the suffering in those around you and the path of compassion is clear, naturally guiding you to ease the pain in others.

You only get bravery after the battle, at the time you are terrified. Anyone who would refute this simple fact has either never risked life or limb, or is basically inhuman, and has never known the joys of love and the pain of loss. Like it or go back to your job as a podiatrist, grinding people's corns off.

I was born in the Chinese year of the Earth Monkey, the same configuration as both Siddhartha Gautama (the commonly known historical Buddha) and Padmasambhava (the Buddha famous for bringing Tantra to Tibet), an amusing fact I have dined out on a number of times. It is always good to have an impressive original blueprint. To summarize the nature of the Monkey, *"I entertain"* and *"I plan"* and the other quotable sound bite of its poem is *"I am put together for my own entertainment"*. Sometimes this entertainment verges perilously close to 'dementertainment' (demented entertainment) but then on the path to enlightenment everything is justified especially if you are a Crazy Wisdom practitioner.

Crazy Wisdom is one of the exotic Tibetan methodologies I have in my arsenal of sadhanas. Put simply, it is the practice where you have no idea about what is going to come next but you run through unknown doors with total abandon – completely trusting that even if your next step is onto thin air it will change into a solid substance as your foot lands. This rather gung-ho philosophy is a rapid and bona fide Tibetan methodology of proceeding along the Path to Enlightenment. It is fraught with peril and definitely not for everyone but if one engages it one can move through mountains of karma remarkably quickly.

Crazy Wisdom practitioners have always inhabited the fringes of society, outside the framework of what is perceived to be 'normal' or 'acceptable'. Despite the disapproval of the Monastic Institutions, they were especially loved and revered by ordinary Tibetans for their wild and unpredictable ways.

To engage reality with Crazy Wisdom however, does not mean one does whatever one wants at the cost of others. It simply means that on the road to Liberation, one might do things that those who do not understand the Path will find confusing, questionable even, and at worst unacceptable or offensive. To abide completely in ones nature, once one has accepted it, is the path. Few seem willing to engage it fully since there is after all always the glare of public scrutiny frowning down upon one, quietly requesting that you behave normally by denying your very nature.

Their way leads to a slow death in the suburbs after an unhappy life frustrated by the thoughts of everything you should have, would have or could have done differently.

Had I not done the things I have done, from smuggling drugs, raising my Kundalini on LSD, experimenting in séances, drinking snake venom, staring at the sun for hours at midday or any of my other seemingly crazy activities, I would not have Liberated myself. It doesn't matter how you get there as long as you get there and stay there.

To turn adversity into triumph is truly the art. If one pulls this off, nothing can ever really bother you as you seamlessly turn the tragic into magic. It is really just a question of people getting their priorities right, seeing what is truly important to them, and throwing the rest away.

Take the jewels that are scattered in front of you and boot the used-dictionary salesman in the face when he comes knocking on the door selling last year's edition.

THREE

Keeping It Fluid

*If you want to play in the fast lane,
better pay attention to your
driving at all times.*

Never evaluate a work in progress – it is wise to let the dust settle to see what you are truly dealing with before you make rash decisions.

In the Carlos Castaneda books, his teacher Don Juan often emphasises the necessity of having fluid assemblage points. He used to traumatize poor Carlos by perpetually keeping him off-balance and in a state of near terror, so that his conscious awareness could reassemble at new places instead of becoming stuck at a fixed point.

An assemblage point is essentially the point where consciousness assembles at any particular moment. It is the view point from which we can engage reality, but when one stays in a particular one for too long, one runs the risk of becoming stuck. Don Juan made a point of constantly shifting Carlos' assemblage points so that each time it would reform at a more useful and fluid place. Once things start moving one can truly begin to work with the fabric of the mind and the illusions that bind.

When you realize that there is no fixed point at which consciousness assembles, because reality is created anew at every moment, then one is free to shift it at will to pretty much any place you want. The mind will perpetually seek to return things to a state of normality in order to maintain continuity and sanity, but the more you shift the more used to shifting you become, and as a result – the more free.

I have always been open to any means of shifting my assemblage point – hallucinogenic drugs, psychosis and putting myself in all manner of extreme circumstances, to name but a few. Standing in a freezing Himalayan lake for half an hour I collapsed when I came out but the resulting shift to my consciousness was well worth the experiment. If you are suddenly taken out of your comfort zone, especially by extremes of reality, you are bound to reassemble at a new place which is for the most part a very energizing experience.

I experienced just this on one of my early trips to India with Lana, my girlfriend at the time. We had been waiting for a Himalayan pass to clear of enough snow so we could travel from Kashmir up into Ladakh. After a while I grew tired of waiting and we decided to make the trip on foot with a group of six other travellers. We were assured that if we got to the top there would be an army base where we would be provided with food and shelter.

Armed only with a bottle of Kashmiri saffron honey we began the long hike. The road was surrounded on all sides by twenty feet of snow and it felt a bit like something from THE SHINING. We were walking in about a foot of melted snow which at times became a small river flowing down the road. At some stage we even came across the corpses of two men and a horse, not a good sign whichever way you choose to read it.

Spurred on by the fate of those who had stopped or been caught in a landslide we marched on, getting more and more exhausted and depleted as we neared the top of the pass. Thoroughly exhausted, we arrived at about 5 o'clock in the afternoon and spotted the promised army base. It wasn't much to look at, but still the only possible sanctuary and food for the night.

On entering a little hut where a small barrel fire was blazing, we politely asked for accommodation and food. A rather rude sergeant informed us that it was absolutely impossible to stay the night because their general was coming to inspect the camp. They refused us food as well.

Fear, indignation, and adrenalin all hit me at once. We were exhausted and verging on the edge of getting frostbite from walking ankle-deep in icy water. To exacerbate matters the next town was 30km away and the sun was starting to set. We had no sleeping bags or even a tent between us.

"You might as well take your rifle and shoot me now" I said to the sergeant, hoping to shock him into the reality of our imminent deaths, but he was deaf to our pleas, and even more surprisingly to the offer of money. Seeing no hope, I changed my socks and began the march.

Darkness was approaching rapidly and the already icy temperature dropped another few degrees. We were marching as quickly as we could manage, nothing like impending death to get the adrenalin running, as we knew that to stop would be fatal. Anyone familiar with the workings of adrenalin knows that it is a short term solution which wears off after a while. We had at least ten hours of walking ahead of us and it provided at best just a momentary burst of fear-induced power.

With the moon's reflection gleaming off the snow banks, it would have been a beautiful night for a walk except that I had serious doubts about making it at all. With the others straggling behind it soon became every man for himself, and so we grimly marched on. Luckily we had completed the 4500 ft ascent and there were no more serious up-hills, but with the bottle of honey long gone we were getting weaker by the moment.

After another hour of desperation running head to head with desolation, I heard a buzz. By this stage I took it to be a hallucination from my exhaustion and resultant sensory agitation, but it persisted, a low rumbling getting increasingly louder. Then I saw a light in the distance from behind us, reflecting off the snow. Still somewhat convinced that it was the play of my mind, fuelled by the fear of approaching annihilation, and desperately reaching out at mirages, I watched the light approach – suddenly there it was, plain as day, a truck.

Shock, euphoria and disbelief, I could not have been happier if baby Jesus and all the angels had appeared playing SWEET DREAMS by Annie Lenox. Remembering our poor reception at the army camp I decided to take no chances. Figuring that money normally gets you through most problems in India, I extracted a thick wad of Rupees from my bag and stepped into the middle of the road waving furiously. They were going to have to run me over or take the money and give us a lift. At that point I was actually beyond caring which of these happened. It slowed down and stopped to avoid running me over and I asked them if they could give us a lift to the next town. With the curious 'yes-no' headshake typical of the Indians which means yes, they put us in the back and took us to the next town.

Drass, known as the coldest place on earth and one of the most miserable as well, was paradise to me. With a bucket of hot water for my feet and a roof over my head I gobbled up the heavenly blessing of some instant noodles. It turned out that the truck we had caught was the first to pass through the snow laden pass in months, bringing through supplies from India.

The looming immanence of death goes a long way to change your assemblage points, but the downside is that it can be tiresome to maintain and often life threatening. If the truck had not arrived most of us would probably have died. One does not have to do this kind of thing daily but it certainly puts things into a new perspective.

I was always consuming any deranging situation or substance, anything I could get hold of just to keep my assemblage point from sticking in one place, which is the surest way to grow old and die. Smuggling drugs did the same thing for me – there is nothing like reading in big bold letters that drugs are punishable by a lifetime sentence, while walking on a kilo of compressed hashish in your boots through a Taipei airport.

Enlightenment is sometimes described as the moment after a small fright, because then one is truly present and aware, and not off in your head thinking about the cheeseburger you are going to have for lunch, or the underwear model you would like to sleep with. These thoughts take us out of reality and put us in some pleasant fantasy which we only wake up from with a jolt as we drive into the car in front of us. This brings us back with a small or large fright to what is actually going on around us, hence the Buddha Brat ethos of using *"everything and anything"* to bring you back to the present.

Scary, frightening, horrifying and exciting situations all keep you very present and upon reflection everything I have done has been Crazy Wisdom Means to ensure that I do not get drawn out of the moment by some attractive fantasy, losing sight of the real goal. When you are walking through an airport with a kilo of hashish in your boots you are definitely present and aware, never more so. Attempts to escape into fantasy are overridden by immanent fear of incarceration and you have no choice but to remain present and hyper aware, trying to dodge the ongoing succession of frights while keeping a straight face.

Coming back from India once, I smuggled opium through in my boots but neglected to wrap it properly before I left. I found myself on the plane back to South Africa with 400 grams of melting opium sliding between my toes while the gay man next to me tried to pick me up. I kept it friendly thinking that if things went bad, I could always rope him into it and diminish my sentence, especially if I got to the airport and collapsed from an opiate overdose. Luckily all was fine though. I met my father at the airport, shook his hand and went home to scrape the sticky mess off my feet.

There is no way to compare the feeling of having done it, although it started wearing on the nerves after a while which is why I stopped. In spite of the easy money, I had a few close calls at customs which put the fear of the lord into me. It always comes to the point when it is time to get out and if you ignore the warning signs you are bound to end up in a very unpleasant situation that you can only blame yourself for.

I have always been good at reading the writing on the wall and getting out while the going is good. Once I convinced some English travellers to hollow out my basketball shoes with the excuse that I had bought them a size too small by mistake. I couldn't help smiling as I watched them carving out space in my boots with Stanley knives, completely oblivious of my intent to use the extra space for carrying hashish.

I used to score hash in Guangzhou, China and I remember sitting on a barber stool on one of the streets where I stuck out like a sore thumb with my hair nearly down to my waist. All the Chinese passing by would loudly comment in Cantonese while I pretended to be wildly interested in the display of agricultural implements in the store opposite me. The Muslims who brought the hash even offered me a greasy comb to comb my hair while they dawdled around in some distant hole getting together my stash. They ended up short changing me, only giving me 400 grams instead of the kilo I came for, but by then I was beyond caring and just grabbed it and left. It was part of the writing on the wall, a warning to get out of the game – when the milk goes sour it's time to find another cow to milk.

While I was smuggling I used to sell to a Canadian electric flute player, an Australian smuggler and Shadow, a Chinese gangster who owned a late-night place called Owls. Shadow became a good friend, but then you never know how far you can trust gangsters. Yes there is honour amongst thieves but then often only as long as you are useful to them.

Once I sold some hash to a new contact for a higher price but he was stalling on the payment, so I asked Shadow for some help. With a nod he summoned three of his henchman and we headed off to collect the money. With these three at my back the guy who owed me money produced it immediately, almost falling over himself making apologies. It was fun to play the gangster for a while. It got to the point where Shadow wanted me to take over his speed business with the foreigners and do a run to pick up some smack in Thailand for him. Both of these offers were a bit beyond my level of comfort, so politely declining, I decided to leave the country.

At around this time my Australian connection told me that I was encroaching on some 'mystery' person's toes, someone who was apparently becoming increasingly unhappy. Having a pissed-off, unknown gangster on my tail was all I needed. I was completely exposed, ultra high profile, leather pants, silk shirts, Italian boots, long, thick hair down almost to my waist, 6 foot 2 in Taiwan of all places, I could not be missed, no blending into the crowd for me.

My gangster connections liked me because I sold them cheap hash. At the same time they were looking at my general utility and I got offers for being a male escort for women, working in a porno movie, and all kinds of strange stuff. I was definitely getting too well-known for my own good so I left, and when I returned much later it was to legitimately teach English, something I had studiously avoided for years.

One useful thing was that the experience allowed me to play out my gangster fantasies and escape in one piece. Shadow eventually got taken down for heroin and did 10 years in jail, the rest of them disappeared. I will always see Shadow putting on his cap backwards, taking his baseball bat and going out to do business. He was known for his violence but I only saw the best of him - always stay on the good side of gangsters.

Taiwan was great. While driving around with my Chinese girlfriend and another friend on the back of my bike, we were pulled over by four short but menacing cops with M16s. They asked for my passport in broken English and I launched into a tirade of irate French, ending in *"I speaking little English"* and they just let us go. I was drunk, carrying drugs, and all this on a stolen motorbike with too many people on it. I had gotten away with it through sheer bravado. They did not want to lose face by admitting they could not speak French, having just mastered English. You have to love the Chinese, as long as you know how to play them of course.

When I eventually left Taiwan, Shadow drove me to the airport at high speed, weaving in and out of traffic in his black Alfa. I had been awake for about six days and was well and truly paranoid. Although I was getting out with a bunch of cash I still had some acid that I had swapped for hash, just a few trips but still, my anxiety and derangement level was about 15 on a scale of one to ten.

When you have been awake for so long reality starts skipping a bit with ten seconds turning into one without missing a beat. You come to with a jolt, finding yourself in a place you don't remember getting to, realizing that you have gone to different places while your mind forced down time on you by catching a quick catnap. Praying we did not get pulled over for speeding or reckless driving, I finally said goodbye to Shadow and waited for the plane.

Using airplane napkins and menus I decided to write my way through the trip to Hong Kong, all divine inspiration and crazed mind space just to keep a grip on reality. I spent my last days in Taiwan in a frenzy of dealing, selling to anyone who would buy my remaining hash. As National Day and its resultant crack downs approached I had to outrun cops on my stolen motorbike, ditch it, steal another and basically offload my hash as fast as possible. I was way beyond security breaches, relying on random movements to protect me whilst feeling the cloak of the law beginning to descend.

The curious thing during all of this was that I never felt that I was doing something wrong. Yes it was dangerous, but wrong? Never...

When I got to Hong Kong I went straight to a hostel to get some sleep, realizing that my mind was becoming dangerously unhinged. I got a bed in some big hostel and next to the door in full view of everyone tried to go to sleep but despite ditching the acid on a neighbouring bed I kept imagining that everyone was talking about me. I believed that they knew my recent history and were just waiting to plant some drugs on me to get at my money or some such paranoid fantasy. People kept coming round the door, looking at me and talking to each other about my exploits. I might have made the mistake of telling one of them what I had just done but even that I was not sure of. Not being able to see very clearly from days of not sleeping and with heightening paranoia I decided to leave.

Gathering my things I went in search of a better hotel but for some reason everything was full, or they just didn't like the look of me. I must have looked like hell, all wild-assed with long hair, tasselled leather jacket, pixie boots, and a 'cornered tiger' look in my crazed red eyes. I couldn't have looked like a safe tenant to entrust their room to. I also could not make eye contact properly to bluff them because I couldn't see their eyes properly. I went from hotel to hotel but there was nothing available, and I became even more disconsolate and paranoid. This was obviously some grand plan by the Hong Kong police to fuck with my head and I even considered sleeping in a park.

I eventually decided to clean up so I went to MacDonald's, changed my shirt, packed my leather jacket away, splashed my face, tied my hair back, and decided to find a five star hotel. Surely money could buy you immunity in Hong Kong of all places, so I walked straight into the fanciest hotel I could find and asked for a room.

"What will it be Sir, single or double?"
"Single".
"That will be $500."
"Not a problem."

Peace, quiet and anonymity, all with a fully stocked mini bar and a lockable door, what more could I want. I passed out and the next day booked a first class plane ticket to Nepal, just get me out of China and into a nice Buddhist country where I can chill and unwind – which is exactly what I did.

William Burroughs said that we do not seek safety, we seek adventure, a credo I have always adhered to. Adventure feeds the mind, safety stagnates the soul.

Sometimes you need to run your own movie so fast and crazily that all restrictions and limitations simply dissolve around you. Of course it is dangerous if you drive off the road, but it is often the only way to propel yourself away from your binding illusions.

FOUR

The **Dance** Of **Emptiness** & **Form**

Anything, everything, whatever, whenever –
as you like, bring it on.

When you go rooting around in the abyss, the abyss always takes a chunk out of you in return.

Lana, one of my early girlfriends who I ended up spending five years with, had the fortune or misfortune of meeting me in my post-Taiwan, first enlightenment phase. She was so entranced by my Crazy Wisdom attitude that she loyally followed wherever I led. We were having a séance, as one does from time to time, and some 'spirit' came through seeking liberation. I, in a fit of largesse, promised to assist it in exchange for a treasure map, which it described in a fair amount of detail.

I was broke at the time and this seemed like an easy way out of my problems. The gangster in me was always looking for a way to make a quick buck without too much effort. What transpired astounded even me, although I was winging it completely and should not have been too surprised by the flies in that particular ointment.

What happened was that the spirit basically entered Lana's body and started to possess her. There was even an extra heartbeat that started in her abdomen, and began to move up towards her heart. This creature had obviously taken the liberation offer as a reincarnation offer in the most available form – Lana.

Realizing this, and the fact that I was somewhat responsible since it was my deal into which she had been dragged by association, I proceeded to try and draw out the ectoplasmic mass oozing from her solar plexus. It came out in pieces, strands of sticky gunge, but not all of it, and it would reform around my hands. It was hard to shake off this sticky mess which had a life of its own. In a flash of inspiration I raided my parent's bathroom cupboard for any aerosols I could find. Armed with a dozen cans of insect spray, deodorants and anything with a flammable propellant I could find, I returned to the bedroom.

She was in a rather desperate state, as was I, but then there is nothing like desperation to get you really inventive. I would draw out the slimy ectoplasm from her body and then proceed to flash fry it with bursts of aerosol which I lit with my Zippo as it came out. I exhausted about eight cans of aerosol trying to incinerate the stuff, with only some measure of success, as it seemed to be endlessly regenerating.

Lana at this time returned to her original Christian default and began praying to God and Jesus for help, which of course did no good beyond vaguely appalling me. Luckily my parents were away, because the house now stank of a bizarre mix of roasted bug repellent and deodorant, and breathing was becoming problematic.

She called on everything she knew, including one of my friend Luc's self-created pantheon, an archetype associated with healing and protection which interestingly enough seemed to do some good. It was at best just a holding action though, as the throbbing mass made its way to her heart, and for some reason we were both convinced that if it got to her heart she would be possessed. Eventually we curled up in the next room to get away from the scene and stench of the crime, and utterly exhausted we curled up in each other and went to sleep.

On waking it had all gone, so I quickly disposed of the empty cans and we never really spoke about it again. She even had the gall to accuse Luc of doing this. I am not quite sure why she chose to pinpoint him as the cause and not me, and felt that he was being a bit unfairly treated since it was one of his archetypes which did her more good than either God or Jesus. Not that Luc was exempt from fiddling with people's minds but in this case he was innocent.

We all get caught in the crossfire but this time I escaped largely blameless despite the fact that we both knew it was my misguided attempts at a free lunch that had pre-empted the whole thing. I never collected the treasure, but it did put an end to my séances, leaving a rather bad taste in my mouth. I still cringe a bit whenever I smell certain bug sprays.

Two days later an equally strange event occurred. Still a bit strung out from events and wired on my last Taiwanese crystal, I was lying in bed next to Lana trying to sleep. Suddenly a great weight descended on me and I remember thinking that, if only I could move my little toe, I could break the force of whatever it was. To my amazement my penis started to rise and I got a full-on involuntary erection which proceeded to orgasm in the course of about 5 minutes. The whole time I struggled even to breathe, but once I ejaculated I could move again.

Maybe the succubus had taken my sperm in repayment for the broken promise two nights before, who knew. The mind tends to fill in the gaps of reality so everything makes sense, allowing one to continue operating – it seemed a cheap enough price to pay to assuage my guilt for what had happened.

Events like this, where I perceived something to be a separate entity from me trying to posses someone, would never happen to me now. I now see everything as *the play of my own mind* and essentially empty, but at the time, before discovering Dzogchen, the whole thing seemed very real indeed. Maybe it was also just a warning to me not to fiddle with forces I don't have a thorough understanding of. Of course these forces all need to be integrated into your mind, but if you start playing into and with Duality it will definitely play with you.

It is good to throw ones sorcerer skills a bone to chew on every now and then though, just to keep them sharp. Molesting myself in order to get off the hook for a careless infraction of my impeccability might seem a bit strange, but then whatever works. I of course never had another séance with Lana, it was not something I would even dare suggest.

My first experiences with séances at university happened long before this event and had always been positive. Jessie and Jeanne, two other girlfriends of mine, were a bit hardier as mediums and less indoctrinated with the whole Christian demonology ethos.

We chatted happily to spirits of the deceased giving them advice in exchange for information on our state of development, banishing anything that was too heavy and moving on. We were all very light and pure of heart in those days and bursting with a desire to know, which definitely protected us from some of the more malevolent forces. We chatted to an Air Elemental once who told us about the time when the dinosaurs became extinct due to a large cloud of dust thrown up from a meteor. This had a powerful effect on me as I realized that the elemental forces were immortal. Why they were then not ruling the show had bugged me ever since, and later led to my Titan Liberation Mission – the beauty of 20/20 retrospective vision.

I often felt more at home chatting with spirits than I sometimes did with people. There was no need to conceal anything or pull ones punches, you could play it all wide open, man to spirit as it were. The combination of my Datura experiences with these séances briefly converted me from an atheist to a spiritualist, but all this got dropped fast when I ran into the Natural State and then found the Dzogchen Teachings, which quite literally just takes all the pain away. It is less a religion than a Science of the Mind so I have no particular fear or love of heaven or hell, and in order to understand my somewhat cavalier attitude to the whole thing, you have to understand a bit about the Buddhist world view.

The Buddhists consider all things to be the play of the Six Realms – hell, hungry ghost, animal, human, jealous god, and god in ascending order. According to conventional Buddhism, one will be drawn to the realm which is associated with the governing emotion at the time of death. Anger leads to the Hell Realm, Greed to the realm of Hungry Ghost, Ignorance leads to the Animal Realm, Desire to the Human Realm, the realm of the Jealous Gods is characterised by jealousy, and the God Realm by pride. The catch is that the God Realm goes back to Hell at the end of their 10 000 years, and the finest God Realm palace will eventually be swapped for a pit of burning lava, so no matter how good the trappings might be one is on the way down sooner or later. This is the traditional interpretation of the Wheel of Conditioned Existence.

From a Dzogchen perspective these Realms are not actual places but states of mind, which generate situations that reflect and perpetuate those very same states as circumstances in our lives. As humans we contain aspects of all of these realms within us, and the only way to free ourselves from their clutches is to make peace with them, firstly by acknowledging them, and then by integrating these as Aspects into ourselves.

When a Hungry Ghost comes to a river it sees blood and puss, when Gods come they see ambrosia, when the Jealous Gods come they see weapons, and yet it is all the same river. It is all mind generated and everyone has been in some, or all of these states, at various points in their lives. These realms represent internal states and it is about integrating and being ok with all these Aspects of your 'self', without being bound by them. This way you become free to dance in the world without getting caught in the swamp of desires and aversions, two of the things that bind us into form, and make us suffer.

Many of the Tibetan and Tantric Deities are depicted with five or six skulls around their necks, showing their mastery of the Realms and their associated passions. The passions overcome are worn as adornment, proving that one can henceforth play in, and with the Realms, without getting trapped in them.

Hollywood is definitely the God Realm with the beatific figures of Angelina Jolie and Brad Pitt beaming down upon us from on high. This contrasts with your average ghetto which is an interesting fusion of Hell, Hungry Ghost and Animal Realms as people try claw whatever they can from the weaker and more vulnerable. The Jealous Gods would be the 2nd rate actors or the middle managers trying to dethrone the CEO's and take their position.

Hungry Ghosts constantly chase after things, seemingly never satisfied. Once they give up their incessant grasping, they revert to their true nature of satisfaction and abundance, which is happily shared with the rest of reality. The Hell Realm symbolized by intense anger, once satisfied, turns into diamond-like clarity, with the ability to see clearly into the heart of a situation. The Animal Realm of ignorance turns into the pure instinct of knowing, or feeling, exactly what is right to do in any situation, without having to intellectualise it. The Jealous Gods, free of the need to claw their way into heaven, become content in their role as guardians and protectors of reality. The Gods' cold pride turns into benevolent blessings as they shower goodwill down upon reality, no longer feeling the need to be worshipped – something that always struck me as a rather parasitic paradigm anyway.

Once we have embraced all these Aspects we can wear the passions as adornment, and play in any Realm we like, without fear of being trapped. The passions, once conquered, turn into our fine colours, our individual rainbow display of reality. This is a lifelong task and at different times we are definitely more in one Realm than another. This said, they all need to be visited, befriended, and then allowed to play out in their purest form, for the benefit of all sentient beings.

All the archetypal forms of reality are there for us to play with, building the field and adding depth and colour to our movie, further fuelling our process. Knowledge and understanding of ones true nature banishes fear, and then where one goes is inconceivable.

The skill is to realize that all of these are Aspects of your Nature, all need to be expressed in their own unique way, and if we deny any of these Aspects we start to suffer. Conversely if we get stuck in any one of these roles, we also start to suffer - all Aspects of our Nature need to play out and they do not take well to being ignored.

Dzogchen starts from the basic premise of Non-Duality where *everything is self* and yet *self is empty*, so one avoids the complicated ego traps one might fall into if everything was just Self. Starting from this view one then proceeds to abolish all other dualities, i.e. time, space, god, and society, quite literally anything that implies an external permanent reality. The Non-Dual state means no 'self' and no 'other' – just the dance of reality or awareness, whichever syntax appeals to you more. It is all simply the spontaneous arising of images, sounds, and sensations that make up reality.

If one can maintain this view, one eventually dissolves, breaking down everything that separates you from reality, and one becomes the very fabric of reality. If one successfully completes this stage, one turns into rainbow light. Pretty damn sexy, and it beats the crap out of praying to a god, or worshipping some poor bastard who got nailed to a cross and in whom one is pinning ones hopes for salvation.

There is no need to deify anything or anyone, no particular conduct to keep. All that is really required is that you dance with reality, shifting in and out of faces and form, always returning to Emptiness, which is your essential nature. Once one is no longer bound by form or concept, it is basically the multi-pass to the universe and beyond. If you can dissolve yourself, you can reform in any shape, place, or time, and theoretically be and do anything – like I said, terminally sexy syntax.

The scary thing is that most people seem to like being bound into one or two fixed forms - the bank teller only has three expressions, *"yes"*, *"no"*, and *"I have to ask my supervisor"*. You would think that people would get bored of being so limited when there are so many options, but it gives them a sense of continuity which keeps them safe at night, although it eventually turns them to stone.

To be yourself or your 'selves' completely is the ideal that we all strive for, and I instinctively felt that one should surely have access to any and every form available. To dance between faces at will, according to the situation, and never drop the ball – seems a worthy goal, and I have yet to find something loftier to strive for in this world. Shifting seamlessly from persona to persona without the tedium of ever getting caught in one, surely must hold great appeal to anyone.

Athena manages to do this as an entertainer, going into different aspects as the mood takes her. Unfortunately she also gets stuck in some fairly heavy ones from which she has a hard time shifting. We all have our crosses to bear, and certain powers entail certain restrictions and possible dangers, and this particular ability is often a hard one for people to engage. That is why Clarity is one of the main tenets of Dzogchen, to be in any form but aware of the true, empty nature of the manifestation at the same time, thereby never bound to or by it.

This is the 'extra cherries and nuts' version of reality and the easiest way to access this is to embrace the feeling of emptiness. If one tries to break down fixed forms by deliberately shifting out of each state, every time, it is automatically more difficult than if you just crack the mould at the source. This is done by not letting ones concrete identity assemble for too long, but rather allowing it to be free-floating and without any definite fixed position.

To do this successfully requires a strong grip on reality from the start. One need only look at mental hospitals full of people capable of shifting who then get caught in one particular Realm. Unfortunately for them it is often an unpleasant one from which they spend large amounts of time trying to escape.

If you are everything and nothing at the same time, there is no face or persona you cannot go into in a moment, and then exit in the next. Not as easy as it sounds but it is doable, it just takes perpetual reminding that whatever form you are in is just a dance of pretty coloured lights, and whatever you see is just the *play of your own mind*.

I used to sit in the bath with Cat, one of my girlfriends, and show her my thousand faces, all me, and there were plenty more which I did not show her. At the time it was suitably entrancing. Some of these faces are definitely not for public consumption, but what one shows to ones lover in the bath and what face you put on when you visit your grandmother, is often very different. The point here is that it is everyone's birthright just waiting to be claimed. If I can do it then anyone can, you just have to want it enough.

The whole concept of multiple personalities is little understood and often feared. As long as they do not fight with each other, the more personalities you have the better. Why be only yourself when you can be everyone else and a whole lot more? The more faces you have, the less chance there is that one will usurp the throne, claim dominance, and banish the rest. When this happens you get stuck with a dictator who refuses to relinquish power, and it eventually solidifies and starts to age you.

We have the capacity in us to be a god, a demon, an animal, a human, or a Buddha – literally anything. The easiest way to embrace this is to make peace with all of these Aspects and realize that we are all of them, yet none of them.

The face is a muscle and the more you exercise it the stronger and more versatile it becomes. At this point the whole façade of ones discreet identity falls away completely. The people that have a problem with this are those that have not made peace with the various facets of their True Nature, and seen the whole thing as empty.

What face we put on for the day is actually arbitrary, and has no more meaning than flipping through the channels on a TV. They are *all self* yet *none of them are self*, and if we lock ourselves in one or two personalities we are severely limiting our true inheritance, which is All Form. The implications of this are huge. Anything, everything, whatever, whenever, as you like, bring it on.

To prevent abuse of this we have to bear in mind that the way we come to the party is the way we will be received. If you come with a sour face, everyone will look at you with dislike. Come with a smile, and everyone will be smiling back at you. Not brain surgery, yet it applies across the board to everything.

Since everything is Self, the way we treat reality is the way it will treat us. We determine the way the movie plays out. You are essentially playfully interacting with yourself all the time and it is useful to play nicely, unless you are looking for pain, because if you brutalize reality you are only brutalizing yourself.

FIVE

Method In The **Madness**

Anything you can walk away from, or
get a good story out of, is worth something
in the long succession of moments
that make up your life.

To pluck the lotus from the lake without falling in, is the ideal we all aspire to. To dance in the mud and remain untarnished. We do not stand upon ceremony, we dance upon it, and if we engage the movie in this mood we definitely have more fun and take less damage.

Carlos, my good Argentinean friend, ditched his shark diving business to go to Peru and do a documentary on Ayahuasca armed only with a Sony handy cam and a solid dose of charisma. He had done his own 'heart of darkness' trip into the jungles and came back with some staggering footage on what the locals call the *"Vine of the Soul"*.

His plan was to do a series on medicinal and hallucinogenic plants with himself as both subject and cameraman. What Steve Erwin the crocodile hunter had done for reptiles, Carlos would do for the plants, and the crocodiles he was hunting were the various Demons and Hungry Ghosts in his own head. He planned to do a series on Iboga in Gabon, San Pedro and Ayahuasca in Peru, Salvia Divinorum in Mexico, and Amanita Muscaria in Mongolia, basically whatever he could get his hands on.

Using the medicinal plants for awareness, while getting high off them, the Hungry Ghost in Carlos was being fed until it popped and became satiated. Not a bad way to spend ones time. Getting paid for cruising the world, looking for exotic botanicals to tweak ones skull with, seemed like a suitably appropriate Buddha Brat pastime to me. He was always dragging me off to sweat lodges and San Pedro ceremonies and he always held it together, something that cannot be said for everyone who dances the fine line between sanity and madness.

Carlos was always consuming something, another burger, more San Pedro, more cigarettes, whiskey, and women, whatever the Hungry Ghost took a fancy to. It took a lot of feeding but he was good value, being generous and with a big heart, which counts for a lot. Carlos was an Earth Rooster, in Chinese Astrology, and the Realm assigned to earth was that of the Hungry Ghosts, the same Realm as me. I knew it well, although I have largely conquered mine, having become satisfied with what reality has brought me.

"Have no desire for desire, desire not", the Teachings say. Sounds simple, and yet not something you can fake or fabricate either.

Every drug he took and woman he slept with seemed to diminish his Hungry Ghostliness, so I guess his sadhana were drugs and women. If Thor's little maze was to help Thor 'find the beers' then Carlos' was to help him find the *"womens"*. From a Dzogchen perspective, if desire arises in that moment you engage it, but until then you do not spend your time hankering after it. This was something that Carlos was definitely learning, but some old habits die harder than others.

One of the things that characterise Buddha Brats is their insistence on making up their own versions of reality, and playing it to the max, let the chips fall where they may. This is not to say that they just make up escapist fantasies and then proceeded to live some lukewarm reality where everything is beautiful and safe. On the contrary, they take great pride in the finer trappings of their realities, inventing crazy but intelligent paradigms, backed up by various theories to re-format whole new levels of understanding.

Athena is one such Brat who lives a world entirely of her own creation, and in addition to which she has the same commitment to liberating sentient beings that I do. I have a love-hate relationship with her, or more accurately, she has a love-hate relationship with me. I mostly have a huge amount of respect for her, tinged with a bit of trepidation, because she is rather prone to extremes of behaviour which I am often at the receiving end of.

The first time I met her we were both about twenty-two. While I was dancing on some stage at a club she walked up to me, dressed in a snakeskin catsuit, and asked for my number so she could give me obscene phone calls – very cool. Of course we ended up together that night.

Athena was the original mad hatter, with five planets in Virgo which is aligned to Mercury, the Anarchist's Remedy in Homoeopathy. She actually made hats, and mercury was originally used by hat makers to stiffen the brims of hats, and so the saying *"as mad as a hatter"* was born. She made fabulous costumes of all her personal archetypes and then embodied them. She went into these forms in order to gather their wisdom energy and add another face to her repertoire. Everything from black sunbirds, various embodiments of Pan, fairies, aliens and lions, you name it – she played relentlessly with reality.

She loved speed and the Apocalypse, and was the original 'why-not girl', which also drew us together. There is nothing like crystal meth to bring you to a fever pitch of apocalyptic frenzy, excitement, and exultation. There were titans to unbind, new structures to be set in place, systems to be hammered out, and of course some 50ft speakers to be procured to play the final soundtrack, details, lots of details.

I made her a bottle of Theist Swine Spray once to put in her bubble gun, showering it down from on high on the unsuspecting punters who had come to her for entertainment. As the bubbles filled with homoeopathic antimatter, hydrogen, nitrogen, and plutonium rained down upon them, she would go into aspect and break their attachments by challenging their conception of reality. She was as relentless as I, if not more, although she somehow seemed to take more damage from the whole thing – the 'brutalizing of reality' principle perhaps.

Athena was my Vajra sister and also an Earth Monkey, born in the same Chinese year as me, and we went through a range of interaction scenarios. I also introduced her to Asher who was dealing Acid at the time, and they eventually got married. It didn't last long though, and when I dragged Asher off to India as a comrade in arms for my enlightenment holiday, Athena was furious. She felt that I should have taken her instead, but then it was a boys' trip, and precisely what I needed at the time to rebuild my psyche in the archetypal image that I wanted. No one throws a fit like Athena, and yet I still have more respect for her than I do for most people because she truly walks her talk.

One of the central Crazy Wisdom sound bites is *"hide nothing in your house"*, which I force myself to adhere to. There is nothing to fear or be ashamed off as everything comes out in the wash sooner or later, and the more upfront you play it the less you have to concern yourself with the vagaries of self-examination, doubt and lies. Hide nothing in your house and play it wide open, then you don't have to watch your back or conceal little secrets that might get you into trouble later.

Luc is one such Buddha Brat and has been one of the more insistent ones in regards to making up his own world. He showed me this with his writing, exposing all his fears and grandiose plans for all to see. You've got to respect that. Having your mother read about your 'Spray and Cook' (and aerosol cooking spray) habit is not something the average punter is showing up to do. Revealing everything is immensely liberating, nothing to hide and nothing to fear, everything played wide open.

Luc was a prolific writer albeit less successful at publishing but he was honing his craft until such time that the world would recognise his talent and love him for it. When I first met Luc he was living with the rest of the 'Guild of Illusion' cohorts and his girlfriend Shannon, and their standard meal would be sugar sandwiches. He somehow transformed himself into a gourmet cook during later years. That is one of the things I like about Luc, he is always willing to listen and learn if something good can be gotten out of it. Rats are relentless at seeking out information and of course love the company of Monkeys because we are on par intellectually. Monkeys enjoy the little sweetmeats they bring back from reality to show and share with us, and this appreciation in return, encourages them to keep hunting for more.

Luc was also the only Rat who did not betray me, and the only one I still have around. Betrayal is one of those deal breakers for me that is just not negotiable. I take the 'banishment or death' view on it, but banishment is usually enough. If you stop playing with someone they cease to functionally exist in your reality, and eventually become forgotten.

I met Luc 15 years ago, in a dark and rather menacing looking quarry where I had gone with Asher to take acid. We bumped into Luc and Gregory, dressed in ninja suits, complete with ninja frog boots, ostensibly for scaling walls. I wasn't quite sure what to make of them, especially after Luc brought out a can of Letra Air to inhale, which is an airbrush propellant containing carbon tetra chloride. Immediately after taking it everything turned to molten rubber, thick, dense, and heavy – quite simply horrible. I leapt back from the fire as if I had been poisoned and started imagining that I was being lured into some strange cult. The effect soon passed and we ended up becoming the best of friends, although I never really got into the Letra Air thing, too déclassé for my tastes, way too grungy.

Luc styled himself as a ninja for as long as I could remember, probably as a way to make him feel tougher. He was quite light of build when I first met him. I had to respect the magical mystery tour detail that he had generated along the way. It was truly epic and I loved it. He had cooked up his reality while on acid, Letra Air and 'Spray and Cook'. Eddie, one of his friends, once told me that Luc had his final vision of emptiness sitting on top of a cupboard, high on his particular cocktail. He basically made up a whole world with adjunctive structures, divisions and levels, plus a wide array of exotic weaponry. He had also written a treatise on time and how to manage it, which he never published, but just the act of doing it demanded respect.

Luc first started his 'Guild of Illusion' with some of his school friends, complete with clothing, emblems, and detailed tripping parlance. This was his world, the Loricelean world, where the blades were sharper, the armour slicker, and people developed into super beings who went to war with each other. Rather strange I thought, for such an advanced civilization. But then Luc never allowed reality to get in his way, even though some of his tech and spells had been pilfered from Carlos Castaneda and Dungeons and Dragons manuals. In spite of this he somehow concocted an extremely elaborate world, complete with archetypal deities, which he was always trying to entice people into it. *"Make yourself a religion"* is his motto, it worked for Jesus or didn't, as the case may be, but the dream needs to be dreamed nonetheless.

I always respected and loved him for it – not everyone has the balls and the gall to cook up their own religion to lure unsuspecting humans into. I always pleaded other elemental allegiances to avoid being directly drawn into the Guild but I was an honorary member by association. It was a funky enough dream to be a part of and certainly one of the more interesting things going on at the time.

One of the central credos of Dzogchen, the *"Great Perfection"* and the highest of the Buddhist schools of conceiving reality is - *"Give up the disease of effort"*.

Why? Because everything is already perfect and to change it would be an error. It is also known as *"the Effortless State"*, so any personal movement into struggle or effort is automatically wrong, and not in tune with the true nature of reality. You wash the bloody dishes when, and if, you feel like doing them, and only then, as only at that time will it be effortless.

If you force yourself to do them, you are deviating from the real mood of reality, which is Effortlessness. At this point one is truly undisturbed by reality and one just enjoys things as spontaneous uprisings of reality in that moment. This view obviously makes it a lot easier to live day by day, although one of my friends Anri, another *dzogchempa* (practitioner of Dzogchen), often gets accused of being a selfish Buddhist because of it.

Another very important and often overlooked tenet of Dzogchen that goes hand in hand with this is *abiding in one's nature*. If Dzogchen is essentially the path of effortless ease, all you have to really do is follow that which you are naturally drawn to, provided of course that you do not get stuck in Dualistic Fixation.

Realising that you are empty anyway and that there is no real meaning to what you do, you can proceed to simply do whatever it is that interests and amuses you. You always return to your essential nature, even through the skein of trying to be all 'adult' about things, certain things one cannot go beyond, nor would one want to. To try to avoid it or be something else, immediately falls into the bracket of making an effort, which is essentially a deviation from the Natural State of Perfection, and therefore quite simply wrong.

The South Americans will always sing about *"me courasonne"* (my heart), *"la veridade"* (truth), and *"la tristesa"* (sadness). It is not in their nature, it is their nature and certain things are unchangeable. Hunter S. Thompson in an interview with Mohamed Ali, on being chastised for drinking and smoking around the champ, claimed that they were both first nature actions for him and hence incurable, as much a part of him as breathing or eating.

Whatever you are drawn to and suits your nature can, and should be used as Means for Liberation, and what this is for you is completely personal. It is even conceivably possible to reach enlightenment by watching TV if you can see everything as just *the play of your mind*, and hence realise it all to be self-generated illusion. If you use your visions to guide you, follow your intrinsic nature, remain present and aware, and slowly cut away all binding obscurations, you can greatly accelerate your journey on the Path.

If you choose the path of your wildest dreams and be yourself completely you do risk public ridicule, disapproval, and possibly insanity but it will bring you everything you ever wanted and a whole lot more - surely a small price to pay for all your dreams coming true.

Luc was definitely entirely self-created and one of those rare creatures that I would put a bullet in the skull of Samsara for. Luc and Eddie were both vying for the top spot in the Guild to guide and control the hapless sentient beings who went along with their vision and version of reality. Luc eventually won because most of the visionary stuff was his, and so became the leader of the Guild.

Gregory, one of their most fervent devotees, flipped out after a while trying to live the 'Loricelean Blade Warrior Ethos' in real life. He was always carrying multiple knives around and 'stalking' animate and inanimate objects alike. Unfortunately after a while Luc had to have him committed for his own, and everyone else's, safety. It was a bit sad because Gregory was quite a beautiful creation in his own way. It certainly highlighted the hazards of going too deeply into one's own magical world, but then if you are not willing to take the risk in the first place you should not get in the water.

My grip on reality has always been quite strong and my attempts to actually drive myself mad failed, in fact the more I pushed the boundaries of my own sanity, the saner I became. I had come to the conclusion early on that mad people had more fun as they were less bound by society and structure than normal people, but tweaking the head often leads you deeper into sanity, and not the other way round.

SIX

Triumphant Return

Hard, fast, effective, and fun,
lest we forget why we play this game
in the first place.

When you start to doubt your visions you are truly screwed. They exist at your most precious core and turning your back on them is like flushing your dreams.

Life can only be hell after that.

A number of years after the psychosis in Taiwan, which gave me my first real taste of Enlightenment, I had become a Homoeopath and returned to South Africa. The first time I could not maintain the state permanently so I resigned myself to chopping away residual aspects of my psyche with Homoeopathy, until maybe I got back to my earlier beatific state. It was during this time that I ran into Asher. Asher and Athena had gotten their hands on the Dzogchen Teachings while I had been away, and these teachings pretty much exactly described the state I had been in before.

We embarked on a speed binge as we were all in the habit of doing at the time. We were aware of the immense potential inherent in the substance, which has less to do with the drug itself, than the fact that you are staying awake and not eating for extended periods of time. This is what yogis would do to themselves with deprivation (fasting) and staying awake for long periods of time. Given the shortage of caves in India, we saw this as an invaluable tool for the modern seekers of wisdom.

Most importantly though, is that you remain sufficiently lucid so that the unconscious obstructions in ones mind can be observed, and then ideally be nailed down. By this time I had the hammer of Homoeopathy to bash the crocodiles as they appeared from the waters of my psyche. This allowed me to cut quickly through a wide range of residual mental and emotional conditioning from childhood.

Using Homoeopathy this way allowed me to rapidly accelerate the process and very soon I found myself on the verge of returning to my original enlightened state. For a moment I hesitated, remembering the pain of returning to mundane existence after the first time, but then my usual gung-ho nature threw caution to the wind and I plunged headlong back into the Natural State. It all returned - the bliss, the joy and the ecstasy, especially when I discovered that the end point of the Dzogchen Teachings led to the Body of Light - surely the highest spiritual achievement of any discipline and a most worthy goal to strive for.

One way, full-metal-jacket, nothing could and would stop me now. Seeing Self reflecting everywhere and devouring Buddhist texts, I embraced various Dzogchen practices and hurled myself back into the current of reality. We would sit for days trawling through our psyches for subtle nuances of dysfunctional and aberrational states. Cleaning, purifying, and heading always towards the Body of Light, we danced our way through space and time.

Around the same time I bought a bottle of homoeopathic anti-matter, which was made from 1000 000 000 decaying particles of sodium-22 captured over 24 hours in water. It was a brand new remedy, recently released. When I opened the bottle, in true anti-matter style, the whole thing shattered. I watched in mild horror and fascination as Asher scooped up handfuls and gleefully devoured it. This was quite different to my normal way of proceeding with Homoeopathy which until then had been far more cautious. Once

I took it, I discovered the fabled Emptiness that the Buddhists drone on about ad nauseum.

There it was in a bottle – nothing going on in the head, nothing at all, silence, nothing manifesting.

Reality is the dance between emptiness and form, but in order to see form as *"originating from emptiness"* it is valuable to have experienced this Emptiness. In order for the birth of Form and its return to Emptiness to be seen as distinct but similar states, one has to have a direct taste of them both as separate. Of course this is not emptiness in its ordinary sense, but rather something that is pregnant with pure potential and awareness, just waiting to give birth to the myriad of forms that shape our reality.

Emptiness in a bottle, who would have imagined it, yet there it was. If *emptiness* is 0 on the Periodic Table and therefore represented by anti-matter, then hydrogen, number 1 on the Periodic Table, is *ceaseless manifestation* and this is the binary that we dance within. The definition of Enlightenment is *"empty like space, but aware and manifesting ceaselessly"* and this suited the Anti-matter - Hydrogen combination to perfection.

This became the binary mix, 0 and 1, in perpetual states of interplay. I eventually added Nitrogen, number 7 on the Periodic Table which is about enjoyment, and thus it became *"emptiness, alternating with ceaseless manifestation, in the mood of enjoyment"* in a bottle. This affectionately became known in our group as the XXX road show to which I later added Plutonium, to give it a bit of a punch.

Most Homoeopathic remedies are diluted millions of times beyond the point where there is even one atom of the physical substance left, so one can safely play with substances that would be poisonous or even deadly in their raw form.

Plutonium as a Homoeopathic remedy represents the underworld and facilitates the waking up of the Kundalini and its movement up the spine. It is not a very predictable substance at the best of times, but it definitely gives people a bit of an energetic boost on the path.

If you are riding the whirlwind you need a tiger in your tank, and to use potent methods to facilitate a process which is largely inconceivable, is not only desirable, it is necessary.

One evening at a friend's house, day two on speed and half a trip of acid later, I decided to raise my Kundalini. The teachings say that men need to be driven and women need to be contained and this is in line with the notion of the Kundalini. The masculine energy, situated at the crown chakra represents Skillful Means and Compassion, and the feminine energy situated at the base chakra, represents Intuitive Wisdom and Power. When these two are separate we either use our skills but derive very little satisfaction from it and it is merely a cold, analytical function or we are constantly experiencing rollercoaster emotions as we cling to people or concepts, consumed by passion.

A good analogy is that of a car – the engine is the Skillful Means and the fuel is the Intuitive Wisdom. The car without the fuel is not going anywhere and the fuel without the car burns out of control. Therefore, men need to be driven by getting in touch with their Intuitive Wisdom which will supply the fuel for their actions, and women need to be contained by directing their volatile energy into Skillful Means. There is in fact no getting away from this, and I maintain that the raising of the Kundalini is of paramount importance if one wants to progress on the path.

I did not know much about it at the time but had a very strong urge to raise it so I plunged right in. I had read texts where it said that to get it moving one had to visualize two channels, one on the left and one on the right, *Lilana* and *Rasana,* flowing into the base of the spine. One then sees the red and white mix together at the base chakra, and when that's done one starts contracting the anal sphincter, as if interrupting urination. One does this a number of times until it undeniably starts moving up the *Avadhuti* (central channel).

I remember Asher saying to me before I began *"Don't expect me to scrape you off the walls"*. In spite of this I was buoyed up by the spirit of Crazy Wisdom and would not be deterred, especially by any residual fears for my own safety or sanity.

The texts also spoke of dropping *amrita* (nectar) from the lotus of the crown chakra down the spine to lure the serpent up. Cute, yet it seemed to work, and as the drops descended from my lotus, I was rather surprised when I felt the force at the base of my spine beginning to move. Quelling my trepidation with enthusiasm, and reminding myself that it was all my own energy anyway, I watched it beginning to rise.

It was like feeling a river of tingling lava beginning to ascend through the chakras, from the back and up the spine. Raw power – you don't do Kundalini, it does you. It was unlike anything I had experienced before, and anyone who claims the Kundalini rising is a sexual experience, has obviously not done it.

It took a while to come up and I remember quite distinctly that it went through various smaller channels, clearing them out. This lasted about two hours and to protect the Kundalini from leaving the top of my head I put an eagle, one of my personal archetypal forms and the traditional enemy of the snake, at the crown chakra. Such naivety in retrospect, as if anything could stop the Kundalini from doing what it wanted to anyway, but fortune sometimes favours the ignorant and the inspired. I quickly drew it up to the crown chakra and forced it down back into the heart chakra which is where, from my understanding at that time, it was supposed to reside. Another of my archetypal forms that appeared to me in a vision once was a giant tree that grew all the way through me up to the sky. When I returned the serpent to my heart I let it wrap itself around this tree, gazing at the sky, where I thought it would be safe and secure.

On opening my eyes from this experience I was full of energy, a dynamo of activity, dancing around supercharged with the joy of existence and the power of Kundalini. By this time Athena had arrived at the house and as I said we are a bit competitive. She was so pissed off that I raised my Kundalini before her that she proceeded to do it as well. Hers lasted somewhat shorter and she will hopefully tell her story of it herself.

I was so juiced by this whole thing that I was literally dancing in supermarkets, riding high on a supernova of inspiration. I really had no idea of what was to come and I thought that having raised it that would be it. I began to notice over the next few days that my heart was enlarging and I was starting to get some strange twitches in my left arm. As this grew more intense I realized that I could not continue the way I was going without risking some sort of heart attack.

I moved the Kundalini from its place in the heart and put it in my solar plexus, which is where the Chinese generally focus their *chi* (energy) from. This became even more unpleasant because it seems to be the storehouse for a lot of dream memory. I watched thousands of seemingly unconnected junk images, things I had never even seen before, flash before my eyes. All kinds of random images of old boathouses and driving around in the backs of unfamiliar cars had been unconsciously stored there, taking up space. I decided to embark on a cleansing jihad, tearing apart these images in a fury of dissolution, trying to return things to emptiness.

When I opened my eyes I was in a very wrathful space. This was all happening while at James' house and so I averted the fury of my gaze from his eyes out of politeness, and to avoid the wrath pouring out of me being directed at him. He was a bit of a two-faced creature and probably deserved it, but I was honour bound by the rules of hospitality not to upset the applecart. The result of suppressing this state put me into a truly deranged mood because the energy had to go somewhere, and I started to spin out.

Upon quizzing Asher further on such matters he revealed to me that in Dzogchen they normally keep the Kundalini in the throat chakra, which is what I proceeded to do. This helped a lot and although it felt a bit overcharged, it was definitely manageable.

As the Kundalini rises and clears through the chakras, a lot of suppressed energy is released. I was not eating or sleeping much, high on my own supply, riding the whirlwind without a clue beyond an innate faith in my own ability to find my way. It would not go away and I could not return it to the base chakra because once it rises beyond the heart, the chakras peel back and dissolve into each other, and then the only place for it to go is up. After a few days it started to become more uncomfortable in my throat, my voice became stronger, and I was less able to suppress anything that came out of my mouth.

At this stage a Buddhist text just happened my way and it described the final stages – joining the Kundalini with the Lotus at the Crown. Apparently at this point the two dissolve into each other and the released energy goes everywhere in the body in a shower of golden light. It is also said that upon the final dissolution of Base into Crown one could expect to lie like a stone, almost dead for a week, with the heart barely beating. I had not experienced the shower of golden light just yet so it was clear to me that the procedure was not finished. This whole Kundalini process had so far taken about three weeks and it seemed that until completed it would not leave me in peace. I was staying at my parent's house at the time. God knows how I managed to keep a lid on the whole thing but then my parents were used to unusual behaviour from me so maybe they did not suspect anything How could they after all, it was something so completely out of their range of experience.

Asher had had it with reality so he abandoned his flat and was staying with us, along with his daughter, who was definitely used to strange behaviour from us. On that day we were doing some Sky Gazing, a Dzogchen practise whereby one draws the sky down behind ones eyes and makes it ones mind, becoming *empty like the sky*. We were on the grass in the garden with no one home, so I decided to finish this Kundalini story.

I raised the Kundalini from my throat to my crown, without the eagle this time. As the two joined there was indeed a divine meltdown, everything turned into golden light showering down my body. I felt numbness in my feet and it started to ascend up my body until it was at my stomach. Remembering what I had read, and uncertain of the terrain I was entering, I told Asher to put me in the abandoned greenhouse in the garden if I went out, cover me with a blanket, and tell my parents I had gone away somewhere until I woke up, even if it took a week.

I then realised – why should it take a week, what was time anyway? One could surely be reborn into ones new state in ten minutes if you wanted to. It would definitely be inconvenient and most probably ease-breaking for all concerned if I was paralysed for a week. So as the paralysis moved up to my chest I surrendered to the process and lay completely numb for what must have been 15 minutes or so, hard to judge time in that state, hard to even breathe. And then the process reversed, the paralysis drained out of me down through my whole body and out my feet.

It was done!!!!!!!! Having gone way beyond my conceptual framework I had no idea what to expect. Things were remarkably normal but somehow more effortless. I was moving faster through reality, my memory was instantaneous, I was feeling great and my intuitive and rational skills, especially with Homoeopathy were working as one. I was finding remedies for other people and myself in a moment, the 'silver platter delivery service' of whatever information was required, whether it was related to the *Dharma* (teachings), Homoeopathy, or quite simply anything.

I was finally enlightened, although I realize now that Enlightenment is an ongoing process of deeper and deeper enlightenments, which echo ones degree of non-duality and the breaking of conceptual structures that bind one into form.

So, since I was still in form I put in a mental wish for a Vajra Body, an *"indestructible vehicle"*. Having no idea what it actually was, as if they just dished them out at the 'Vajra Body Shop' in a stunning array of diamond shades, complete with all sorts of funky teleporting and flying upgrades – whatever it was and whatever it looked like, it sounded good to me. I included this and another hundred wishes Asher suggested I write out and then burn, a trick he had picked up from THE ARTIST'S WAY.

I wished savagely for a diaspora of exotica, the 64 million *Dakini Tantras* (an ancient body of teachings and skills), all the *siddhis* (powers), you name it - whatever I could think of and a whole lot more. Some of the wishes have already come true and some are still in process, but when you wish so large it is inevitably going to take a while. There was no rush. After all, I had all the time in the world.

That night in a fit of stupidity I joined Asher in a dose of Hydrogen, the *ceaseless manifestation* substance, and things went crazy. I was assailed by everything and I could not turn my mind off, it was racing in all directions and Asher was in a weird space of wanting to round everyone up and exterminate them, which pushed me deeper into madness.

Every trick in the book that I could think of, mantras, meditation, remedies, wishes, yoga, visualizations, you name it I tried it, and none of it worked. Nothing happened until I gave up trying to do anything, collapsed and went to sleep. It returned to semi normal again in the morning, to my relief. Sleep normally sorts out most things and it did in this case. *"Give up the disease of effort"*, just let go because sometimes there is nothing to do but surrender to the process and let it be.

"Surrender the 'self' and inherit the universe."

Fuse with everything that is in fact you, and as you become everything, what is there then that one cannot do?

SEVEN

Honey
On The Tongue

*I have always been a sucker for
sexy syntax, and Dzogchen is the rock star,
supermodel, and movie star of all philosophies
and teachings on the Nature of the Mind.*

The king of a small kingdom in northern India caught Padmasambhava teaching his daughter Mandarava, who had gone off to a nun-
nery to practise meditation. In a fit of rage he made a huge fire and
burnt him. The fire burnt for seven days and when it finally went
out, there was Padmasambhava, sitting on a lotus in the middle of
a small lake, relaxing and looking at the king. The king of course
grovelled and begged apologies and teachings from Padmasambhava,
realizing his error.

Such was the power of the *"Lotus Born"*, born enlightened
to spread the Tantric and Dzogchen Teachings throughout India
and Tibet.

The best place to begin is to run the Non-dual View – the view that
everything is self and that *self is empty*. Then, practicing Zerbu which
means *"nailing down"*, begin the task of integrating the things you
like, the things you don't like, and the things you are indifferent
to. If you cannot accept the Non-Dual View at first, pretend it is so
until you see it to be so. This is the 'fake it till you make it' view of

reality which works surprisingly well. Do this for long enough and once you see it to be so, integrate everything under this banner. Dissolve all concepts of self, other, time, and space, and gradually dissolve into rainbow light, the natural constituents that make up a human being. At this point you get the multi-pass to the universe, and you write your own ticket out of here, or stay and do whatever you like.

Why Dzogchen? Because it works, and it works fast, and there is clearly no time to waste. We no longer have the luxury of waiting for five lifetimes or of sitting in a cave for ten years meditating and drinking nettle broth till we turn green and enlighten ourselves. It has to be here and now, or not at all.

Giving up the disease of effort sounds like a great ethos to start with, and even just doing this will accelerate our path because we are no longer wasting time and energy fighting our own Natural State. There might be a faster way but after searching long and hard I have yet to find a superior teaching. Besides, once one has experienced the depths of these Teachings and seen the speed at which it liberates, it is hard to imagine a more beautiful paradigm.

In Buddhism there are different schools and whichever you choose is dependent on your nature, level of courage, discipline, and stage of awareness. The outcome is essentially the same but the methodology changes according to which View you hold.

The first Buddha originally taught Hinayana, *"the lesser path"*, where you have to take vows of celibacy, non accumulation of objects, and avoidance of certain foods and drugs to learn how not to be enslaved by your senses. He laid out hundreds of rules regarding conduct, which covered everything from diet to sexuality, because essentially he was dealing with people who admitted to not being able to control their impulses and passions. Therefore he had the eight illegal vegetables declared, of which garlic headed up the charge as the antichrist for raising the sexual passions. Included in the list were chilli, onion, tamarind, and a few others which apparently have a deranging effect on ones energetic state.

As for sexuality, he went so far as to put in place injunctions against rubbing oneself up against trees, to prevent monks from indulging and giving in to their passions. The passions, from this View, are the enemy that can lead to getting caught up and carried away from ones state of detached meditative calm. On the other hand from the Tantric View, the passions represent powerful forces which can be transformed in order to fuel ones process toward Liberation.

From a Dzogchen View however, one abides completely in whatever comes up in the moment, but with the caveat *"have no desire for desire"*. If you feel desire in the moment one should engage it, realizing it to be a *play of the mind* – just another aspect of reality, and perfect as it is. Free from the need to renounce or transform it, it is the perfect play of the Five Lights (the emotions) which are responsible for creating this illusion around us that we think of as 'reality'. You do not become attached to it because it gives way to the next moment which is of equal value, and also to be experienced, engaged in, and left behind.

You also need to renounce nothing because by knowing that *all is illusion* one cannot become attached in the first place, leaving you free to play in reality with impunity, without becoming trapped. The very things that can bind one, sex, drugs, and the rock 'n roll lifestyle, have immense potential for bringing up a host of emotions to play with and nail down. They are in essence the fine colours which make up your adornment, and which you can use on the path to greatly accelerate your process into light, and complete freedom from *the bondage of form*.

This presupposes that you understand One Taste, which basically states that whatever arises in your sense field in any given moment is perfect yet empty, and equal to any other moment in reality. If you can view the maggoty corpse of a rat with the same equanimity one views a beautiful feast or a fine sunset, then you have really conquered Duality and the idea that there is actually any difference between the two. If you are equally happy sitting in a desert chatting to scorpions, squatting in a sewer in Calcutta, or sitting in a palace surrounded by dancing girls, you have mastered the One Taste. To arrive at this point is not as easy as it might sound though, and requires the genuine dissolution of conceptual structures around good and bad sensory experiences.

Once one has gotten to the point where one realises that *all is empty and the play of illusion*, One Taste meets Discriminating Wisdom. Realising that it makes no difference what is in front of you, one is free to choose what you like over what you don't like. At this point you might as well be in the palace with the dancing girls because it makes no difference either way. A lot of people try and jump this gun. The senses are always trying to lure us and entrap us in a web of aversion and desire but one only gets to sit in the palace once one is content to sit with the scorpions. To achieve this you have to relinquish everything, or at least be willing to, in order to get everything you have ever wanted. Of course by then you don't particularly want anything because it is all the 'same taste' anyway. No one ever said that enlightenment would be without its own cruel little jokes.

Cruel jokes aside, if one is free from attachment and aversion one is able to rise above reality and truly enjoy the play of ones senses without being plagued by suffering. To me this is a gem without price. All said and done, it is never easy to contemplate the structural annihilation of ones entire reality.

My motto has always been *"why wait?"* and when I heard that the Hinayana path is supposed to take five lifetimes I decided that it was definitely not for me. It takes this long because you are perpetually fighting against your natural impulses, which is never an easy thing. You have to nail each passion down one at a time until you have none, and are content to sit in equanimity.

The Tantric path requires at least one lifetime, maybe two. It is risky to count on another lifetime because there are many unknown forces at play and you might not have any control over your next incarnation. Another problem with this path is that you are dealing with transforming powerful energies into pure states, which require a lot of fairly strict and hidden rituals. These protect the practitioner and the teachings from abuse. A *tantrika* (practitioner of Tantra) will embody an archetypal form of anger for example, in order to overcome that particular emotion, and the rituals are there to prevent them from getting caught up in the illusion. If you lose the plot by identifying with the archetype as yourself and as being real, you can end up becoming the very thing you were trying to conquer.

There are a lot of 'ifs', 'buts', and potential pitfalls. Furthermore, true Tantric teachings are often very hard to come by as they are so closely guarded by their Lineages and hardly ever revealed to the public unless specifically sanctioned. Most importantly you have to be lucky enough to find someone with enough experience and impeccability to guide you through these processes and keep you on the rails. This is no easy feat, considering the scores of dodgy characters preying on gullible students just looking for a Guru, especially in the West.

From a Dzogchen perspective one needs not worry about transforming anything. It is all perfect anyway, and the more you see the perfection of everything, in everything, the faster you move along the path. A great Dzogchen master once said, *"Whatever you are doing just remain present and aware"*. You do this to prevent yourself from getting caught up and holding on to the moment, which is a very real possibility when emotions are powerful.

When you are hungry, eat. When you are thirsty, drink. When feeling angry, be angry. It sounds simple but the trick is to not stay angry afterwards because then you are generating fixed patterns in yourself which will have to be unbound later. When you bear in mind that the natural state of the mind is ease, all you have to do is maintain this state regardless of what arises.

This *maintaining in the state of contemplation* is the Dzogchen ideal, since one maintains the meditative absorption of things at all times. This ensures that one does not get drawn into the drama surrounding one. One moment concludes and gives way to the next, which does the same thing, and any sense of continuity is merely illusion. A duality which implies a 'this' and a 'that', a 'past' and a 'future', is from the non-dual perspective simply rubbish. The only thing one truly ever knows is the Now, the one and only moment you will ever know. The past is just a memory which is subject to colouring in retrospect. The future is even worse, it is a theoretical

construct that we make about something which has not even occurred, and when we get there it is always different anyway because
our mind space has changed in the meantime.

Continuing in the State of Contemplation one eventually becomes so familiar with it that one enters the State of Presence, or
Rigpa in Tibetan, without having to watch the mind too much. The
mind knows its own natural condition and it engages all things as
they appear and disappear equally, simply enjoying the dance of the
Five Lights. Once one is in this State of Presence, one can effortlessly cut through any remaining dualities that bind one into form.

One can then engage the final process called Thogal, which
means completely letting go of everything, resulting in ones dissolution into light. There is proof that it is possible to dissolve back into
the Five Lights that make up our physical form, literally vanishing
into thin air and there are many modern day accounts of such events.
These are often accompanied by tales of magical happenings like
rainbow lights in the sky, the blooming of flowers out of season, the
raining of petals and other such extraordinary events.

Since it can be done, surely the challenge is to do it. There
can be no doubt as to ones ascension then. No getting nailed to
crosses, just dissolving back into the light from whence we came.

Dzogchen is the only tradition I have found so far that gives
such detailed instruction on the means to achieve this Body of
Light. These techniques include sun, moon and sky gazing, yogic
postures which free up any remaining memory stored in the muscles
and joints, and much more. Descriptions of the actual final dissolution process is however, often veiled in what is called 'Twilight
Language' and even when blatantly stated in a text, requires a
certain understanding to unlock its true meaning. After searching
for more information I realized that they were either so secret that
very few people could access it or that much of this process is only
really understandable once you get there.

It might even be that when you are on the brink of Dissolution,
you just have to wing it, making it up as you go along. One thing I
have realized with time is that one can often read or be told certain
techniques, but when you are experiencing something directly it

will be completely unique to you. This seems a very fitting finale to a Teaching which incorporates a principle such as Crazy Wisdom. Each individual chooses their own particular way of going out in style – just the way we like it.

For me, liberation is the Complete Unbound State, the ability to assume any and every form at will, seamlessly come out of it, and into the next most appropriate face. This view is echoed in a pack of playing cards as that of the Joker, playing any form yet no form, automatically being whatever you need and simultaneously the best card on the table.

If you apply this to every situation in your life, always being or doing what is appropriate at the time without any effort, you basically get the multi-pass to the universe.

At the same time one must relentlessly break down old constricting patterns as they will bind you into form as surely as a straightjacket keeps you in place. Dzogchen, aptly translated as *"The Great Perfection"* is like assuming that you are in the best *feng shui* position possible at all times and dancing your dance as you see fit, for the benefit of all sentient beings of course, lest we forget.

There were some enlightened masters who chose to just lie around. This benefited numerous sentient beings in inconceivable ways. There is even one Buddhist master of very high lineage who has chosen to shoot heroin on the streets of New York. The Buddhist orthodoxy will not say a word in judgement as he is considered to be of such a high level of attainment as to be beyond rebuke. I am not advocating any particular lifestyle, it is just that once one has reached a certain point in the *dissolution of duality and the illusion of self,* one will benefit others regardless of how strange ones actions may seem from the outside

All said and done it is perfect and will unfold with an intricacy, patterning and beauty that beggars the mind. If everything is perfect this means everything, no coincidences, no accidental happenstances, no arbitrary events, no crying in the soup and bewailing ones fate, it is all good. Takes a big person to stomach this, you can't blame your parents, your wife, the weather, bad drivers on the road, the political state at the moment, it is all your own manifestation and it is perfect as it is. If you don't like it then change it but there is no need to change anything, unless you want to, and blame is definitely out of the picture.

No god, no demons, no government, no Illuminati watching over you and controlling your existence or demanding obeisance or offerings in exchange for a place at their feet in a second-rate heaven. You have total freedom to do, make, or be whatever you choose, total responsibility as well but one is free from the need to prop up a 'self' and maintain an identity separate from the rest of the world. If *everything is self* and *self is empty* then who did what to whom, and where?

Everything must go, bargain basement sale. How fast you choose to do this will be determined by your own nature. Personally I take the Jihadic view on this, going full-metal-jacket straight at the slugs and beetles in my psyche, as they are the enemy.

This is why Dzogchen is considered to be a teaching that is not for everyone. Some people like having others to blame for their woes or bow down to for their salvation. Take it all back as Aspects, everything, every male and female superhero, mythological figure, god or great teacher, are all aspects of your Self. A rather huge concept to embrace, but oh so sexy, and the potential if one embraces this view is limitless. One is prevented from the excesses of egotism and self-aggrandizement by the realization that the movie as well as the 'self' is all empty.

Dzogchen takes the sting out of reality, but you are on your own, just you and the rest of reality which is also you, so one is never really alone ever, and who said that anyway?

There is a story of a Buddhist monk meeting a Dzogchen practitioner on a road and saying to him:

"So I hear you Dzogchen practitioners meditate a lot."
To which the Dzogchen practitioner replies,
"What is there to meditate on?"

The Buddhist practitioner then responds in triumph,
"So then you don't meditate!"
To which the Dzogchen practitioner coolly responds
"But when am I ever out of the state of contemplation?"

Case closed.
　　I see the pair of Aces in your hand but I've got a full house.

EIGHT

Reclaiming The Holy Land

*The Non-Dual Nature of the Mind
renounces nothing.*

We were Buddha Brats relentlessly using and adapting the Teachings as we saw fit, as well as developing our own means to hack and slay our way to Enlightenment – Body of Light or bust.

We propelled ourselves so fast that we had no time to turn back or look down as we swam headlong into the abyss. No sight of the other side, beyond a sense that there was another side to get to.

Now that I was Enlightened, the question was what to do? In keeping with the Buddha Brat ethos – quite simply whatever one wanted to do. The joy of this state had to be shared with all and sundry so I went on a binge of attempting to enlighten sentient beings, as all good enlightened beings do when they reach enlightenment.

Garab Dorje, founder of one of the the main lineages of Dzogchen, liberated the whole of Oddiyana (his homeland) and they had all gone Body of Light, so this is what I aspired to. If he could do it, then it could be done. When I had taken the *bodhisattva* (enlightenment warrior) vow of enlightening all sentient beings I took my job very, very seriously, but not without a fair amount of glee.

To be honest I could not have stopped myself even if I wanted to. I talked to whoever would listen about the joys of Dzogchen and the benefits of Kundalini, this time with the added benefit of my large black box of Homoeopathic remedies. I began doing extended sessions with people, often over a period of two or three days, clearing years of memory to allow them a glimpse of the Natural State. My faithful bottle of Anti-matter was always close at hand to offer them a real taste of Emptiness once they were sufficiently open enough to recognise it, paving the way for them to understand or accept it.

I ignored Asher's doubts about the validity of what I was doing. He was rather hung up on the lineage thing, needing an official stamp of approval from the orthodoxy in order to spread the Teachings. Either way I was going to do it and nothing could have brought me more pleasure. Hacking and demolishing the residual patterning from people's heads, accompanied by liberal doses of Dzogchen, I proceeded to cut a swathe through a sea of sentient ignorance. I was totally in my element – this was truly what I had been designed for.

Before my enlightenment I had initially planned a trip to India to enhance my Homoeopathic repertoire, so after a few months as we were running out of willing sentient beings to work on, I convinced Asher to come along for the ride. We decided to turn it into my official 'enlightenment holiday'.

As part of my enlightenment manifesto I took to heart one of the core Dzogchen precepts of Zerbu, which is to *"engage the things you like, the things you don't like and the things you are indifferent to"*. I once fantasized about retiring to a cave in India to sit in contemplation, eating nettle broth like the great Tibetan yogi Milarepa, waiting for enlightenment to favour me with its presence. Upon investigating the cave situation in India I found them rather oversubscribed by on the most part, fake holy men. It is not hard to contemplate emptiness as a chillum smoking *saddhu* (holy man). In my opinion it is far more of a challenge to experience true emptiness when surrounded by the pressures of modern life.

Besides, I never quite had the extremes of ascetism required to share a cave with nothing but snow lions, yetis, and ice drifts. There is after all only so much emptiness one can handle and buttered tea one can drink. Since *all is empty,* one might as well be lying on silk sheets with ones choice of music, tasty edibles, and access to exotic stimuli. The Non-Dual Nature of the Mind renounces nothing.

This always made a lot of sense to me and if *all is illusion* you might as well have your choice of pretty and enjoyable illusions. Needless suffering falls under the banner of breaking ones ease, which would be a direct violation of the core Dzogchen ethos, and heaven forbid I did that.

What followed was a spree of indulgence, engaging all the things I have always wanted but had previously denied myself. I procured three pairs of leather pants, intricately embroidered Kashmiri shirts, emerald necklaces, Buddhist *thankas* (religious paintings), bone jewellery, Nepalese *kukris* (curved blades), stones, sculptures and simply anything that caught my fancy. We hired a car and a driver to take us around, blasting Marilyn Manson, Nine Inch Nails, Soundgarden, Cardigans, and Tricky through our little tape deck. Quite simply behaving like brats, we were indulging our every whim as we went along.

I hooked up briefly with a cute British nuclear physicist. I tried to convince her to design me a bow with plutonium-tipped arrows to blow up dams with while hanging from a helicopter Rambo style, freeing the elementals and allowing the rivers to run free again. She played along for a while until we parted ways and I realized that the military aspects of the Apocalypse were best done covertly, if at all.

A good friend once said to me, *"If there is anything in the empti-ness then it is just not empty"*. Walking through a forest in Kashmir with Asher, we resolved to eat every mushroom we came across without exception. Holding firmly to the view that it was all Self and could not harm us unless we deviated from this view, we began our baptism by fire. After an hour and twelve different species of unknown mushrooms, not only did we not poison ourselves, we did not even get high, much to our disappointment.

This story contrasts with when I was quite happily swimming in Dal Lake in Shrinagar, the capital of Kashmir. Holding the view relentlessly every day that the water was pure, one day I saw a whole load of raw sewerage being poured into the lake in an area we were visiting. Dropping my clarity and belief momentarily resulted in me getting sick as a dog that night, and I resolved thereafter never to doubt the perfection of my reality.

Suspension of disbelief is nine tenths of the law, and if one can hold a thought strongly enough and suspend belief seriously enough, one can quite literally walk through walls and fly.

To test the belief in my own indestructibility, when I was in Daramsala I decided to buy some Indian Cobra venom and drink it. It is after all only conceptual structures that limits us from doing pretty much anything, including surviving possible fatality. When the venom arrived it was a rather suspect looking yellow liquid in a dirty bottle, and I decided that I would wait till I found a fresher and more authentic source before I put it in my mouth.

I did find a Cobra skin though from a serpent which, the resident saddhu of some holy island in Kashmir claimed, circled the island three times a day at dawn, dusk, and midday. It was a charming story and he recommended that we mix the skin in with oil and apply it to our hair for long luxuriant locks, which we duly did.

While still in Srinagar, along with my two Indian sidekicks who carried my large Homoeopathic case, I marched into the mental hospital announcing that I was there to help them cure the sick. They politely refused although you could see they were deeply curious about this leather-clad foreigner taking such an interest in the mental health of their countrymen. They cited the fact that it was an Allopathic institution and they would have to get permission from a superior in order for me to be allowed to practise there.

The usual Indian story, although there were people there that could have seriously done with my help. They were clawing at their cages, frothing at the mouth and howling, it was like something from Dante's INFERNO. India is not a good place to get help if you lose the plot. The upside of India though is that you can propose the most outlandish course of action to a *walla* and he will blithely reply *"why not?"* The foreigner is always right even if he is mad. He has money and although it may seem like he is clueless, as long as he is willing to pay it is enough.

While on a boat trek through Kashmir I saw a Datura flower and promptly plucked and ingested it. We were paddling through a sea of lotuses to one of the islands, and entranced by the place or maybe inspired by the Datura flower I had eaten, I decided to declare a free clinic for all the inhabitants. I was immediately deluged by a swarm of locals all clamouring to get their airtime from the strange foreign *"doctorji"*. I set up three locals as my bouncers to filter the crowd, as a hundred people arrived to be treated all at once. With two translators I proceeded to write out prescriptions and dose them all in the space of about four hours.

I could have easily taken up residence there as the neighbourhood doctor, they were lavishly grateful for the treatment and stuffed me with mango slices and spiced tea. In spite of this gracious reception the movie needed to continue because there were larger and fatter fish to fry in the future. It is always good to leave on a high note - swoop down, save the day, and exit with a flourish, definitely my style.

We returned from the boat trek to Dahl Lake, which is quite simply paradise on earth, overflowing with lotuses, cherries, carpets, sweetmeats, saffron honey, and floating food islands. All this while you relax on your own houseboat with literally anything and everything brought to you.

The ecstasy and absurdity continued as we carved our way through Kashmir. I was hell bent on getting a tiger skin for a pair of pants. Traditional yogis are drawn sitting in meditation on a tiger skin, but one has to modernize and adapt everything, making it practical after all. Make no mistake I love tigers, and *Panthera Tigrus* happens to be one of my core Homoeopathic remedies. I use it at times when I do a lot for people and then when in need of help myself it is withheld, resulting in anger.

Added to this I had once let a tiger out of a cage in one of the suburbs of Taipei in Taiwan. When I saw the glorious beast for the first time they had it in a cage in some tiny backyard gambling den, feeding it dogs. I gathered, Jason my cohort at the time, to pull off the great escape. Jason was an American ex-cop who was exiled for having broken the arms of some guy who tried to rape his girlfriend. The judge said it would have been fine if he had broken only one arm, but two was a bit excessive and advised him to leave the country for a while.

Since it was my plan, it was up to me to open the cage. Having broken the lock off the cage with a small metal bar, an action that had woken the beast, all that remained was to open the door. All I could find was a short piece of string which I tied to the door to pull it open and ran. Jason was waiting for me on the street keeping the revs up on a stolen motorbike. We went round the block and there it was, all twelve feet of unleashed power, walking down the street at about two in the morning.

With a quick mental projection to the tiger that it should head for the forested hills without eating too many Taiwanese in the process, we sped off, never to see or hear about it again. The sight of the tiger walking down a grubby suburban street revelling in its newfound freedom will remain etched in my memory forever. I figured the tiger nation owed me a pelt, but it never came my way. I had to content myself with smoking Chinese Golden Tiger cigarettes which I bought by the carton, and a tiger claw which turned out to be carved from buffalo horn, but entertained me nonetheless.

In Ladakh I picked up a skull bowl (a ceremonial bowl made from the top of a human skull), the nuclear physicist, ceremonial daggers and generally wrecked Dzogchen mayhem on the locals. Asher picked up Charlotte who he would later marry and proceed to torment in various inconceivable ways. It was quite convenient for me since I had been picking up most of the tab for the trip and he then became her problem.

Our little party soon moved to Nepal because Charlotte needed to renew her visa and so the physicist and I parted ways.

Anything is available for fifty dollars in Nepal. I wanted a human skull, and managed to procure one from the charnel grounds. The drug, and part-time skull dealer, brought it to me wrapped in newspaper. It was very, very fresh, in fact it still had a bit of meat on it, which was perfect. I used it to meditate on Impermanence so the bit of meat was actually fine, good for the *chodpa* (practitioner of Chod) in me. I remember giving an hour-long Teaching to the skull on traversing the bardo (in between spaces after death). I explained how to move to the other side and on to the clear light while not being distracted or drawn into any of the Realms, which are all illusion and pathways to further suffering and incarnation. This speech acted as a practise run for when I gave the same speech to my mother after she died.

Everything fitting flawlessly into place is what one has to love about the Natural State, total perfection and yet completely inconceivable. It is designed for you to allow the most enjoyment from the movie, just the way you like it. You just have to reach out and grab it, and then have the balls to play it, something a lot of people choke on.

One day I went down to the burning *ghats* where they cremate bodies by the river and probably where my skull had come from. The more one destroys the *illusion of self* the more fearless one becomes and sitting next to a burning body I experienced total calmness and bliss.

There is a Tibetan symbol for this called the *gaykil* or *'wheel of joy'* which is depicted as three spirals bound together in a circle, *"the three that are one"*, Emptiness, Clarity, and Bliss – the aspects of your Natural State. When you realize that it is all the play of sound, light, and sensation, it frees you from a lot of fears.

Who determines when you have conquered them? Quite simply you do, you are the enlightenment inspector who stamps your own passport on arrival, and only you know for sure. When texts on the Natural State correspond to what you are experiencing in that moment, you know have arrived.

There is a practise called The Lion's Roar which entails kneeling and roaring at the heavens to announce ones arrival at the Natural State. This is another benchmark moment on the path but not the end, in fact it is the true beginning. Then one can play out the rest of ones karma without hindrance. I did the Lion's Roar at my family's farm on a weekend away with Asher and some other friends. I remember his daughter Sophie sitting and watching with approval, the minds of young children are to be disregarded at ones own peril, often they see the clearest. The Lion's Roar happened around the time of the Kundalini episodes and after this there can be no doubt as to ones state.

Enlightenment is a process of degrees of dissolution into light, yet beyond a certain point, one can no longer be drawn back into the matrix. You are officially unplugged and one is free from the Wheel of Karma. How fast you complete the final steps is largely dependent on personal choice and of course 'reality', which is you anyway.

You cannot really accelerate the process beyond the speed it is meant to be going. God knows I tried, with every ounce of my being I tried. One way, full speed, Body of Light here I come, but certain things cannot be rushed and the lessons one learns along the way aid in your ability to benefit other sentient beings.

Then it's a matter of having the weaponry and just spending time on the playing fields, sharpening and mastering the art.

"Awareness, first and last and always", you can't go wrong. If you put anything in the priority list above that, one risks becoming entrapped in Samsara and suffering like a dog with mange and worms. Any way you slice this pie guarantees that you will suffer, but if you choose to exit the matrix at least you have a shot at immortality.

What was never born cannot die, and when one breaks up into light one is free to choose whatever path or reality one wants. Seems like a good choice to me, but then I always had a hard time playing daily life and doing the things one is expected to do like suffering, children, and mortgages.

Those that share this view with me, or have suffered enough to risk dancing through the minefields of their minds, are my cadre, my Vajra brothers and sisters.

The rest of humanity seems a bit like another species.

NINE

Shattering The Mould

*Take the jewels that are scattered
in front of you, and boot the used-dictionary salesman
in the face when he comes knocking on the door,
selling last year's edition.*

Homoeopathy is indeed freedom from suffering at ones own hands and is quite simply a jewel that has no price.

When I took Nitric Acid as a remedy I was literally dancing in the streets, no longer having to keep up my 'long hard struggle' with a reality that had done me wrong. Why exactly I had gone into this state in the first place is unclear but it was possibly to make me feel stronger at certain junctures when I needed to feel strong, of which there have been many. It gets very draining on the system however, keeping up an ongoing battle with reality, and is also appropriately one of the main remedies for family feuds.

I had been in a homoeopathic Dragonfly state most of my life which meant that I had an excuse for non-achievement. The core of this remedy is about feeling that the world is coming to an end anyway so what is the point of doing anything beyond accelerating the inevitable end. After I took the remedy I became more active in figuring out how to optimize the people around me, so that by the time we do move beyond this paradigm, everyone would be ready to roll with the new program.

Everyone has multiple states that condition them and it is like a poison garden with beasts, rocks, and serpents. It is in this garden that one needs to go hunting in order to clear the weeds and the noxious beasts. After this you can plant the garden that you actually want, with birds and deer, and not scorpions, rattlesnakes, thorn trees, and jagged rocks.

The idea behind Homoeopathy is that it introduces a similar but stronger medicinal force to the body, to which the body responds by producing exactly the opposite effect and through this process the disease is removed. For example, we use homoeopathic coffee to combat sleeplessness because this is what the raw substance produces, so if a person is sleepless from excitement a dose of *Coffea* will often send them to sleep. Therefore the principle that Homeopathy is based on is that of *"like cures like"*.

The problem with Homoeopathy is that there are just so many remedies. I have 2000 next to my bed and there are probably 5000 in total. If you do not give exactly the right one there is often little or no effect from it. Homoeopathy is actually harder than Allopathic medicine because with each case you have to start from scratch. There are no protocols and few specifics for particular conditions, and you literally have to reinvent the wheel for each case.

I used to think that when one got to the bottom of ones own barrel, having found ones core remedies, then the barrel would miraculously disappear and one would turn into light, but this just did not happen. What I now believe is that we are the bottom of the barrel and it is held together with five or six remedy states that represent the core of your true nature, and one can no more go beyond these than a cat can stop itself hunting birds.

The trick is to tag and recognize these individual states and then have the appropriate remedies on hand to dose them away till they become so mild that it is no more than a cloud in the sky. This is the ideal and it is definitely achievable, it is just a question of finding a homoeopath insightful enough to see the full potential of Homoeopathy, and to dig deep enough into ones superstructure to spot the struts that prop up the whole building.

Once this is done one can sit back and happily dose away any residual ease-breaking states, realising them to be just temporary fluctuations in form. They only have meaning if we attach to and follow them. By identifying with them they become real and start to hurt. Early warning is definitely the way through because if you can spot the baby crocodile you can defang or kill it, but if you leave it there it will grow into a critter that will want you on its plate sooner or later.

I have no intention of ending up as croc food and neither should you. There are ways and means to forestall the meal and the warrior is always proactive. You dive into the water and start the hellswim for the Island of Jewels before you get pushed in. This way you have some momentum to carry you through, and you might at least evade some of the crocodiles en route.

The Armies of Ignorance arrayed against you are legion, and the sooner you begin the strategic advance and start taking down their forces, the better. The warrior's only true battle is the battle within and it is a fight that will require all of your resources and courage. Once on the other side every scar becomes a badge of honour to be proudly displayed to the other denizens of the Island.

This is why I now generally confine my actions to the Buddha Brats as they are mostly across the river already, having jumped in out of foolishness or desperation. At least they are trying for the ultimate goal. My narrow-focus policy is not due to selfishness but to pragmatism.

Working on people with no potential, commitment and guts is quite literally a waste of everyone's time and not something I indulge in. My previous all-comers policy of engaging anyone who presented in front of me is now a thing of the past, although I am always open for viable new candidates, if they meet the criteria.

One of my patterns was *Lyssinum* which is a remedy made from the saliva of a rabid dog. It has the feeling of being tormented by someone you are dependent on. My father would keep taunting me on my spiritual and metaphysical beliefs until I would fly into a rage, at which point he would stop. It was a perfect response to a situation and was designed to maintain my integrity and sense of self-worth and it worked, he generally backed down. Of course this made for messy dinners because he would not stop until I reacted.

This all changed when I found the remedy and dosed myself with it. After that he could taunt me on my beliefs as long as he liked and it was like water off a duck's back, I just wouldn't respond. The pattern of snapping at a tormentor had been broken - high praises for the saliva of the rabid dog. It had been useful when I was a teenager but later on as an adult it was more of a burden, because I would automatically go into this state, since I had done it so often that it had in fact become a hardwired response. But what is hardwired can be un-hardwired, and this is exactly what I did. After this he grew bored of trying to torment someone who was not responding and stopped.

One of my major remedies is Diamond or *Adamas* in Latin, which is made from carbon and homoeopathically has a lot to do with the father. If I had not had such a problematic relationship with my father as a child I would probably not have gone into the Diamond state as compensation to deal with it. I probably would not have left my fairly comfortable home so early and gone off exploring the world.

Diamond has periods of incredible lucidity and clarity with a sharp cutting intellect, alternating with states of extreme depression and fogginess. I am not that susceptible to the downside of this remedy any more but I used to be, and it gets very frustrating to fall so low when one has risen so high. Diamond also has lethargy in the morning, a state I have always been prone to, to the extent that I swore as a child that I would never have a job that required me to wake early.

Even my early attraction to speed as the drug embodiment of clarity makes perfect sense viewed in this light. Like after all seeks like in all formats. Diamond even has dreams of friends betraying him, something I manifested to perfection in real life with Asher and to a lesser extent Jona, a tale I will tell later.

Homeopathic diamond even has the interesting delusion that

it is a Tibetan deity, a fact I have derived a lot of amusement from. Homoeopathy leaves nothing out, tells you the colour of the underwear you are going to wear next week, feeds the cat, takes out the garbage, and even makes you tea in the morning.

Corvus Corax, which is made from the raven, desires cheese and salty things and gets greasy skin. When I find myself living on only cheese and olives and my skin starts getting greasy I just pop a dose of Raven and I return to a more normal diet and the skin miraculously dries up, sometimes within minutes. It also cures self-consciousness, something that plagued me as a child – that horrible feeling of being conscious of a self separate from everything. Anyone who says that Homoeopathy is slow obviously hasn't had a correctly indicated remedy because when you find said remedy it works far speedier than any Allopathic drug, often alleviating mental symptoms within minutes.

Another remedy that seems to keep recurring in me is Palladium which has the feeling of keeping up brightly in company and afterwards being completely exhausted, and when I take a dose of this it bounces me back for another twelve hour talking session.

China, made from the bark of the *Cinchona* tree from which quinine is derived is also one of my core remedies. The theme of this remedy is about having obstacles thrown in ones path just before you are about to bring something to fruition, somehow there is always a spanner in the works. Everyone at some stage experiences this and once you have taken the remedy everything just seems to work smoother. The car does not break down on the way to the important interview, the geyser doesn't burst in midwinter, and everything runs as it should, without hiccups. It is useful in treating malaria which has periods of being fine alternating with periods of intense fever, striking you down when you least need or expect it.

The snakes are another group of remedies that have benefited me immensely. *Crotalus Horridus* (rattlesnake) with its aversion to family members and difficulty swallowing solid things is typical of some of my behaviour. I even wash my cheese down with olive oil straight from the bottle, because things never seem to be juicy enough to get down my throat with ease. The rattlesnake is also the most social of all the snakes and threatens to strike before it actually does – something that has always seemed only fair to me.

Lachesis (the bushmaster) is a South American snake that does me a lot of good. It has great loquacity, often finishing peoples sentences, which is a habit I am always trying to break in myself. It 'desires solitude to indulge its fancy', which is when I go to ground and ignore the world. It is a strongly left-sided remedy with all its organs on the left hand side and most of my ailments seem to occur on the left, even injuries.

The last few snakes that benefit me are *Naja* (the Indian cobra) and *Elaps Corallinus* (the coral snake). Naja feels obligated to help people who have treated you badly, when really you just want to cut them off or punish them. After taking it I felt quite fine not treating people who had injured or abused my trust. The coral snake has a playful attitude with a desire for travel, is often multi-talented, but with an unintentional haughtiness which can alienate others.

Each of these remedies represent an aspect of my psyche, one could say one's initial blueprint that one was stamped out of initially, and to which one inevitably returns at times of stress. Having dosed the crap out of myself with all of these remedies I find myself sometimes still returning to these different states although they do not last long and are easily liberated with just a single dose of the remedy. I am bit like Obelix and the magic potion cauldron when it comes to remedies now, having thoroughly immersed myself in them. There is not that much left to dose away anymore, but reality continues to manifest new things nonetheless, and it is hard to get around your blueprint.

Last but not the least of my remedies is *Falco Peregrinus* and to understand this remedy the falcon's early training has to be borne in mind. The young falcon is kept hooded and half-starved and then let out on a leash to hunt, but never quite far enough away to escape. When I was born my legs were curved, in order to ride the Apocalypse of course, and had to be put in braces to straighten the bones. I was literally starved of my freedom to crawl around and allowed out on short forays only, exactly like the falcon.

The falcon prefers hunting exotic birds over normal ones and as a child my father gave me a pellet gun which I used to hunt birds, taking great pleasure in bringing down the most exotic birds I could find. It is also the fastest bird and I have always felt that if I could move fast enough I could stay ahead of the storm that was about to break, and is probably why I enjoyed speed so much because it gave me the sense of being fast enough to never get trapped. Despite this the falcon always maintains a state of persecution in its psyche from being drafted into human service to hunt but always forced to come back. Sometimes it breaks free and escapes which is precisely what I did but some patterns run very deep in the unconscious psyche, which is why I occasionally still have to battle my tendency to flee when I feel particularly restricted.

The remedy also has a fascination with spirals, spiralling up to gain height before it plunges down at high speed for the kill. The spiral has always been one of the motifs that run through many aspects of my reality. It forms one of my models of how we spiral inwards, clearing old patterning as we go, getting smaller and smaller until we hit the center, at which point all bets are off, multi-pass, Body of Light. Another aspect of the spiral is that certain remedies form the base and structure of the spiral which keeps perpetuating throughout our energetic bodies and we need to revisit them a few times before they are completely cleared. The final incarnation of the spiral in my reality is the feeling that time is spiralling inwards, speeding up as reality goes down the drain in order to be reconstructed on the other side. This ties in with the Vedic view of the Kali Yuga (Age of Destruction) coming to an end in order for a new 'yuga' or age, to be born from its ashes. Yeats' poem THE SECOND COMING goes:

Turning and turning in the widening gyre
The falcon cannot hear the falconer;
Things fall apart; the centre cannot hold;
Mere anarchy is loosed upon the world,
The blood-dimmed tide is loosed, and everywhere
the ceremony of innocence is drowned;
Surely some revelation is at hand;
Surely the second coming is at hand.

There is more but it encapsulates the sense of breaking free from the states, and people, that bind us into being less than we are, denying us our true inheritance as limitless beings.

Certain things one cannot, nor would one want to, change about oneself but the excessive behaviours which bind or incapacitate us can be removed by the correctly indicated remedy.

If your visions of what you want to be do not tie up with what is around you then the only thing to do is to sacrifice reality. There is really no choice, and even if you become an outcast at least you have remained true to yourself.

There will always be those that love you for it and that alone makes it all worthwhile.

TEN

Baby Buddha Syndrome

The path does not end with waking up.
It is just the beginning, so if you
don't have the drive to fuel your
own liberation, don't
even bother.

They say that the road to hell is paved with good intentions, and one of the pitfalls on the road to enlightenment is the Baby Buddha Syndrome.

I have seen this happen to people as they woke up to the Natural State, finally existing in the moment, only for the excitement to abate and to find themselves pretty much back where they started.

I would watch them run around sprouting off about the joys of enlightenment, not realizing that without consolidating the state with concrete teachings and practises they would quickly slip back into the Illusion of Duality. Worst of all, is that they would be oblivious to anything you say because they were running so high on their own supply that they did not bother to find out about fuelling stations down the road.

The smart ones listened to my injunctions and held onto the Teachings. That's why few of them are still in the Natural State, but the willful ones just sped off in the first direction, only to find themselves running out of steam, and the only thing left of their great enlightenment is but a bittersweet memory of what it tasted like.

You can only help people to cross over to the Island of Jewels, which is their Natural State, but you cannot hold them there if they do not make their own attempts to stay there. Enlightenment is not a singular event but a process of increasing awareness and requires total commitment. There is very little you can do to stop people from exiting the Island of Jewels and returning to the mud flats and the suffering of Samsara (conditioned existence) on the other side.

If you don't have the drive to fuel your own liberation, don't even bother because the sacrifices are simply too intense. However, if you have the drive go for it, reality will support you and a way through will be found, it is worth every minute of pain which just becomes a memory thereafter.

The further I went down the road, the more I came to realize that certain people were worthy vessels for the Teachings while others simply were not. They just did not have the heart that it took to lay everything on the line, no matter how gentle I made the process, and I pride myself on my gentleness, having suffered enough myself.

When I first began I would spread the Teachings to all and sundry, defragging their old patterns as an expression of my essential nature, exercising my compassion and honing my skills. But after dealing with certain weak people, I realized that it was actually doing them a disservice by helping them in this way, as they did not really proceed deeply with it. Even though it honed my skills, it made me realize how important the Buddhist concepts of *"appropriate student, teachings and timing"* in fact were.

Certain tools should not be allowed into the hands of the uninitiated but then I have always had a strong educational policy of showing people how to do it themselves. This said, it is generally better for them to learn to walk before they try flying but there is just not enough time to devote to everyone. I encourage people to get acquainted with the tools and run their processes themselves, and if they listen, there are generally no problems. So we learn, so we grow, and if people are not willing to risk something they really don't have a hope anyway.

There is nothing I can do for people if they don't want to

travel the path in the first place. It takes a lot out of me, requiring plenty of concentration and can be very time consuming, all of which I am willing to engage if they are, but the dilettantes should just stay in their shadow palaces. I no longer have anything to do with these types of people anymore. Live and learn, onwards and upwards. The Discriminating Wisdom not to throw pearls before swine was my lesson and I see the perfection in it, not one morsel of reality out of place.

You can only drag someone so far if they are not already swimming. To unpack all someone's stuff, if they have not done a lot of it themselves, almost always backfires due to their lack of commitment. If they do not meet you halfway to the Island of Jewels you cannot drag them the distance, and lagging around in the waters in between can only be dangerous.

I found that as I tightened up my criteria regarding who was really appropriate, more appropriate people started showing up. Most of the people I work with now have done a lot of the work already themselves, with yoga, meditation, drugs, or psychosis, whatever their chosen sadhana is. From my experience if one in a million people actually get Dzogchen and run with it to its completion, I will be more than amply rewarded.

Many people hit the Natural State when they are doing what they love, in moments of divine inspiration, on drugs or in extreme or life-threatening circumstances, but one needs to stay there and keep staying there till it sticks and becomes the default. Once we have been there we can always get back there, eventually. After how long and how many bouts with the Demon of Despair only we can choose, and this is an adversary that will win unless we slay it first.

I have a .45 silver bullet with its name on, and when this particular beastie comes knocking at my door I do not ask questions, I just shoot it on sight. It is never welcome in my house, especially if I have opened the door to it myself. One does not negotiate with terrorists and this is one of the worst that exists. I don't care if Jesus is descending in a cloud of sparkling light or if the Apostles are here to anoint me with rare Kashmiri saffron, you can't come into my house and spread your dissent – door closed, end of story.

It always starts small as a little bit of doubt and quickly builds if it is not nipped in the bud, and from a temporary doubt you are suddenly looking down the barrel of your own .357.

Keep killing Doubt until it stays dead and as you deepen into the natural state of the mind, which is ease and perfection, you will see that it is truly the default setting for reality and anything else is just the play of Mara (the illusion), designed to distract you on the path to the Body of Light.

The Baby Buddhas still have a lot of this to experience because the path does not end with waking up. It is just the beginning and then you have to deal with all your accumulated patterning, which will be painful, any way you slice it. Certain illusions are glued to your heart and ripping them out will make you bleed, there is no way around it.

As you start clearing out your old programming, old karmic memory comes flooding back and there are techniques for holding your space when it hits you. It is very tricky because it comes without warning and it is totally personal, but someone who has been down a similar road is definitely worth listening to. Many of the potholes that they had to deal with might be in your path too. Everyone needs support and direction on a path of many roads travelling to an inconceivable place, and this is why some guidance is useful. We have many teachers, all *aspects of self* of course, but a wise man listens to the mistakes and successes of others and modifies their behaviour accordingly.

Everyone's path is different but there are certain junctures along the way that everyone shares, regardless of what your particular belief systems are. These benchmark events and landmarks along the road are definitely worth paying attention to. If you are on the road to enlightenment you will always – be faced with your attachments, find yourself in a situation where you struggle to hold onto you clarity, and most definitely will at some stage have to battle the Demons of Doubt and Despair.

I watched the Lilys and Tom's of the world prancing around in the flush of initial enlightenment, confident that they had arrived and would never leave. Sadly this is not the case because the Armies of Mara are still lined up in battalions, waiting to test your resolve and commitment to your own state.

As I have said many times before, it is not the getting there but the staying there, that is important. To stay there you have to want it with every ounce of your being as you watch the Six Realms begin their assault on your psyche. The Illusion doesn't like it when you escape and it has many tantalizing and horrifying tentacles to draw you back with.

It is imperative that you draw on all your residual practises and skills to defend yourself at this time. You might even survive a few small skirmishes at first without many solid practices, but sooner or later the big guns will come out, and everything you cherish will be used against you. It is one thing to learn to eat a meal you don't like with equanimity, but it is quite another having someone you love torn from you.

You use whatever you have to build up your own sense of self-worth and strength. Whether your practices are sitting meditation, yoga, chopping wood, swimming, singing or listening to your favourite music doesn't matter – as long as you can use these techniques to drag yourself out of the pit before it devours you. When the bombs are falling it is only important that you survive, worry about the reconstruction on the other side when you get there.

The problem is that with most people there is just so much that needs to be done and most of them have barely started. Some people have a whole lot of mental obstacles or emotional blocks preloaded from previous lives or even this life. In contrast others have, for the most part, managed to free themselves from the traps of their conditioned identities. This can sway the swim either way but since it is not quantifiable any more than is luck, you just have to wing it and hope that you make it through.

It is beneficial to begin the process or continue it as speedily as possible as there literally is not a moment to lose. When I look at all the defragging I have had to do on my own head to get to this point, it can be a rather long process. Of course this does not take into consideration the person's position in reality and their relative advancement on the path, which is largely inconceivable except sometimes to themselves.

Everyone knows deep down where they are sitting in this particular equation and whether they have what it takes to begin and complete the journey, this is just my story. Enlightenment is clearly not for everyone, at least in this life, and that is fine too as you can't turn a kitchen knife into a Katana folded a hundred times. On the other hand though, you can sharpen the kitchen knife to a point where it starts slicing through *the matrix of illusions,* and begin to unbind yourself from the things that hold you in form.

Besides the obvious dangers of the complete upheaval of your life as you know it, the road to Enlightenment comes with a warning: *"Better not to start, once you start better not to stop".* One can never be completely prepared for what awaits, hence why a good dose of bravery, insanity, or desperation is useful. There have been many cases of people who at some stage in their lives have a glimpse of the Island of Jewels only to return to the shores of Samsara, damned to always remember the taste of nectar while having to feed on frozen pizza.

Despair of ever reaching the state, or of returning to it, is a demon that we all have to face as it taunts us with glimpses and then pulls it away. I went through that myself out of loneliness, for about 2 years like a zombie, mechanically carrying out the vagaries of reality, barely feeling alive. I abandoned all hope of ever getting back there, and resigned myself to chopping off residual bits of homoeopathic programming from my psyche as my only available means, until I might, if ever, taste the nectar again.

I eventually returned to the state, unconsciously driven to it anyway. You never really lose it, but it can be so far away that it can seem to be gone forever. A lot of people reach the State of Enlightenment at least once in their lives, but they do not stay there due to a lack of understanding or good teachings. In my case, it was out of loneliness at not being able to speak to anyone on the same level. You can only run the one-man-show for so long before you wonder why you are even doing it in the first place.

With company though, one will play forever. This is the value of Sangha or *"community of enlightened beings"*, as it allows you to communicate your state to others that know it as well. You get to share experiences which reinforce your own understanding and deepen the colours of it. It was my total pleasure to build a Sangha, realizing that I did not need it but liked it, and that made it worthwhile. Having faced the Demon of Loneliness before and conquered it, I was free to have or not have fellow Buddha Brats around me.

I love entertaining and being entertained, so in my opinion the bigger the party the better. The only problem is that there are very few people one can really party with once you have crossed the threshold into luminous awareness. On the other hand it just takes a handful to have a great party and it is handful more than the first time I hit the Natural State, it seems like a sea in comparison.

Everyone will have to deal with the Baby Buddha Syndrome when they first reach the Natural State. It is largely an ecstatic phase full of visions, realisations, inspiration and joy, but there are a range of stoves and toasters that can scorch you if don't watch where you're going. On the other hand with a pure heart and the will to drive through, there is little that can deter you for long. If you have been anywhere once it is a lot easier to get back there because you know what it looks and tastes like, and to return is just a question of dredging up that memory back into consciousness. This is why Dzogchen talks about *"direct introduction"* to the state in the first place, because if someone can give you a taste of your own Natural State, it is a beacon that one can pin things on in order to get back there.

Traditionally the process of enlightenment was done by yogis in the mountains, away from friends and family because the resulting disturbances to your psyche can be quite deranging to the people around you. Especially if they want you to keep playing the everyday games of reality, it becomes quite hard to break down the ego.

In Dzogchen there is no need to change anything though so one can do it from the comfort of your own home if that's what you want. You should just get good at hiding your inner processes because people might think that you are mad, and for a while you will be, until the new improved super-deluxe special matrix reforms.

Everyone knows suffering but there is a way out. I don't really suffer anymore. If I do, I realize that I am just indulging in the Illusion as real, and I get out of it as quickly as possible. It is a pit full of crocodiles. Basically if my easo-meter goes into the red, I pull out all the plugs and sort it out. *The Natural State is ease,* and if I am struggling or suffering I am no longer in the Natural State, and it is wrong. No ifs, no buts. Ask no questions. Shoot the crocodiles on sight, they are not to be played with and do not have your best interests at heart, ever. Following your ease goes a long way to liberation. One sees people who follow this principle instinctively and they are often remarkably clear, even without access to good teachings on the Nature of the Mind.

Of course those of us who apply this are often perceived of as selfish, but then the actions of Buddhas are inconceivable and therefore beyond rebuke.

All is unveiled for your entertainment – you just have to be willing to pay the price of the 'self' at the door, a price a lot of people are unwilling to pay. The door is open to everyone and the party has already started, and yes we do have dancing girls, and the finest French wines and cheeses, so come on in.

This is of course why I love Dzogchen as much as any woman I have ever loved, as much as life itself. She is a demanding mistress in terms of sacrifice but she gives you the world in return, which seems more than fair to me. She also doesn't get pissed off or jealous if you go out with your friends and come home drunk late at night. And the cherry on the top is that at the end of the ride you get to dissolve into light.

I have always been a sucker for sexy syntax, and Dzogchen is the rock star, supermodel, and movie star of all philosophies and teachings on the Nature of the Mind.

ELEVEN

Warrior Born

*If you start playing into
and with Duality, it will definitely
play with you.*

If we fail to take the exit from the highway of Duality, there is a whole load of pain just waiting to come down the chute at us. On the other hand, if you are perched on the springboard waiting to dive in, I strongly suggest that you take the plunge.

In the words of one of my more vicious ex-girlfriends *"he who hesitates, masturbates"*.

Of course one can never completely predict the outcome of ones actions but then this is the essence of Crazy Wisdom – doing it anyway and trusting that it will all be fine. If you take the wrong turn or when it feels wrong, you often just have to retrace your steps a bit. There is never really any permanent harm done and you just learn where not to go. The closest word the Tibetans have for guilt is 'something that could have been done better'.

What I have found is that one recovers from painful experiences remarkably quickly, as reality continues to manifest nevertheless, and new entertainment or reasons to continue are always around the corner – nature abhors a vacuum.

When you buy into Duality the body starts throwing you warning signs because we are just not designed to function that way, trapped in a single physical form or mental construct. There are signposts to direct us in the right direction, and if we heed them, we don't have to wait until the melanoma reaches the brain, when it is often too late.

I first heard about Thor from one of my students who brought his story as part of a case study, and it was quite a story. A lot of his problems stemmed from indulging in magic, and he believed when I met him that he was possessed by Crowley. He believed he was to blame for all the misery in the world, even for the spots on the sun. Having bought into the dualities of good and evil, 'self' and 'other' and believing it to be real, he came to the conclusion that everything was his fault, and became caught up in a vicious psychosis of his own creation.

The Buddhists consider the mind to be the Wish Fulfilling Gem, but what they often omit is that it will just as easily bring fears into reality as wishes. They talk about a channel that runs from the heart and exits through the eyes, so the movie plays out from within you, according to your moods. There is no external reality to perceive and instead, one projects reality onto the perpetually changing screen of space. This impersonal fluid matrix that we perceive of as reality is called *Dakini* (sky dancer) by the higher Buddhist schools. Dakini reflects the *illusion of duality* in order to project *the play of life* back to us. This means that whatever the Wish Fulfilling Gem generates gets played out through Dakini, to create the dense array of phenomenal existence.

The screen and you are one and hence the definition of the Self as *"empty like space but aware and manifesting ceaselessly"*. One is of course never supposed to take this illusion or dance too seriously because it is always just the play of light, sound, and sensation which changes from moment to moment. There is in fact nothing to hold on to, and when we get caught up in emotional responses and deviate from the state of Empty Awareness, we have succumbed to Mara.

Mara represents that part of ourselves that wrongly perceives a duality between 'self' and everything else, and in the guise of something beautiful or terrifying will lure or trap us into bondage. Therefore, if the Wish fulfilling Gem is generating fear, Dakini will reflect those very fears. If we neglect to see these appearances as just an empty, changing light show, it changes into the face of Mara and binds us into Conditioned Behaviour which results in fixed response patterns.

In a deranged mix of compassion, invulnerability, and curiosity Thor had invoked all the demons plaguing the world to take into himself, and purify for the rest of humanity. This is why Tantra is so carefully protected and has so many safeguards because unless you see *everything as self,* and more importantly *self as empty,* you risk becoming caught in a powerful archetype which ends up possessing you.

Of course any concept of gods or devils has to go, unless one sees it as the impersonal Nature of Reality which one is a part of, and which is in fact your very Self, and essentially empty. If you can suitably overcome the *Demon of the Illusion of 'self',* you get to ride the whirlwind because then whatever comes up into your mind will be seen as an impersonal projection of light and sound. As a result you will not be bound by it, as it attempts to drag you down. If you are able to sit and watch them as *aspects of mind,* you stand a chance at Liberation.

Thor would not have been a Buddha Brat if he had not done what he did though, because it is the very gall of doing such things that distinguishes us in the first place. He is a complex character and he had managed to well and truly fuck himself up. His natural invulnerability allowed him to relentlessly punish himself without backing down. Everyone has their Achilles heel and his was his mind, which took me a while to unscramble, but I love a challenge and he was definitely worth it. I threw my Homoeopathic wall at him, a good 30 remedies in different combinations and in rapid succession. Now he is a happy and healthy functioning creature once again and I consider him one of my finest works.

The remedy that helped unscramble his head best of all was *Taxus Bacata,* the Yew tree, one of the holy trees of the druids. The core behind Taxus is the feeling of being thrown out of heaven through no fault of your own, because of a contract one had signed without realizing the implications. One then rages against heaven at the injustice.

Some time later when he started renting a room from me, he asked me once why I had allowed a psychotic schizophrenic to come live with me. I think I just smiled. Certain manifestations are simply too beautiful to waste or ignore. To live ones dreams and heroic fantasies is part of the enlightenment methodology, and a lot of our inspiration, joy, and power lie there. One cannot but respect someone who completely runs with their own created world, and the beauty is that Dakini tends to meet them half way anyway, rewarding them by fulfilling their dreams.

Thor is a very curious creature with deep insights into reality and an immense sensitivity, contrasted with bouts of indulgent drunkenness. He is an embodiment of the archetype of Thor though, so what can you expect. He spends a lot of time exploring strange and unusual phenomena which he then brings back to share with me. He is also completely fearless which is definitely a trait I appreciate, and essential when exploring the backwaters of the mind. He can pick up a remedy and tell me what it feels like, describing it in terms of mood and sensation. This receptivity is something that few other people have and his taste on it is unique and very useful to me. I have a different sense of the remedies, more a vibrational sense of what it does to the molecules in my body.

Certain shared experiences bind you to people forever and the dosing of the water supply especially, was one of those for me. He had shown me where the central water supply was and helped me to make the final dose that hit the water. It was a very bonding experience in itself, but more so when he started coming apart at the seams at the same time as me. It warms my heart because even though I never doubted it, it is encouraging to have solid confirmation that the whole thing had not just been a fabrication of my mind. There is always that little voice in the background telling you that maybe you just made the whole thing up.

Whether it is mushroom picking, drugging, or partying, we

share many similar interests from music to comics, and it is always good to have a companion at arms around when I need one. Added to this is the fact that he is a Fire Dragon, and I am an Earth Monkey. Monkey-Dragon interaction is 10 out of 10 and Fire feeds Earth so there was no way we could not be fabulous friends. We have a lot of fun all in all and that tends to get one through the bad times. No one has time to dwell on the negatives of existence, after all the party must go on.

Thor also carried the Norse, the Chinese, and the magical traditions in his DNA which drew him to things that I connected with as well, and this was possibly also why we got on so well, so many common interests. Thor had a vision once of everything that was not beautiful enough turning into ash – skyscrapers, oil-rigs, warehouses, and even the majority of people simply dissolving. You have to love the Dragon for his vision, and this mix of sensitivity and derangement is what characterizes most of the Buddha Brats.

On the whole it has been a very beneficial interaction so far and he has been living with me now for five years. We have clocked up at least 5000 chess games in this time and he is like the younger brother I never had. Not that I was looking for one, but it came anyway.

We even had a mutual eating pact, that whoever died first would be eaten by the other one as a sign of respect. Why waste good meat, surely if you respected someone enough you should have the balls to eat them if they die. I envisaged sautéing his brain and spinal cord in olive oil, garlic, black pepper, cream, and some forest mushrooms, washed down with a good Cabernet Sauvignon. When I told a friend about our pact she joked and said that she saw Thor with a serviette tucked around his neck, a large knife and fork, and a quart of beer, tucking into my roast leg doing his best to finish off as much of the meat as possible.

He once appeared with a fresh porcupine roadkill which we proceeded to skin, cut up, and then cook in a pot with some red wine and potatoes, to the horror of some of our more sensitive friends. He has a knack for blending the brutal and the beautiful and it is this strange mix of savagery and sensitivity that makes him an interesting character to go on adventures with.

This is not to say that he does not piss the hell out of me at times, especially when drunk. I bail him out of shit on a regular basis and he seems hardwired to attract trouble, but then what are friends for if not to bail you out when the shit hits the fan...

Thor told me once he had vision of coming back to this planet to get more wine and somehow getting stuck here as a result. That pretty much sums him up. *"En Vino Veritas"* is Latin for 'in wine, truth' and alcohol certainly tends to bring out the best and worst in people, showing who they really are. Sometimes one doesn't necessarily need or want to see the whole truth though and certain pretty illusions are often better than seeing the demons that lurk in people's psyche. Give me good illusion over a crap reality any day.

Thor once chased down some guy who tried to break into the house, caught him, cut his clothes off and then burnt them, which was when I arrived to complete the beating. Luc just watched somewhat bemused and a little appalled by the whole thing. When I asked Thor why he stripped him naked and burnt his clothes, he said that it was not that easy to sneak off through town if one was naked and bleeding – I couldn't argue with that.

It was a perfect example of Zerbu, nailing down aberrant aspects in ones reality, thereby stopping them from manifesting in general. One should apply this same principle to the aberrant aspects of ones own mind, go in with a flamethrower and burn it all out. You cannot destroy something that is eternal and if you can, it probably was not meant to be there in the first place and best that it be destroyed.

He cut his finger in the process of cutting the guy's clothes off so we ended up at the hospital for stitches later that night, all in a days work with Thor. He regularly returned from a weekend with some new injury or tale of being maced, locked up, electrocuted, burnt, bashed, cut, sprained, you name it he did it, on a regular basis. He had a few bad ideas running around in his head, but this was mainly due to irritation at his personal circumstances. Once in a fit of frustration at having to photograph frozen chickens at work, while trying to court a supermodel, he stabbed himself in the leg. He certainly challenged the truism that only he could destroy himself.

I think there is some self-destructive hardwire in his head that just refuses to go a week without indulging itself, but then that's the fibre from which he is carved. He would have been perfect on the battlefield swinging his battleaxe, happy as can be. However at times we find ourselves in paradigms that seem at odds with our natures and the trick is to be ourselves without damaging ourselves, or others, in the process. 'Respect the mood' is the Buddha Brat ethos, and when he finally gets tired of trying to destroy himself he will probably stop.

When Thor was still in his psychotic state he once said that I had gotten the right program while he had somehow managed to get the wrong one. What he failed to realize was that I had paid in blood, sweat, and tears to find Dzogchen and Homoeopathy, and only found it after hunting through myriads of imperfect programs.

I often feel like a sculptor, bringing out people's Natural State by chipping away the rough edges, smoothing the gashes and bringing them back to their true form. I do this not only as an exercise of my skill but because it brings me great pleasure. It is very satisfying to see someone shine as they were meant to, and not lie all broken and cracked by the side of the road.

Anything you can walk away from or get a good story out of is worth something in the long succession of moments that make up ones life. All one often needs is an introduction to the state of Emptiness and the realisation that everything is just a Play of your Mind.

My first taste of Emptiness happened in Taiwan long before I found the Teachings or Homoeopathy. I had smuggled marijuana into Taiwan to swap for speed, and in the process had most of it stolen from me by someone I considered a friend, though there was no way I could prove it. With my money gone I lived on practically nothing but speed, which amongst my group of friends at the time we were never short of. I spent the next seven weeks in an increasingly warped and hostile environment. I must have slept four times over this period, and eaten maybe six, putting me in a thoroughly deranged state.

To envision the level of sensory extreme experienced, you have to understand that on about the second day of not sleeping you begin to trawl through your subconscious. Basically you start dreaming while you are awake. All of your subconscious and unconscious patterns start rising to the surface for observation – all the fears, paranoia, doubts, guilt, and resentments, you name it, bargain basement sale, everything comes out to play. I started looking progressively wilder and thinner with the people around me giving me increasingly strange and suspicious looks. The situation was only further exacerbated by my increased paranoia at my so-called friend's betrayal which resulted in even more erratic behaviour on my part.

One night towards the end I went with a friend to a sauna to chill out for a while and he just suddenly disappeared. In my already paranoid state I believed that he had sold me out, so I climbed up onto the roof of the building and hallucinated all night as Interpol agents, Chinese gangsters, and South African mercenaries complete with grenades and mortars conspired to remove me from the rooftop. All my worst fears played out in one night.

When I was on the rooftop I was firmly convinced that the South African mercenaries were coming up the stairs to get me, and I seriously considered jumping off the roof as a last resort, believing that I would be resurrected in the body of a random Chinese person passing by. It was a time of strong and powerful delusions – the shattering of ideals and the actualization of fears brought up and played out in form.

At the end of the night I was eventually enticed to come down from the rooftop because my mind concocted a scenario whereby Interpol realised I was actually a good guy who was just a bit down on his luck. All was forgiven and they were going to give me some speed to take home to celebrate the happy resolution of the day but when I got down to the street, there was of course no one there. When I walked back to my hotel room and turned on the TV to soothe my rather frazzled mind, every channel was speaking Afrikaans, my second language. At that point it all became too weird and I forced myself to sleep to reassemble my reality. The psychosis in

Taiwan so cleared my mind space that when I eventually returned to South Africa I went into a state of total ecstasy and all I wanted to do was heal people and share the bliss I was experiencing.

This was my first experience of the healing power of extreme emotion as a result of psychosis.

Sometimes the only way to rid ourselves of our attachments is to face it and have them all destroyed in a fit of grand psychosis. The lucky ones survive it, managing to clear large chunks of their neurotic behaviour in the process. This however, is not a thing that most people willingly jump into, in fact most run a mile to avoid it. There are of course the normal paths of meditation, yoga and tai chi, but in my experience nothing clears the archives faster and more thoroughly than a good meltdown. When all your major preconceptions are lying in ashes on the ground in front of you, there is little alternative but to reform, clearer and cleaner.

Since this is just the beginning of the path very few of the New-Agers stand a chance because they are generally the day trippers, just dipping their toes in the murky waters before withdrawing to consult their animal totems, or hold space in some corner.

Sheltered by his father from the brutalities of the world, the Buddha only became Enlightened once he left the comforts of the palace and saw the suffering caused by old age, disease, and death. This drove him to find a way to move beyond suffering and had he not experienced these things, he probably would have been just another ordinary prince until his death.

Take the cross you are bearing, hammer it into a boat, and sail across to the Island of Jewels. Be willing to put a bullet through the skull of Samsara, with a smile.

TWELVE

Breaking Through **Disease**

If we choose our suffering, we can also choose our freedom.

Garab Dorje said that if a thousand people ask, to tell them is not enough, yet if one person doesn't want to know and you tell them it is too much. I stick quite rigidly to this credo. I am not going door to door, trying to flog bibles after all.

Which came first, the chicken or the egg? Is it the mental state that creates the disease, or the disease that creates the mental state? I would argue that it is always the mental state that comes first, the mind being the finest and most sensitive instrument we have. Disturbances always manifest there first before moving down to plague various organs in the body. The search for viruses or bacteria to pin the blame on for a lot of these diseases is actually a red herring. Although they exist, it is the mental state which makes one susceptible to their influence and allows the infection to take root in the first place.

We have inherited mental patterns and emotional tendencies to go into certain disease states, even for those illnesses that are genetically inherited, and many of these can be dosed away if caught early enough. Even if all of the mental or behavioural patterning cannot be entirely eradicated, judicious dosing at the right time can certainly prevent one from actually manifesting the disease. The Delusion Chapter in Homoeopathy is huge. They are all erroneous views on reality, which after being maintained for a while become hardwired in reality and this sooner or later leads to disease.

Based on my experience with patients, my view is that the 'ego' is actually a collection of different homoeopathic states generated as response patterns to specific situations, which then solidifies into conditioned behaviour. We become so used to it that we start believing we are the beaten dog, the resentful child, the avenging angel or the hard done by punter. You start living these roles as if it were actually you, and not just a defensive strategy which you went into in order to survive a particular event. I see it as an *"assumed identity"* – something intrinsically insubstantial but becoming real because we buy into it. From a Dzogchen perspective it is just another face of Mara.

When exactly this so-called 'identity' assumes sentience and takes over the person depends on the individual, and is hard to predict. Some people manage to resist its call better than others, some have had fewer traumas, and some are just more sensitive and more likely to go into defensive states than others. How long is a piece of string? Well, you listen to the story, and you measure it.

Basically the average ego is made of a handful of core patterns precariously glued together, although people often later reinforce it with superglue. This piecemeal thing takes over the system and starts running the show as it sees fit. Its only imperative is to stay alive and reinforce itself. Sooner or later it has you chained up in a little corner of your mind, telling you that the whole thing is pointless and painful and you might as well kill yourself.

The problem is that it relies on previous experiences as reference points for behaviour in the future. This in turn is what binds us into form, deluding us that we don't have any other options, and no way of changing or altering our behaviour. One goes into these different defensive strategies consciously or unconsciously, in order to survive a cruel world. The catch is that the longer we stay in these states, the more we are tricked into thinking we are them. In truth they are just a hat or cloak we put on at that time in order to deal with a certain weather condition.

An example would be if you pass a dog every day for a few months and it bites or tries to bite you. When this happens your 'fight or flight' instincts kick in and you either run away or cower down to avoid being attacked, or alternatively you might get aggressive with the dog to chase it away. Both of these states are situational and appropriate for someone being attacked by a dog. If years later you still feel fear whenever you see a dog, or became aggressive to compensate for this, you are literally in a state of delusion because not every dog you encounter wants to attack you.

These response patterns, which you take on at a time of real threat, are never designed to be long term, but unless we disband them they become part of the *"I"*. *"I am a person who is afraid of dogs"* or *"I have to get aggressive to protect myself from dogs"*. If you take a whole life of response patterns like these, what eventually happens is that they stick together and this becomes ones idea of oneself. By believing that *"I am a person that does 'xyz' in 'pqr' scenarios"*, you define yourself as a fixed responsive entity and all spontaneity is lost. It is said that love is better but fear is stronger, and the ego thrives and feeds on fear, allowing it a good justification to continue being in control.

Certain defensive patterns like *"righteous indignation"* are very alluring and easy to become attached to. You are the good guy and reality has done you wrong, and you are rightfully entitled to take revenge on the perceived miscreant. This is a particularly hard pattern to shed because it feels good to be righteous. These patterns have names like *Staphysagria* and Nitric Acid. When you give people these remedies all of a sudden they stop playing this game and the gold-stitched straightjacket comes off. You begin to laugh again and just let stuff go, which before would have put you into apoplexies of indignation. I talk about this from experience. They were some of my states and as Homoeopathy is the book of karmic deletion and unbinding, old patterning can happily be dosed away.

If left untreated these patterns pile up. Your typical ego is made up of about 8 to 15 homoeopathic remedies, stuck together with chewing gum. Mine had more but then I am a complex character and it was part of my journey as a homoeopath to unveil and discover them for myself, so I could better understand how to benefit sentient beings.

If you can pull a strategic takedown of these states all at once or in quick succession you free up a lot of space which results in a tremendous burst of energy and freedom. If one were to view the mind as a computer, the average person would have Windows, Explorer, a game, Photoshop, a movie player, and a 3D animation package all open at once. Why then be so surprised when the computer pleads lack of memory when you want to send an email, or does it so slowly that it might as well not have done it at all.

What the remedies do is they close all these different programs down one by one, restoring them to their proper places as icons on the desktop, to be used individually at the appropriate time. If you consider in addition that most people have installed Windows 95, 98, 2000, and XP on top of each other, it is actually amazing that they can function at all. If you imagine that your mind is your house, it is like opening the front door and seeing garbage stuffed to the ceiling in every room. This garbage of old memory, old patterning, and old resentments, are stashed in the body until you release it with exercise, yoga, meditation, dance, or psychology, the list goes on. Alternatively you take the remedy and the garbage gets taken out for you effortlessly, which happens to be in line with the ethos of the Natural State of the Mind. This is why I consider Homoeopathy as the ultimate complimentary tool to Dzogchen.

I used to do strategic ego takedowns over three days, which involved lots of remedies and lavish doses of Dzogchen. I loved these events because it allowed me to take out my diamond sword and perform soft-sculpture on people's minds. It always left them infinitely lighter and much cleaner. If you can demolish most of people's patterning at once, the assumed identity is left with nothing to cling to, and starts disintegrating. It is at this point that the person realizes the true nature of their mind as an *"empty dance of pure pleasure"*.

The goal is to interrupt the continuity of the harmful patterns that people harbour about themselves. Continuity is the act of blending one moment into the next, based on ones assumptions about the nature of oneself and reality at large, so that it fits into a neat little picture that makes sense.

Mind-altering substances or extreme states like sleep deprivation can be very useful during processes like these. When in an altered state, one has less power to maintain the continuity of a largely false reality, as one watches oneself scrambling from one assemblage point to the next. At one stage, speed was one such a tool for me. I could run it hard and fast, keeping up my snappy Dzogchen monologue to entertain them for long enough to sweep the house clean before they even noticed. Only by the time they went home trying to reconstruct their former identities would they occasionally see me as a threat to their little world, which I was tirelessly trying to upgrade.

In some cases during this process their egos would become aware of me, perceiving me as an intruder, and after playing along for a while would try find any spanner to throw in the works. They would lose their remedies, suddenly need to attend to more pressing business, or lash out at me. This very rarely happened though. I am very gentle, very cunning, and very, very swift, but sometimes the monster sees me sweeping out the cellar and in a panic tries to stop the process. I find this unfortunate but understandable, and I maintain that it is only their inherent weakness of spirit at the time which stops them from overriding their conditioning, and allowing me to do my job properly.

When I did these combat cleansings of people's minds I was always amazed when people turned their back on the process to start piling up new junk once again. Some people just don't have the guts for Realisation at the end of the day. I do not blame people for this, I would be the first to espouse free will, but it does sadden me to realise that so much potential in people never gets actualized. That's humanity for you – so much potential but so much suffering.

What matters is the fact that everyone has the potential to get out. If we choose our suffering we can also choose our freedom. The ego is a curious beast, it will play along for a while believing that you are actually going to give it more strength. It thinks you are feeding the tick sucking on your skull, but when it realizes that you are actually plotting to rip it, out it goes ballistic.

The Homoeopathic Maxim for cure is *"rapid and gentle"* and fusing these two is what we strive for. With enlightenment there literally is no time to dally in the water as the crocodiles of ego are always attempting to hamper the process. Therefore rapidity is definitely more important than gentleness, for unless you get to the Island of Gems you are fucked anyway. I am always honing my tools in terms of elegantly removing the various ticks and leeches from people's psyches. It is instinctual in me to avoid needless suffering in dealing with people, I consider it sloppy and I abhor sloppiness.

I have always gone for rapidity on myself trusting that I can piece myself back together when it's over. Besides, nothing is truly breakable since our minds reform reality at every moment. As I get older I am definitely favouring gentleness though, it is just more elegant so when I work with other people I marry the two. Having suffered enough myself, I am committed to not subject others to unnecessary torment in the process. This is the core of Compassion – seeing the suffering of others as if it was ones own. Anyone who has suffered and sees someone else suffering will do whatever they can to help them through this process. Suffering sucks and there is no need for more brutality in the world. We are already traumatized enough as it is, just living in it.

THIRTEEN

The **Earth Church**

*For my part I am just playing out the role I was
born to, and those Buddha Brats who choose
to join me on this adventure
are as precious to me as my own,
rather battered, heart.*

When the inconceivable becomes the norm, you know you have
arrived.

Part of my commitment to Earth came from when I was studying
in Australia and met up with Eron Earth of the Earth Church. His
mission was to ensure that this planet did not get destroyed and he
goes way beyond the call of duty to do this.

His story began while he was playing pool as a student in some
bar when an elderly man came up to him and basically recited Eron's
entire life back to him. It was all stuff he never could have known,
even where and when he kissed his first girlfriend, names of his
parents, and things he had never told anyone. He claimed that he
and Eron had been passing the lineage baton to each other through
successive lifetimes. As the one got old he found and trained the
new one, passing on the teachings of the Earth Church between
them for centuries, if not millennia. This is very similar to the
Tibetan reincarnating master paradigm, and thus seemed more
than plausible to me.

They did this in order to ensure that a lot of the ancient earth magic was preserved. It included a whole battery of interesting techniques such as healing lodges, working with ley lines, and Trees of Connection. Eron was suffering from an enlarged heart at the time, totally appropriate for someone with more compassion than I had ever met.

His teacher basically made up what Eron referred to with fondness as, a 'homoeopathic bomb'. Eron claimed that he shat and puked for a week and at the end of that he was able to throw away all his allopathic medicines, requiring only the odd dose of cannabis to keep the heart in check. From this story I learned that it was in fact possible to mix multiple remedies in one bottle and clear lots of patterning all at once, monkey see monkey do. If someone else can do it or has done it, then it can be done.

As a result I have spent many years refining the technique of dosing people with multiple remedies at once. It is very contrary to the existing homoeopathic ethos of 'one remedy at a time'. The single remedy is a bit of a Holy Cow to the Institution, something that always strikes me as odd considering the revolutionary attitude of the founder Hahnemann.

I would counter in my defence that I am not only trying to cure disease. I am trying to purge all residual memory from the body, and if it took 40 years to build up it needs strong medicines dosed repeatedly to clear. I maintain that I actually get less aggravation when dosing with multiple remedies than I used to get as a young homoeopath dosing with single remedies. People get better much faster, although getting better is still just the tip of the iceberg in terms of the potential of Homoeopathy, which is really a tool for enlightenment, used for karma deletion.

All physical and emotional memory that gets stored in the body, whether it was from being beaten as a child or a prolonged state of unhappiness, can be flushed from the body using remedies. If we are ninety percent memory and we are reacting according to old residual defensive patterning then when we remove it we become a lot more free in our actions. We stop playing out old patterns and it opens up the space to play whatever we like.

I studied Homoeopathy at a college in Australia and I also enlisted the help of Hank, an elderly Dutch homoeopath, who came to live in the same house with Lana and me. I had met him at a festival and he immediately began upgrading my knowledge. He drilled me in old-school conservative Homoeopathy which counterbalanced nicely some of the more liberal techniques I was learning at my college. As a result I was way ahead of my classmates and they used to come to me for advice on remedies and even tuition.

It is said that the sons are greater than the fathers and although Hank would definitely upbraid me for my more liberal dosing regimen, it works. I am merely continuing the development of the science and its philosophy which has become a bit hide bound. Its true potential is not being exploited, except of course by me and Eron's teacher, but he has since died.

I once treated a white trash family in Australia as a favour to Eron. The father was an alcoholic ex-biker and the mother was a speed freak. They had their herd of wild brats rampaging around their council home, punching holes in the cardboard walls, and scrawling in crayon on every surface they could find. At one stage they had built a moat of old diapers one had to cross to enter the house. The father would drink until he passed out and the mother would fuck anyone she could find, the four kids probably all being from different fathers. Amidst the cursing, shrieking, pounding on the walls, and empty cigarette boxes, I took the whole family's cases.

The little daughter had such a strong craving for salt that she would steal into the kitchen and pour it directly from the salt seller into her mouth, until the mother caught her and beat her. The homoeopathic remedy she needed, *Natrum Muriatricum*, is made from salt, and it is typified by a strong craving for it. It is caused by ailments from anger, fright, grief, and worry, and no doubt she had mountains of all of these.

The English are very 'salt' as a remedy, literally being surrounded by it all the time. It is seen in the attitude of keeping up appearances of normality, not showing emotion, and having an aversion to being consoled. Once I gave her the homoeopathic salt she improved markedly and stopped raiding the salt seller. Sadly though, she probably regressed back to that state, due the fact that her environment was a breeding ground for misery.

The father had such bad allergies that he could not touch any plant matter without going into anaphylactic shock, requiring a shot of adrenalin. Such was his allergy to anything natural that he would pack dope into his pipe with tweezers. It all started for him after being stung by a bee when he was twelve and hence reacted with the same degree of intensity to anything associated with nature.

After I gave him the remedy made from bee venom, *Apis*, he proceeded to sweat for three days and when he finished he was cured, and even his vision improved. I was still a student in those days and had felt a large degree of trepidation on dosing him, a housewife going postal on you is one thing but an alcoholic trailer park biker was something entirely different. All was good in the land afterwards, thankfully, and I could do no wrong in the small town he lived in. He would not have been surprised if I had walked on water after that. If I ever needed convincing of the power and brilliance of Homoeopathy, the Divine Science, this was certainly it.

To return to Eron, he had the task of rewriting the BOOK OF RE-FLECTIONS which was their lineage text. As they passed the baton from the one to the other, master to student, they kept upgrading it with new tech. He introduced me to sweat lodges, took me cross country skiing, hiking down abandoned mines, rock climbing, anything that would get us closer to the earth. He once did a one month long vision quest, alone in the mountains without food, until he received a vision of his wife to be to whom he is now married.

We also smoked mandrake, *(Mandragora officinalis)* which he got from some witches in the area. Mandrake puts you into a fairly wild state of mind being something that warriors took before battle, putting them in a type of berserker space. It has increased mental activity, euphoria, and driving restlessness. It is a great painkiller and has been on the coat of arms of Anaesthesiologists for years. There are all sorts of strange and exotic mythologies associated with it. The story goes that it was originally created when hung men ejaculated at the point of death, and the mandrake sprung from their seed spilled upon the ground. It was supposed to kill you if you pulled the root out yourself so they tied dogs to the roots to pull it up for them.

Eron's teacher had a field where each of his students planted a Tree of Connection when they began their journey, and he could tell by watching the tree grow how the person was doing in their life. He would then medicate the tree homoeopathically and the person would get better. It ties in with the use of voodoo but in its cleaner form – no hexing of people, casting bones, or sticking pins into wax effigies. It was clean, very clean and pure, and quite simply just good earth magic.

There is a homoeopath in India who runs a full clinic from a distance using people's hair. He gets his patients to send their complaints by letter with a strand of their hair. After diagnosing the state he puts the remedy into a bottle containing their hair, and heals them that way. The parts contain the whole, holographic universes and all that new age and quantum physics parlance, but it works. The only thing that really holds water is the grinding mill of experience.

One of Eron's ideas to create food in the desert was to truck away all the green waste from markets, pile it about two feet thick on the ground, spray it with lime to deal with the acidity and then surround it with a moat. The moat was to keep fish in and also to prevent animals from getting to the crops. Then you just sit back on your island and wait while the tomatoes, potatoes and carrots sprout around you.

Eron made me Master of Homoeopathy for the Earth Church, a job that I take very seriously even though I am a total maverick, but that is my essential nature after all. I won the prize for Best Clinical Skills at my college, so I had the official approval from the establishment and a mandate from the earth itself to do whatever it took to heal the planet and remove disease. Not really necessary, I would have done it anyway but it is nevertheless nice to have stamps of approval from various lineages so you can go on your merry way and develop global healing techniques to your heart's content. Not that I am a 'save the dolphins' kind of guy, fuck the dolphins, they get far too much airtime in my opinion. Go to the root of the problem, fix the people and they will stop killing the dolphins, and even more importantly, the trees.

I continue to spread my particular brand of Homoeopathy to anyone who pays attention. Once again this is not for everyone as it requires a detailed knowledge of Homoeopathy and a fearlessness which most people aren't courageous enough to engage.

There is a lot more information that I never got from Eron but then it is all there if you go find him. He is one of the purest people I have ever met, yet a total renegade at heart – just my kind of friend. More important than anything though, he was a comrade and an equal. He was someone to share the joys and pains of The Path with, someone who understood. His brief was slightly different to mine but we all play our parts, the smart ones play it with a smile on their faces, and the others suffer by denying their real nature.

Eron held a clean but powerful energy, yet was very humble in his own way. The earth shapes you to its will and then breaks you apart to be shaped again, stronger and clearer. A Dzogchen saying *"be yourself completely"* encapsulates this, and if you express your unit potential then you are happy, and if you don't then you suffer. Certain paths are more extreme than others but there is no judgement either way. Don Juan says that all paths are meaningless so you might as well choose a path with heart because this is what nourishes you during those dark nights of the soul.

When you deny the mood of feeling you go down a dark hole very rapidly. If one just follows the mood of enjoyment, and conversely avoids the mood of non-enjoyment, there is nothing that can really touch you. You become one with the flow of reality, which is the State of Ease.

Ease is not laziness it is just doing what feels right, when it feels right, and not before. The other alternative is to do things that you don't feel like doing and then everything becomes an uphill battle. You engage what feels right and stop when it ceases to feel right, a lesson it took me a long time to learn.

Insist on following the mood of Ease and Perfection, nothing less. Lay down the Self on the steps at the door and enter the magical mystery tour.

Awareness first, last, and always, as you forge on toward your own Liberation.

FOURTEEN

Divine Science In Reflection

Without our binding illusions we are free
to resurrect in a purer, more
adamantine form.

To take the reflection of ourselves as *"The Path"* is *"The Means"*. If there is no self, then there clearly is no other since 'other' is just a projection through the eyes of the 'self'.

Having a correct Dakini View is of utmost importance and something that helps greatly on the path. Dakini who is the very Nature of Reality and that which reflects ourselves at all times, is perceived by the Buddhists to be feminine. No man was ever born except from woman. All foetuses start out XX and are then modified to XY if they are male, masculine being a modification of the feminine within the feminine.

The Teachings even say *"do not question the actions of women"* who are seen as the natural expressions of Dakini at large, just by virtue of the fact that they are women. This does not say that you should do whatever a woman says. Some women embody Dakini more than others but it is said that ones degree of Realization is indicated by the degree to which one sees Dakini in the actions of all women. This is a hard one for both men and women to swallow, men for obvious reasons (pride being foremost). For women it is even more complex because they have to see the perfection and infallibility in their own, as well as other women's actions. I have often seen men who simply love women deeply have fewer obstacles in their path than men who have a bad attitude toward women, even when they have more knowledge and information on The Path.

This is only one facet of the dance with Dakini but ones relationship to women is truly the fundamental basis for how one treats reality at large. I talk here of Dakini as something separate but she is not. She is me as I am her, and my dance for her is for my pleasure too because at the root we are One. In contrast to Dakini or *"sky dancer"* is the masculine *"sky flower"* or Daka, which is an Aspect of Her.

This is why a wrong view on the feminine is so damaging to people, male or female. They are essentially fighting against their very Self and that is a war that can never be won. Treat the feminine, which is everything, as the Nature of Reality itself – follow its directives and you cannot go too far wrong.

Dzogchen leaves nothing up to chance and all one really has to do is keep ones eyes and ears peeled, and recognize the messages that Dakini is delivering. Since everything is your own manifestation anyway, every bit of information that comes to you is designed for you and by you, to facilitate your own process of Liberation.

I saw this clearly driving through Johannesburg one night. In the early days, still believing that the radioactive remedies might do me some harm, I drove past a signboard which said "RADIOACTIVE SCARE". Once you realize that it is your own movie playing out for you, you can begin to navigate through it. The answers are everywhere, and the more you see the reflection as the totally personal mood of the moment, the more exciting and entertaining the movie becomes. Then every newspaper headline, song on the radio, or global event is there to inform you on the status quo of the moment to aid you in better navigating through reality.

The more aware you are of this, the more you can literally pluck signs straight out of thin air. It has been proven to me time and time again when taking people's cases. My patients often blurt out the name of the remedy that they need in the consultation without even realising it. I have had many of these seemingly arbitrary but totally succinct messages delivered to me by different Aspects of Reality

One such instance was a message left on my answering machine by a woman inquiring about goat's milk. How she got my number or came up with this request is hard to fathom. I phoned her back thinking that maybe she was looking for some Homoeopathic *Lac caprinum* (goat's milk) that I could sell her a bottle of, but she was looking for five litres of raw milk, which of course I did not have. Coincidentally one of the Buddha Brats was due to visit me that afternoon. Ming was born in the Chinese year of the Goat so, given the fact that such a strange request had come down the tube in my direction, it was clearly an indication to take Goat's Milk so naturally I gave her some. It suited her well, having lots to do with competition and who would come out on top in any power struggle, which is one of her control dramas.

This was by no means an isolated event. While busy searching for *Bitis Arietans* (Puffadder) for myself, a friend came to my house and told me how just a few days back she had almost stood on one while camping.

Nila, my hairdresser and friend, once described a colour she was referring to as the colour of tungsten. My ears immediately sprung up at the mention of a word that very few people even know let alone use in a sentence. Tungsten is the Superhero remedy with the theme that nothing is ever a problem, and that one will make a plan to succeed even if there are seemingly insurmountable obstacles in ones way. It is not surprisingly one of my remedies and it turned out to be one of hers as well, delivered right to me by her, to reflect back for both of us in remedy form.

Athena went a step further by actually naming her son Raven twenty years ago, a remedy that suited both of us. Whether it reflected an aspect of herself at the time, or in a moment of future lucidity wanted to ensure that I gave the remedy back to her twenty years later, is inconceivable. Both are beautiful explanations and probably contain a measure of truth. It doesn't really matter exactly which one it is, and all one can do is stand back and appreciate the magnitude of the dense array, as it reveals its own Perfection.

One morning a patient blurted out in the consultation room that they felt like they were made of granite, which is an element very prevalent in Cape Town, and turned out to be exactly the remedy that she required to jack her out of her entwined state. Another time, a friend of Anri's was describing the cramps he got in his calf and he said the muscle went flat, *"like a cuttlefish"*. My attention was immediately piqued as I have never heard anyone describe it like that. It turned out that *Sepia Succus* was the exact remedy he needed. The cuttlefish ejects ink when it is in danger and the remedy centres on not allowing other people to come too close, to avoid getting hurt by emotional entanglement. He had spent the previous two years avoiding any close emotional contact with women, and almost immediately after taking the remedy found himself willing and able to engage a serious relationship.

People often come to my office wearing turquoise, amber, amethyst, or seahorse pendants, and then it happens to be exactly the remedy they require to cure them. Thor came home one day with a bottle of potassium bichromate for some photographic project and this was exactly the remedy I saw reflecting in many of my patients that week.

I also often prescribe for myself and other people based on numbers which align to the Periodic Table. If one is drawn to certain numbers or if they keep repeating in your reality for no apparent reason, it is a sure indicator that it is required in remedy form. The number of my house for example is 7, which on the Periodic Table is nitrogen. The central theme around this remedy is about enjoyment and enthusiasm which echoes my mental state. A friend of mine used to live at number 17 which is Chlorine, a remedy around the theme of the mother. This was an archetype she most certainly embodied, looking after all the broken children who come into her reality. Whether we choose the house or it chooses us is mostly a question of semantics. Your manifestations are always a reflection of your Self.

There is an old Polish proverb which says *"show me your friends and I will tell you who you are"*. I could not agree more and I often apply this principle in reverse, giving my friends and lovers the remedies that work well on me, seeing the threads of similarity running through us both. A lot of my friends have Diamond as a core remedy and Athena was even born in Kimberly, which was the largest diamond producing area in its time.

Generally if I get on really well with people there will be a lot of shared remedy states. Naja for example, has done many of my girlfriends good. Conversely, when I see a particular remedy reflecting out there, in either patients or friends, I see it as a clear indication for me to take it as well.

That is why it's best to pay attention and learn to shape it the way you want it, consciously. Dakini is always showing you the way - how to free yourself from stagnation and what negative situations need to be changed. When something is too complicated to see in yourself or too fine a thread to spot, it will manifest as an experience, person, or sign in your reality, so you can become aware of it.

In the same way we are often drawn to certain numbers because they reflect and express a part of ourselves that needs to be taken note of. Often the age that we date ourselves from, or experienced our first trauma, is the age we get stuck in. When people start their sentences with *"when I was eight"* (oxygen) or *"when I was sixteen"* (sulphur) it is for a reason. The reason is that they want you to reflect that age back to them as a Homoeopathic remedy. Sometimes even the corresponding remedy of people's current physical ages can be useful, as they might be stuck in that particular phase and in need of a little prodding to move them along.

The reflection can be spotted inside or out, it makes no real difference. It is all the *play of your own mind* and whether you choose to manifest something in your head, or externally in reality, is pretty much the same thing. Why something shows up in your reality in a particular way is largely irrelevant. What does matter is that if you pay attention you will come to realise that you are constantly communicating with yourself through signs.

Kama once came to me with the story that they were getting broken into every night which was something that had never happened before. It transpired that a good friend of hers was about to give birth while the father had gone off with another woman. This is exactly the homoeopathic picture of *Panthera Tigris* which is made from the urine of the pregnant female tiger. Although normally strong, she is extremely vulnerable just before giving birth. At this time she is not even able to hunt, and since the male has left her alone she cannot protect herself from harm either. After I gave her friend the remedy the break-ins stopped the very next day. The increased energetic intensity of her pregnancy was of such magnitude that it even manifested as reality in the lives of her friends.

Got to love Homoeopathy, it takes all the pain away if you understand its real nature. If you cut the delusion at the root it can no longer manifest as your reality. The problem is that there is often not just one state in a person, instead there are many layers woven together over each other, which complicates the picture. Ceaseless vigilance becomes a necessity in order not to perpetuate this state into further manifestation. Imagine peeling an onion while the skin tries to reform as you peel, so you go in hard, with many knives, and hope you can get as close to the core as possible and cut out most of the main roots before it reforms.

Some remedy patterns are often archetypal and common to many people. In particular there are a group of remedies that are almost a blue-print for love relationships. With Cat I had learned all the relationship squabble remedies.

They are all based around Sulphur which is about the partner. Iron Sulphide is about laying down the rules in relationship. Magnesium Sulphate is around conflict with the partner, and Copper Sulphate is an intensification of this conflict, with the feeling of each person entrenched in their respective fortresses, attacking each other with malicious intent. The unavoidable result of this squabble is Zinc Sulphate, which is the feeling of complete exhaustion to the point of being willing to just call the whole thing quits. Then there is Ammonia Sulphate which is the acrid residue of a relationship gone bad with all its bitter acrimony.

This was the sequence of remedies I would revolve around with my girlfriend Cat, and I would antidote one state, only to be forced to put out another fire with another remedy shortly after. So the merry-go-round went round and round, again and again until it just had to end – you can't ignore the bitterness in your mouth which keeps resurfacing, regardless of how much one tries to sweeten it up.

Every marriage counsellor should have a set of these remedies on hand, in fact anyone in a relationship should have them. They definitely calm the waters and put out smouldering fires. This said, they can only help correct states that are unnecessary, but they cannot force people to love each other when things are just not meant to be.

It got to the point in our relationship where I even procured the remedy made from the Gila monster for Cat, in the hope of eradicating her tendency to chew poison slowly into my wounds. She had a thing for lizards, but even the essence of this beast was insufficient to annihilate this particularly nasty trait in her. Maybe it was her nature and hence incurable or maybe I had not given her enough, who knows. Everyone plays their part to perfection – certain movies are just more pleasant to watch than others.

For treatment to be truly curative it is better to treat not only the initial patient, but those close to them as well. If someone comes for treatment, I often encourage their partner to come in also. In the same vein I prefer treating whole families instead of just one of the members, because one can certainly treat a person but if the situation that generated the disease in the first place keeps perpetuating, it's only a matter of time before the patient returns. This is unfortunate because all it does is unnecessarily delay the completion of the curative process.

Proper homoeopathic treatment often requires a complete overhaul of a person's lifestyle or behaviour. I once treated a cop with haemorrhoids and although I got rid of the haemorrhoids the remedy also took away a lot of his aggression. This made it harder for him to do his job as an enforcer of the law and so in the end what is cure anyway? Sometimes the curing of a particular state will also prompt a change in life style so that a new paradigm can be forged.

This is something that people are not always willing to do either because the sacrifice is too big, the implications too large or the old ways of doing things so deeply entrenched that they prefer to stay in their diseased state. Some people would rather stay in their comfort zones and familiar reference points no matter how painful and potentially deadly they are.

Dakini asks a lot from you – your heart and soul as a gesture of commitment to the cause, but the beauty she reveals brings tears to the eyes, and the bounty she returns is more than you could ever want.

FIFTEEN

Treasure Hunting In The **Mind**

When you step into the inconceivable,
it steps into you, and then
all bets are off.

The higher Tantric teachings talk about the *Karma Mudra* (action form). This involves union with the archetypal partner who will bring out more than the sum of the two people. These are hard to find yet well worth the searching. It is further said that if there is no Karma Mudra then there is no *Mahamudra* (grand form or gesture). This is basically the state where one finds oneself completely in tune with the grand Play of Reality – the highest goal in Tantra.

In modern western Astrology *"they"* say that the way one engages relationships is dependent on the position of the asteroid Juno in your birth chart. Juno was the wife of Jove, the head of the Roman pantheon. My Juno is in Sagittarius and it makes a lot of sense to me personally. Sagittarius is about exploration and spiritual advancement and I have always found that as long as the relationship is centred on these aspects, I remain interested. When it descends into daily life and cooking meals I soon become bored.

This is my pattern and I seem to stick to it. This does not mean that it cannot last for a hundred years, it just never seems to. I am always a romantic at heart though, and I remain open for surprises.

And so we start the story of Cat. She entered the picture when I was living in Cape Town, just under a year after my enlightenment holiday in India. She was a spunky, sexy, wild, bright long red-haired Aries Earth Horse.

Luc had told her about me and she had apparently had visions of me in her dreams. She came to see if her fantasies were based on something real and we got together almost immediately. She had been running her own little magical mystery tour, being interested in magical traditions both modern and ancient, and her visionary capacity was exceptional – it was fatal attraction.

The Horse's gift is vision, but they are very difficult and a bit self-absorbed in my experience. I have known a number of them and should have learned when I got kicked in the stomach by a real horse when I was ten, but then a crucial part of this story would never have been told. Perfect from the start, no need to change a thing.

Cat lost no time diving straight into my homoeopathic box, especially when she learned that you could get high from them as well as cure disease. The body will always seek to return the organism to its naturally healthy state, so when the patient experiences disease as a result of a distortion of their Natural State, the correct remedy will assist the body in permanently deleting the disease.

On the other hand if you want to generate a frequency in the body as opposed to removing a disease, one can do it just as easily. In this case it is only temporary because it is just a momentary rearrangement of a healthy body's matrix, which will rectify itself fairly quickly. This is what I used to do with Anti-matter, Plutonium and snake venoms, introducing these substances into my body and getting high, although the effects could often be more than just a little deranging.

None of this deterred Cat and she demanded all the nastiest remedies, Mercury, Scorpion, the snake venoms, and the plant poisons. I managed to get hold of some raw Cape Cobra venom from a zoologist friend of mine, and Cat and I each took two drops. You have to love a woman who will take raw snake venom with you, it takes more balls than most men have. I remember trying to document both our symptoms while my vision started blurring and the venom scrambled our nervous systems.

Documenting the effects of poisons is one of the main means of finding out what a remedy does, and this process is called a *"proving"* in homoeopathic circles, although one normally takes it in dilution so that the effects are less intense. What a substance causes it will also cure and sometimes one has to singe ones tail feathers in the name of science to gain a deeper understanding of the remedy.

We had a bottle of raw *Androctonos* (scorpion venom) which we took more often just to tune us up a bit, as it was definitely more manageable than the Cobra venom, but then we were both of the 'baptism by fire' school of reality, so we loved it. The difference between a poison and a medicine is the dose, and getting high is somewhere in between.

One night after about a month of being together we were having a speed binge with some of our friends. It was day two and Cat had disappeared off to the bathroom with some of her girlfriends. What transpired was that her Kundalini started to raise itself in the bath. She thought that she was overdosing from too much speed and felt too embarrassed to call me. Instead her friends became rather traumatized by watching her writhe around in the bathtub as a process which normally takes hours, if not days, occurred in the space of about fifteen minutes.

Cat was not prone to wasting time on anything and that included her own processes. It came up unbidden partly from our energetic interaction, and partly from her taking such a large number of remedies that had cleared various blocks in her, which would normally have slowed the process down. In addition to this, she also had the benefit of me speaking Dzogchen most of the time. When she came out of the bath she curled up in my lap like a cat that had just been in a fight, and proceeded to sleep it off.

After this she started having visionary spells where she would describe, not really knowing them, a lot of the Buddhist archetypes. She had visions of *Garuda* (the lightning bird), *Simhamukha* (the lion-headed dakini) and of course *Ekajati*. Ekajati is the principle guardian of Dzogchen and is portrayed with one eye, one tooth, and one breast, to signify her commitment to Non-Duality. She has a wrathful expression, and she dances on the corpse of a perverter of the Teachings. Luckily I was on hand to guide her through certain things though I was largely in the dark myself, but in the land of the blind the one eyed man is king.

There is a Buddhist tradition that talks about something called Terma (teaching treasures). These are *"secret, hidden, or undiscovered teachings"* stored by various teachers in physical or ethereal form. These Terma include various texts describing previously unknown practices, or giving insight into already existing practices. They may also be objects that are sacred to specific lineages or of particular significance to Buddhism. Most of the physical objects were hidden by Padmasambhava and Yeshe Tsogyel in Tibet, Bhutan, Ladakh, and Nepal, some of which have been found by various Tertons (treasure revealers).

There is a lineage of Tertons whose job it is to find or be led to certain hidden Teaching Treasures and this lineage continues to this day. Often at the time of stashing the Teachings verbal predictions were made regarding the name of the Terton destined to find it, and the time at which they would be revealed. However, many of the Teachings were supposedly hidden in Mind Space and these can be accessed by anyone, if you can get there, and provided that the Guardians allow you access.

What started happening was that Cat began discovering and revealing various Treasures which were hidden in the *secret space of the mind* to which she for some reason had access. She would go into states for up to six or seven hours on end as these energetic tantras (weaves) were being written into her body. I would watch as she went into spasms on the bed, unable to do much of anything, while the air around us became so thick one could hardly crawl across the room, let alone stand.

This extra-heavy-gravity-honey air, which we called 'Dakini States' for want of a better word, became a regular phenomenon and we became used to it as part of our day to day experience. Sometimes reality became so intense, the thigle so bright, and every molecule in ones body vibrating so actively, that it was hard to even breathe, let alone speak to each other.

She would often not be very communicative in these states and she would do little but mutter snippets of her visions to me. Sometimes I would get shards of it, like when the whole of Table Mountain was unveiled as a camping ground for all manner of magical beasts waiting for a time when they would be able to return, either once The Wave hit, or perhaps before.

Of course we were speeding through a lot of this, but this just allowed us to get into a fluid enough state so that we could access these visions. When in altered states ones conscious logic and disbelief are pushed to the background. This allows better access to the subconscious mind which is more creative and visionary, allowing it to receive and accept things that it would normally reject.

When we experienced these types of states things got so far out there that it was hard to even imagine returning to normal life and continuing daily affairs. Eventually we would just go to sleep to wake up and find reality close to normal again, yet somehow changed forever. I still see dancing light when I look at space, but then that is the true Nature of Reality, the dancing spirals that make up the universe. My sight has never really reverted to normal since I raised my Kundalini.

Cat would share some of the Tantras with me but most of the time she chose to re-stash them. She decided, as was her prerogative as a Terton, that the time had not come for them to be shared with reality. You can't argue with that, given the state of ignorance in the world. She once had a vision of Ekajati in which, from what I could glean, she was basically threatened with annihilation if she gave the Teachings into the wrong hands. This seemed to have suitably impressed upon her the seriousness of revealing the Tantras to inappropriate or unprepared folk.

Cat was studying Chinese medicine and Shiatsu at the time and she did use some of the psychic surgical teachings she received. One night she was trying to raise a friend of ours' Kundalini, an action I just barely approved of. Shanti was a bit of a dilettante in her own way and Cat asked me if she should remove Shanti's brain, since she was obviously not using it, and it was clearly getting in the way of her process. I quickly told her that it was probably better left where it was. Whether she could have done it or not is a matter of speculation, but I'm sure the implications for us would have been very messy, so I was relieved to be spared from it. That same night she looked at me in pure wrathful Dakini form and I felt not a shred of Cat in there, just a destroyer. I did get nervous at this point, but managed to wing my way through, it although I am sure she saw my fear. She was like the angry sky looking down on an insect and wondering if it should be eaten or not. She returned to normal after this, as normal as she ever got anyway. She was rather prone to extremes of mood, which became a major challenge later in the relationship.

At that time though, we were still lovers dancing through the intricacies of mind space, intoxicated by the newness, the beauty and the sheer Crazy Wisdom of the weave that was unfolding before us. We had no idea where we were going. We just followed the threads as they presented to us, running them to the ground and then trying to figure out what it all meant. I think we both realized that all that was really required from us, was to play our parts in the Cosmic Dance.

One day I stole some flowers from a lamppost where someone had died in a car crash, thinking that she would appreciate the morbid romanticism of the gesture. Instead I got a rather withering look and *"don't bring me flowers bring me drugs"*. That was the kind of girl she was, no picket fences for her. As a child she even used to push snakes around in her pram – how could I not love her for that?

Cat used to date a guy who translated Sumerian texts for the Dutch government and a lot of the stories she told me made sense to my cosmology. She relentlessly trawled the internet for interesting mythological titbits, primarily Dzogchen, Sumerian, Egyptian, and mystery school texts. There was a similar thread running through these mythologies in regards to opening the Gates of Earth, which resonated strongly with my personal mission to unbind the titans from wherever they had been bound.

We constantly searched for ways to do this, her I think out of curiosity and mischievousness, me more out of a strong internal urge. We went through the Dakini downloads a number of times together. They had at first been completely unknown to us but after a while it became a bit like, *"oh this again"*, and *"how many hours is it going to last this time?"*.

There was always the thick air and heavy gravity and Cat was the only person I experienced this with besides Athena. Athena was a creature unto herself, yet during that time it was me at the centre of the download. The only other person I have heard of that has experienced the same thing is Anri. She received her first Dakini download on the border of Lesotho near Sangoma Valley, after a baptism under a waterfall, signalling some kind of initiation onto the path which finally led her to Dzogchen. The nature of the Teaching Treasures differs for each Terton and is unique to their natures. For me it mostly involved tech on liberating bound forces, for Anri it often involved a type of sensory experience of the fabric of reality.

Why certain people are deemed appropriate to receive this kind of information is inconceivable, but it happens and can happen. In this way nothing is lost, all the Secret Teachings are kept safe. These Terma are potentially available to anyone as long they carry the right genetic and ethereal keys to access the *twilight world*.

I often think of Cat with her shocking red hair as the packhorse designed to seek secrets, find, and then stash them in her mind space, in order to carry them across into the new Yuga. Waiting for the appropriate time when she could unpack and spread it to whoever could, and would, use them the best. That time has not yet come, but it is coming.

SIXTEEN

The
Left-Hand Path

I had often been accused of arrogance
but when you know, you know,
and need no excuses to justify
your existence.

All the secrets are coming out of the woodwork, but whether people pick them up and run with it is another story entirely. If it can be done it is doable, and if someone else can do it so can you. I am telling this story back to you as inspiration to spur you on, because everything I have done so too can you.

To do this you have to strangle the Demon of Disbelief every time it sneaks into your bedroom at night and keep strangling it until it stays dead.

In traditional Tantra they often talk about *right-hand path* and *left-hand path* as two different ways of approaching awareness. This distinction originated in India, predominantly to distinguish between two different approaches in methodology. Left-hand practitioners would participate in rites, or partake of substances that were considered taboo for the traditional priest caste, like eating meat or drinking alcohol. Similarly, when honouring or exploring the Union between masculine and feminine, a right-hand path practitioner would use symbols to represent the masculine and feminine aspects, whereas left-hand practitioners would actually have sex.

Left-hand path practitioners were, even then, viewed with some suspicion by their more moderate counterparts, however the stigma of 'evil' associated with it in modern times, was only later attached by misguided western esoteric practitioners.

In truth, the left-hand path literally means being willing to use powerful but volatile forces to accelerate your process, as long as you are willing to take the consequences, which are never entirely defined. These consequences, if used improperly, can range from psychosis to schizophrenia so if you want to play in the fast lane you need to pay attention to your driving at all times.

One uses anything and everything to spur you on through the waters so that you arrive at the Island of Jewels in one piece. An ex-girlfriend of mine shot nail polish remover into her veins, passed out and woke up twenty four hours later with the worst headache of her life. Not all roads need exploring but one often has to travel to dark and desolate places to find out where not to go.

I knew I had taken the pursuit of Clarity too far with speed when I stopped smelling the roses along the way and shortly after that I stopped, yet I always pay homage to the powerful diamond knife that crystal methamphetamine represents. It was a tool that greatly accelerated my process and one that complimented Homoeopathy beautifully.

Another one of my practises in the pursuit of dissolution of form is Sun Gazing, where one gazes at the sun for up to an hour. The texts recommend sunset but I always favoured mid-afternoon and after a while everything breaks up into swathes of colour. This was quite at odds with my father's grave warnings of imminent blindness to be visited upon one for such a practise, and my eyes are still hale and hearty. Another belief to cast upon the pile of erroneous human notions, yet if one flinches one will burn one's eyes. If one does this, one first sees the sun turning into a giant black and red revolving disk, and after having done it for a while, you realize that you could do it for ever.

Like with most things it is just getting over the initial fear of damage that is the greatest hurdle and after that it is all downhill.

The trick to this practise is to see the sun and Self as one – you would not hurt yourself after all. If you are going to try this I recommend starting at sunset, and then building up to the afternoon, as the Suspension of Disbelief generally takes a while to master.

One of the Thogal techniques is to stare at the dancing rainbow spirals and to see the Pure Lands and the Buddha in each one. When you see yourself as the Buddha looking back at you at all times, you cannot ever be bound into a concrete form again. Truly going beyond, the universe is you and you are the playground so what else is there to do but play?

On the path one stands to gain certain seemingly magical abilities, which to the Enlightened becomes just another part of ones unique display. Naturally, the supreme siddhi is that of complete Awareness, but there are several lesser siddhis that have made their appearance in the annals of history. The obvious ones like turning water into wine or walking on water, are familiar to the Western mind, but these powers can include anything from recollection of past lives, psychic healing and living on air, to name but a few. As with everything one often just needs a taste in order to set the execution of it in motion.

One of the interesting ways I have found to introduce a taste of these powers are the radioactive remedies, homoeopathic remedies made from substances like plutonium, uranium, americium, and others. These remedies represent the 'power behind the throne', and theirs is the power to influence the flow of events with raw intent and then watch the stage shift accordingly. In true Buddha Brat fashion I view these as useful tools to play with, in order to give one the experience of those subtle weaves of reality that are above and beyond normal life, if you're up to it of course. The Radioactives are a bit unstable by their very nature and as such are a tad unpredictable, much like the siddhis, and there is not a lot of research into their use and application. There have been a few occasions however where I have deemed it appropriate to stir my, or other people's energetic pots. I find Plutonium for example, to be quite useful in kick starting the Kundalini process, or to add extra potency to certain psychic processes.

As far as magic goes, Homoeopathy itself appears to work on a seemingly magical level because once you take the correctly indicated remedy for the diseased state, it miraculously disappears, as if it were never there. These states are totally personal at the time, they hurt like hell and feel for all intents and purposes real and it often baffles people that something supposedly so real can just simply disappear without a trace.

Yeshe Tsogyel was a princess in Tibet who became a principal student and consort of Padmasambhava to learn the various Buddhist teachings. When he eventually sent her out into the world, the first people she met were eight bandits who raped her. Having conquered One Taste she saw Padmasambhava's face in all of them and proceeded to raise their Kundalinis. They apologized profusely and begged forgiveness after which they became her disciples. This level of control over reality makes Jesus look like a choir boy in comparison. He was never raped by the fishermen after all.

She had so much compassion for humanity that she married a leper when he asked her to and stayed with him as his wife for four years. She had such control over her own body that she would give people her kneecaps when they asked her for them, and then regenerate new ones herself. She recorded all of Padmasambhava's teachings with her photographic memory and most of the information we have about him today was documented by her.

This is why, when the concept of a weak woman is presented to me, I just laugh. With an example like Yeshe, how could you even begin to dispute the power latent in all women? She is a much more powerful archetype than Mother Theresa, Joan of Arc, and Mother Mary combined. She embodies the best of all of them and a whole lot more. She lived in the 10th century which is relatively speaking not that long ago, and she stored a lot of the Secret Teachings all over Tibet to be discovered when the time was right.

These are the lineage strands that I align to and draw inspiration from and they represent some of the more epic potential of what is truly possible. If someone else can do it, so can I – monkey see, monkey do.

The main thing that keeps us bound in this Illusion is the belief that the 'self' is a separate and singular entity isolated from everything else. I want a thousand faces at least, or even better, a million to play with. Being bound in one form is the surest path to old age and death.

As I have mentioned before, there is a practice in Tantra which involves visualising an archetype and then transforming oneself into that archetype, in order to embody it. In *Vajrayana* (diamond way) it is called Yidam Yoga, which literally means *"union with the deity"*. It is a practice that according to traditional Buddhism needs many initiations and relies completely on the guidance of a qualified teacher, lest the student should get it wrong due to subtle dualistic tendencies.

The point is that from a Non-Dual space these archetypes have always been nothing other than *aspects of self*, and should be viewed as such. It is useful and enjoyable though, to find archetypes that represent certain aspects of oneself that one has not integrated yet, and then playing them out for better understanding of oneself.

One of the many unique features of a Buddha Brat is that we all naturally seemed to have gravitated to the incorporation of various archetypes. All Aspects from any mythological sphere are useful to integrate, but it also seems that certain people are drawn more to certain aspects according to their natures. We also embody certain Aspects more at certain times, and the skill is to know which face to go into at which point in time. Then, when to come out of it effortlessly, ready to put the next one on.

All one has to do really is to be familiar with what each archetype represents and put in a mental intent to embody it when necessary. Remembering to do it without straining or struggling, spending a few moments doing this is usually more than enough to activate it. To make it more fun you can incorporate the various symbols, tools, and mudras that the deities are normally pictured with. It is useful for example to embody *Ganesha* when one senses obstacles in ones way for any reason, as Ganesha is the Destroyer of Obstacles.

There is no end to how creative you can be. In Buddhism there is a whole array of sexy female deities like the Bat-headed Dakini who uses a whip to flail Duality with. You don't get better than that in my opinion and in the war against ones own ignorance one is definitely one step ahead if you can enjoy the process.

If *everything is self and self is empty*, then all the Pantheons are up for grabs as personal archetypes to be reclaimed and so on my enlightenment holiday in India we initiated the downloads. We travelled through India downloading *Shiva, Krishna, Saraswati* and *Kali* - you name it, male, female, everything. Naturally the entire Buddhist Pantheon was the next in line and when we got to Ladakh we gobbled it up, absorbing it into our psyches.

Athena told me once that she had seen the face of *Lucifer* (light bearer) over her face for years in the mirror, and she often introduced herself as Lucifer. She did this partially for shock value but primarily because she believed it. I had gone into a pure Kali form, ready to perform the dance of destruction on reality a number of times, so I had no problem with people embodying possibly strange or 'undesired' archetypes. I have no Judeo-Christian background, so having Lucifer as a companion did not bother me in the least, in fact, it somehow seemed appropriate. Athena also styled herself as Kali for a while and on occasion we could get a bit competitive. She eventually grew tired of her destroyer aspects and it was in her aspect as Lucifer that she entrusted the key to the gates of hell to me.

Everyone gets to play out their own archetypes and since *all is self*, which Aspects you choose to embody are largely according to your own personal predilection and perfect as such. If you are going to dream, dream big I always say. Fuck being an embodiment of Marie Antoinette, or Napoleon – go large or go home. Take on your Aspects and play them as the mood sees fit, it's your birthright after all. If you dream small you will have small realities, but if you dream huge then the hugeness of the manifestation clasps you to its beating breast, and the milk of grandeur bathes you in its lustre.

Regardless of all the many siddhis one can gain on the path, if you cannot move beyond the concept of 'self' and 'other', you will continue to be reborn on the Wheel. Machig Labdron used to fly around and walk through walls, having totally conquered the concept of 'self' and 'other' whereby the wall and her were separate. How then could she not walk through them? She founded the little known and rather wild-assed Tibetan enlightenment methodology of Chod, which is one of my all-time favourite practices.

According to the view of Chod, demons are ideas, attachments, and fears that are obstacles to Awareness because they obscure our true empty, Non-Dual Nature. The central tenet of Chod is that *the only demon that needs to be slain is the Demon of the Illusion of 'self'* because it is identification with the 'self' as separate and concrete, that is the root of all Suffering. Once this central demon is slain all other demons disappear, because if you cut the root the tree withers and dies. Chod means to *"cut through"* and in order to cut through this false identity we have to destroy the idea that our bodies are concrete. This is the best way to remind the 'self' of its True Nature – that the mind as well as the body is in fact a pool of pure potential manifesting as sound, light, and sensation.

The traditional practice of Chod involves going to an isolated or scary place like a graveyard or charnel ground where you visualize yourself being chopped into pieces and torn apart by beasts, or any frightful apparitions that the dualistic mind can contrive. This practice is done visually because the human body is seen as a precious vehicle however it is our attachment to it, and fear of damage, that binds us into Form. This is the very reason why we will then manifest situations in which our bodies are damaged or destroyed, because everything we fear sooner or later comes into form to be dealt with.

The idea is to mentally offer yourself to anything you might normally fear. This could be robbers, murderers, rapists, wild animals, or any other form of physical destruction like car crashes and debilitating diseases. The more extreme the visualisation the better it works. You boldly engage what you dread the most in order to overcome it, giving away your physical body to anyone or anything that wants a piece of you. When you have done a million times worse to yourself in your mind than anyone can ever do to you, what is there ever to fear from reality again?

One of the by-products of this practise is that you become immune to disease. Chod practitioners were often sent to plague areas to treat the sick because they would be immune to the *illusion of disease*, having already done the worst they could imagine to themselves. They had such a diffuse sense of 'self' that there was literally no difference between them and the disease, so it had no effect on them. A lot of one's identity is tied up in our personalized visualizations of self and breaking it frees us from a world of suffering.

My favourite Chod practise ground is trance parties with its loud, rhythmic music and an array of strangely garbed people in all manners of twisted states. Add to that a generous dose of San Pedro and you are set for a solid Chod experience. San Pedro allows one to literally see your heart being suspended from a meat hook in front of you, as dogs gnaw on the marrow of your bones, and you annihilate your spinal cord with a diamond chainsaw. I have even visually cooked and fed myself to the humans at the party, either as stew or in pies.

Epic stuff – it clears more memory and attachment in eight hours than years of meditation. This process has the added benefit of allowing one to view everything as an Aspect of Self that needs to be integrated into Self, thereby reinforcing ones Non-Dual Nature. There is nothing quite like watching yourself gleefully offering your eyeballs to a demon (self) and watching it devour them.

It is useful and indeed necessary to personalise the experience. Whether you are religious, scientific, or artistic, one can use the entire gamut of existing references to fuel your process. One thinks that there are only so many ways to destroy your body, but the more creative you are, the more limitless the possibilities become.

Once I peeled off my skin in seven layers, laid it out for the flies to eat clean, and then burnt it with a blowtorch, watching as the smoke ascended to the sky. Watching your brain being put in a liquidizer, and the juice being fed to the vultures and jackals, is another experience I highly recommend. One of my finest Chod experiences was chopping my head off and watching as a spray of blood fountained up from my severed neck into the sky, raining down on all the assembled people, glorious stuff. I remember watching as Micheala's cat licked up the blood from my severed head.

Every party I explore a different Aspect of Reality and I have hacked, sawn, burnt, ripped, and carved myself to pieces more times than I can remember. The pounding music, lights, and mescaline all add to the heroic self-deconstruction. Hard, fast, effective, and fun, lest we forget the reason why we play this game in the first place. The cherry on the cake is that it goes a long way to removing fear from all aspects of ones life.

Afterwards you feel amazingly free and clear. All of a sudden nothing is a problem anymore and things resume their proper level of importance. It is one of the finest techniques for dealing with fear of death or mutilation and even the loss of cherished people or objects, and as a bonus breaks the Illusion of form as a solid thing.

Left-hand path practices are fairly extreme and definitely not for the faint-hearted. It is all good and well calling yourself a Left-hand practitioner when using extreme situations or drugs to further your processes. If however, one is merely justifying bad behaviour or drug abuse, one deserves the full brunt of suffering generated by such indulgent behaviour.

On the other hand some of the more sensitive New-Agers view Chod with a lot of suspicion and I have even heard some describe it as madness. They continue to insist on holding on to their pretty ideals and cushy practices. But this will only last until the wave of global despair finally spills over into their cosy suburbs, yet it is a pity that this is often what it takes.

In my opinion nothing is more dangerous or insane than the suffering of this world so it has always been an obvious decision for me to exit it by any means necessary.

Do you want to take the red pill and stay here, or the blue one and get out? It's not going to be pretty, so better be committed because it is going to hurt in ways that you can barely conceive of. On the other hand, if you stay you will slowly rot and die in the juices of your own mind.

This seems to me a far worse fate so I am of the *"freedom or death"* persuasion. This is just my opinion and I am biased, because

130

for me there never really was a choice. I was driven to it and by it, and I would have had it no other way.

SEVENTEEN

Holy Cow Slaughter

If it is not indestructible
it can and probably will be cracked –
such is the nature of the beast
that is born of Emptiness.

Without our binding illusions we are free to resurrect in a purer, more adamantine form. The most cherished ideals are the hardest to break and hurt the most – we will seldom relinquish them without a bloodbath, but the phoenix always rises from the ashes, and we are reborn, stronger than before.

According to Chod there are 'demons' who come in the guise of 'gods'. This includes anything from *pride in practice* to things like love, honour, and friendship. If at any time one experiences beautiful visions or enjoyable emotions and it binds us into conditioned behaviour, it has become another 'demon' that needs to be slain. This is why I talk of the Armies of Mara and the Daughters of Mara to distinguish between the frightening and alluring faces of Mara. I have found that the Daughters of Mara are often much harder to spot, let alone overcome, and these particular faces I refer to as Holy Cows.

Machig Labdron said that *"when a man and woman get together they are flirting with the Demon of Adverse Conditions"*. It's not that it

132

is not beneficial or enjoyable to have a relationship but it is definitely problematic.

There is so much potential in relationship for transcendence yet it is a major cause of suffering and unhappiness, probably because there is just so much reflection of ones parental archetypes which play into the picture. I see this often in Homoeopathy and still maintain that the major causes of disease are relationships, family and work, probably in that order. There is of course also tremendous potential in these if one can turn adversity to your advantage.

After the Nepal leg of my enlightenment holiday Asher and I went back to India, where Asher and Charlotte got married in Varanasi, and I was once again best man at Asher's wedding. We parted ways with the idea that I would go back to South Africa to pick up Sophie, (Asher and Athena's daughter) and return with her to Paris, where we all decided to live.

Like all good plans there are always a number of spanners in the works. On my return I stopped in at Cindy's, someone I had worked on before I left, and who was begging me to visit. I had made the mistake before I left South Africa of sleeping with her, definitely an error on my part as she was more than a little fixated on me. The plot thickened – she had a very beautiful daughter Natalie, all of twenty years old, who she was quite jealous of. In the ensuing speed binge, after days of working on her mind with my remedies and Dzogchen, she freaked out and threw both of us out of the house in a psychotic rage. Her paranoia was completely unfounded because at this stage I hadn't even looked at her daughter but she could not be persuaded to reconsider.

I returned to my parents' house with Natalie in tow. They were used to my strange comings and goings so didn't say much about it, and I proceeded to work on Natalie's head, as I tend to do. Needless to say it wasn't long before we hooked up. She was good in bed and very cute if a bit opportunistic, but then you can't always have it all.

She had been burnt very badly on the feet as a child and had been in a homoeopathic Opium state where she could not feel much of anything, emotionally or physically. This allowed her to behave with physical and moral impunity without feeling the effects of her actions, which is one of the types of homoeopathic compensation for trauma. She had literally not felt anything of a sensory nature for eighteen years, as her body's sensory receptors had been functionally blocked since she was three years old. This led to her engaging in some extremely hardcore activities without taking damage. She told me about how she used to stick safety pins into herself just to get some sensation.

When I gave her homoeopathic opium all her sensations returned at once, touching silk was almost too much for her at first and petting the cat almost sent her into convulsions. She was very grateful to me of course, but then gratitude rarely lasts forever.

She was born in the Chinese year of the Dog and they are only loyal to one master, as I was soon to find out. Asher had been obsessed with her when he was in South Africa which is how I originally met her. He was with Charlotte this time though, so I figured that one woman was enough for him. I was wrong.

I paid for her ticket and expenses in Paris but when I suggested that she go out and work when I started running out of money, she quickly decided that her future would be better secured with him than me. I loved her in a sense more for her sexiness and openness than anything deeper and more meaningful but it still hurt when she jumped ship. Not having anything pressing that needed to be done anywhere else I stayed around for a while, digging the knife deeper into myself.

One night when we were all on crystal ecstasy the three of them were in the room next door and I could hear them through the walls. Duly broken, I surrendered myself to Dakini – letting all reality in and becoming one with the feminine principle of existence. As I did this I saw the thigle around me turning into giant rotating wheels and I integrated the light particles into me, breaking down any distinction between myself and reality. I realized then that heartbreak was actually a Skillful Means to further my deepening into the Natural State. It hurt like hell, but Enlightenment is an ongoing process of breaking conceptual structures, including ones most precious ideals and fantasies.

I could hardly complain, this was my end purpose anyway and I had always been willing to sacrifice everything for my state. Certain sacrifices are just more painful than others and certain illusions die very hard. Paris, the city of love, was the perfect place for it all to turn to ashes around me, so I could be reborn. It is said that the warrior works best with a broken heart because then it is wide open and he can truly feel, and boy did I feel. Charlotte was going through hell even worse than me, she couldn't or wouldn't leave, and to add insult to injury she was paying for the whole show.

I finally left Paris and returned to Johannesburg, broke and broken. I hooked up with Nina, another Dog, but she was far more loyal. Not as cute but very accommodating, and although I was never in love with her I did love her for her commitment to me and the Teachings. She provided a good distraction from my emotional trauma and took me down to Cape Town where we split up, largely to protect her from the wrath of Athena. I had passed on all the Teachings to her so she had what she needed from me, although it was probably me that she wanted. Our dance was done and I once again had bigger fish to fry.

Years after we met, Athena decided that I was her soulmate. It's interesting how women never tend to ask you if you are their soulmate, they assume that by telling you this, you will suddenly come to your senses, and everyone will live happily ever after. Since we had so many interactions, and her knowledge of Dzogchen was equal to mine, it seemed like a plausible union and we hooked up again. It was great in the beginning but after a while I started feeling trapped as I usually did, and it collapsed. It was almost like we were too similar and just started irritating each other after a while.

I took a remedy called The Tempest once which is basically a captured storm in a bottle. It joins heaven and earth with a bolt of lightning and so I have dubbed it 'soul-mate drops' because of its ability to connect the male and female aspects. She appeared in the picture a few days later and we got together again for the fifth time, and this time it lasted a few months. I did love her at the times when we were together, but it just never seemed to last and she never really forgave me for not loving her enough.

Maybe I am fickle, but you cannot lie about your heart – either you feel it or you don't. There is nothing that you can do about something that is pure mood, and you can no more lie about it than you can fake a good meal.

The higher Tantras say that all women are Dakini and that one woman represents all Dakini, so whether one chooses to see Reality in one woman, or in all women, makes little difference. It is largely just a question of personal predilection that everyone has to work out for themselves.

One is capable of loving any woman yet I have been in love with only a few. If you have to try to love them it is already a problem, and yet love is one of the finest things there is. It is hard to tell someone that you no longer love them, but the sooner one does, in suitably gentle terms, the better it is for both parties.

I have gotten something from each relationship I have been in and each one adds to the picture. Some were sweeter than others but there is always a golden apple to be found somewhere. The highest ideal is learning and growing, and love facilitates this, but sometimes when the applecart gets derailed it is time to move on.

Marpa, one of the great Buddhist teachers and a famous Mahasiddha, was crying over the grave of his son. One of his disciples found him and said:

> *"But isn't everything Empty?"*
> To which Marpa replied,
> *"Yes, but certain things are more empty than others..."*

And on this note we return to the tale of Cat. After a while Cat and I started drifting apart. Ongoing money pressures put a strain on our relationship and we both worked from home, so spending all that time together probably added to the problem. We spent days and days of amphetamine-fuelled exploration, hers of the internet and design, and me of my mind. I took time out from this regime but she was relentless, and at the end she would spend more time with her computer than with me.

I even toyed with the idea of putting some peanut butter into her CD drive to force her away from it, but that would have sparked a war that probably never would have ended. No one did revenge like Cat, she was elaborate, calculated, and persistent, and I often felt that she was directly descended from Attila the Hun. Her downtime would be de-fleaing our two cats, Savage and Tricky, by hand.

Things started breaking apart and getting spiky. She took to passing out on the couch in her study and I just suffered. I still loved her and this just tore me to pieces. I was trying to patch up a leaking ship, but it kept springing more leaks which I kept patching up, until the whole thing sunk on me, taking my heart with it. When the situation had degenerated too far we agreed to split up. We were still living in the same house, and it was then that she started going out with one of my best friends, Jona.

Watching my girlfriend, who I still loved, getting dressed up and putting on make-up to go out with my best friend, was probably one of the hardest things I have ever experienced. I do not wish this on anyone, as all my Holy Cows were being slain at once – love, respect, honour, friendship, trust, mystical connection, you name it, I was swimming in a lake of self-pity, anger, rage, loss, sadness, vengeance, and despair. A more exquisite torment I could not have devised for myself.

I had a brief scene with a bondage model at the same time to kill the pain, but it was not serious, and just a diversion from the fact that I still loved Cat. When she left I went into a continuous psychotic loop, dwelling on the whole thing. I was oscillating between plotting to blow up Jona's house, sinking into fits of deep depression, and having fantasies of her returning. This went on for a month, and I continued speeding through these deep dark days which just intensified the whole thing. If you want to dwell and fixate on something, crystal meth is definitely your substance of choice. She even threatened to take the cats, to which I replied *"swords at dawn"*. I kept the cats – it was the least I could be left with.

Having my Holy Cows all shattered at once was an epic breaking of attachments and it tore the hell out of me at the time. I even begged her to kill me, I was in such a miserable state. The whole thing actually put me into a Stingray space, which has a lot to do with rejection, and wanting to take revenge on the perpetrators of your suffering. I took it at the time, but the state was way too strong for remedies to touch sides, though they helped a bit. It was something I just had to go through, to come out on the other side.

There was just so much pain and heartbreak, added to by the loneliness and the speed, and I languished in a pit for weeks on end, suffering like a dog waiting to be put down. The intensity and duration of my suffering amazed even me, being Enlightened one still has to play out ones Holy Cows and they definitely play out harder and stronger than before, at least in the beginning. I brought it on myself with my intent to free myself from all binding obscurations. Dakini embodied by Cat and Jona just provided the Means for me to go through my own little psychodrama, and it was glorious.

Acknowledging the perfection of things is easy when things are going well, but when everything is coming out of the woodwork and your world is coming apart around you it is another thing all together – just holding onto your sanity is a heroic struggle. Sometimes it overwhelms you, even if you can see the perfection in everything, the pain just overrides it. This is a very dangerous place to be in and something you want to get out of as soon as possible.

When radical action, like petrol bombing your ex-best friend's house starts looking rather appealing just to ease ones own pain, it is definitely time for a reality check. Although I never did it, it would not have taken much more to get me to light up a Molotov. Jona was largely silent during the whole interaction, which was very sensible on his part, as it would have just taken one spark to incite me into a righteous frenzy of revenge.

When the phoenix finally rose from the ashes of my life I realized that I had been fireproofed, and that no one could ever hurt me that badly again. Everyone had warned me about her vicious ways when we got together, but to no avail. One of her best friends even abandoned her by siding with me, which was at least one small consolation victory amidst the desolation grounds of my heart. In the middle of a trauma one grasps at strange straws to rebuild ones shattered sense of self-worth.

Sometimes love is not enough because it has to work on all levels, and if you keep coming around to the same stumbling blocks and choking on them, then maybe it is just not meant to work. Either that or it has had its time, bail out before all the good stuff turns to dust.

The ability to know when to get out is very important. To stay in something despite the feeling that it is wrong, is merely the result of attachment, and it will most certainly be taken away from you sooner or later.

Either that, or it will make you suffer a long time. If I had gotten out earlier at least I might have salvaged something from the wreckage, some sense of self-worth, or even maybe a friendship. Such is the nature of reality – one often needs to suffer before one learns the lesson.

With Cat we had danced our dance and needed to move apart, that was just the way it was, Dakini States or not. When all you taste is bitterness in your mouth, not to leave is suicide.

In retrospect I thank her for breaking so many of my attachments and slaughtering so many Holy Cows all at once. The more that gets done the less there is to do and then one arises newly born from the atomic fires.

If we had not split up I would not have unbound the titans with Athena, or ever met Anri and Gezar. Cat found the Seahorse remedy and the Tantras for me, and this in itself was worth all the pain she generated. In short, other relationships would not have occurred had we still been together, and it is always about having new experiences, at least for me it is.

If you have not experienced heartbreak you have not truly lived, it is one of the purest pains in existence, because wherever you turn it is still there. Once conquered though one joyfully enters the void, illusions unveiled, embracing Dakini in all of her changing forms.

Sometimes even the will to live is destroyed by the Armies of Mara, with the Demon of Despair whispering suicidal suggestions, which can seem like a damn good idea at the time.

When we are suffering everything seems dark, and the light seems like a faraway concept that we have long lost touch with.

Do not sink into despair, skull-fuck Suffering in the eye instead.

EIGHTEEN

Riding The Whirlwind

*You only get to have your cake and eat it once you have
watched it flash-fried to a crisp in front of you.
Then, and only then, do the cake makers start knocking
on your door with free deliveries from all the finest
French patisseries in the world.*

Dzogchen says *"take teachings like a pig or a dog, go everywhere and
learn from anyone, then like a tiger – retire to a quiet place to digest"*.

There is nothing that you discover along the way that cannot
be used as a Skillful Means and when in doubt, follow your nose
and your heart and you cannot stray off the path for too long.

They say that you generate the same karma from kicking a door,
a dog or a person because it is the degree to which one holds on to
the anger, which causes residual patterning to condition your existence. *"Don't change a thing"* is one of the central tenets of Dzogchen
because it is all perfect, one just has to revisit all the old emotional
spaces in order to see them for what they are.

It is always interesting to watch people going through old photo
albums and trash their present reality with memories of how happy
they were at those times. Strange but true, there is something morbid
and masochistic about the whole process. Why people do this is
largely inconceivable, I guess they like molesting themselves with
the Demon of the Past.

On the flipside there is the possibility of flushing these memories by going back through them in detail. Don Juan calls it 're-capitulation' and there is immense benefit in doing it to clear the body's memory of certain events. Like most tools though, it is a double edged sword, and one runs the risk of reinforcing the very thing one was trying to eradicate.

Even the 'curing the sick' storyline is just eliciting aspects of my own nature so that I can free myself further from the Illusion of Form. Not that I am complaining about my job, but in reality, it is just a cover to further my own process of Dissolution. If from a dualistic view I benefit others, which I do ceaselessly, it is just myself in reality that I am benefiting.

The *path is the goal* and the goal is Liberation and you liberate yourself anew at each moment if you remain present and aware in that moment. It makes THE SECRET look like the ramblings of a teenager, the first step in a long game with many detailed processes. By focusing unduly on the material world you risk being bound on the very Wheel you were trying to liberate yourself from in the first place. It is only secondarily about getting everything you want, the primary purpose is to liberate yourself from Suffering and ultimately from Form completely, in so doing you win the ultimate prize.

Every step on the path is different, and just when you think you have a handle on it, it shifts 180 degrees and drags you off in a completely new and unexplored direction. It is quite simply the ultimate trip, your trip, your very own magical mystery tour through your mind and memories. A trip whose end guarantees freedom from all Suffering forever, and what is left then is pure Bliss, which is the fusion of Clarity and Awareness.

There are many turns in the path and this is why some guidance is useful. We have many teachers, all Aspects of Self of course, but a wise man listens to the mistakes and successes of others and modifies his behaviour accordingly. Everyone has their own path to tread, and no two roads are the same. Ones journey is largely inconceivable, even to oneself, but there are certain benchmark events and landmarks along the road that are universal, and well worth paying attention to.

When you are retraining the mind to its original position, it is important to continually reinforce it as the default. We have had our settings altered many times onto dysfunctional pathways. The mind will seek to return to the false default settings at a moment's notice, unless you keep correcting it enough so that it sticks.

The correct position is easily recognized as the mood of Ease, Clarity and Bliss – the true Aspects of the Natural Mind, your mind. This is why Dzogchen talks about *direct introduction to the state* in the first place. If someone can give you a taste of your own Natural State, it is a beacon that one can pin things on in order to get back there.

There are oases and lights along the way to guide yourself by, although of course you have to be willing to venture into the desert of your own mind in the first place. Any journey begins with one step, and there is even hope for the chip fryers and the tycoons if they are committed enough.

The current fad of living in the moment is not wrong, it is just that until one has liberated oneself from the Six Realms, one will merely be going around in circles chasing ones tail. If you can stay perpetually in the moment with Presence of Mind, you are achieving the Dzogchen goal anyway, but this is not as easy as it sounds.

To quote a great Dzogchen master, *"when smoking your cigarette, just remain present and aware"*. To maintain this Present Aware State in the midst of exciting emotions, is the path, and if you can remain *present* even in the middle of the most graphic or erotic events, then you have truly arrived.

I am not talking about detachment here, you are still totally there, it is just that you do not get so swept up by events that you drop your Clarity and get bound by one of the Six Realms. This is the art and the skill.

It is easy to remain undisturbed in your morning meditation or in yoga class but can you retain that level of 'undisturbedness' when you are confronted by a sexy member of the opposite sex? It's not that one does not engage it, au contraire, one engages it completely, and has a great time. If one hankers after it or dwells on it when it's over however, one has been bound by it.

Proceeding deeper into the heart of the beast, the breaking of the concept of 'time' is just one of the many concepts that require breaking. Once the future and past fall away, or melt into The Moment, one immediately starts relaxing. There are no more guilty regrets and nothing to achieve, just a blank page to write your story on.

Breaking the concept of 'space' is another binding obscuration that once conquered, allows one to have whatever you want in that moment. If it is information you're trying to remember or your car keys that you lost, by breaking down this duality nothing you need is ever further than an arms reach away.

Probably the hardest concepts to break are that of 'self' and 'other' but it is the essential tool in overcoming fear. Once you realise that *all is self*, there is nothing that can hurt you because why would you hurt yourself? These two constantly reinforce each other and you cannot really break them down in isolation, as they are inexorably entwined, and the dissolution of one implies the dissolution of the other. If you manage to see and experience the *emptiness of self*, then you are no longer bound by the idea that there is actually anything inside you, except for a huge pool of unlimited potential waiting to assume any form in a moment.

You cannot just talk about the *emptiness of form*, you have to experience it, and this is where the multitude of enlightenment techniques come in. If you prefer to cheat a bit, a good dose of Anti-matter never goes astray.

You can always imagine it to be empty until you see it to be true. This requires a lot of commitment but is a good starting point if one has nothing else. Once you have experienced the Emptiness of Self as a perpetually shifting pool of pure awareness, it is then quite easy to see 'others' as empty. When you can see others in this light, it is a quick hop, skip, and jump to realizing that there are in fact no 'others' out there, ever.

If you do not experience something it literally does not exist and if you do it is just the *play of your own mind* with no more meaning than a pretty picture show. If you experience it, it has momentary meaning as a *movement of form,* but that is it. There is no more continuity between one moment and another than there is similarity between a supernova and a gerbil. Having seen the Illusion of things to be just that, one cannot be bound by it. One moment, one form, one thought, one emotion gives way to the next, and we have no choice but to enjoy the ongoing succession of light shows.

Buddha watched the Daughters of Mara trying to seduce him and he just did not play. They were trying to lure him into the realm of suffering through his own attachment to them, but he remained undisturbed.

To no longer buy into the *illusion of the self* or of an external independent world as being real, is the ideal. If you break the Illusion enough times it stays broken and you cannot be bound by it anymore which essentially sets you free. This is why most people should not even start on the path unless they are willing to sacrifice everything. Why? Because if it is not indestructible, it can, and probably will be cracked – such is the nature of the beast that is born from Emptiness.

When we slice off something we love it is going to cause us pain, unless we have truly transcended it, and even then maybe so. Your special and pretty Holy Cows hurt the most when they die, but they always resurrect in a purer form when they are reborn. Would we have it any other way, could it be any other way? Sometimes, in fact most of the time, one has to descend into the pits of hell to return with the gems, and if people are willing to confront their own personal demons, they definitely have a chance to liberate themselves from suffering.

One cannot play the half perfect paradigm – it is either all totally perfect or completely fucked, and when I look back I know that everything I have done along the way has been to get me here, so I cede to Perfection. You only get to have your cake and eat it once you have watched it flash-fried to a crisp in front of you, and by then you no longer want it anyway. Then, and only then, do the cake makers start knocking on your door with free deliveries from the finest French patisseries around the world.

How people manage to ride this storm without Homoeopathy

I can barely imagine, hopefully they have some other practices that help them out. I just find Homeopathy so elegant, it guards me from the vagaries and vicissitudes of my mind and I don't really have to put in much effort or suffer through the process at all. Personally I am not a big fan of meditation, having realized that one is never really out of the *state of meditation*, if one remains Present and Aware at all times, but of course people will have their preferred means and skills. I have my armoury of ancient Tibetan tech, my homoeopathic books of karma, and my stash of little medicated sugar balls to guide me through, so I can afford to substitute sitting meditation with strategic takedown of the mental processes that lock the Conditioned Identity into form

The very nature of living creates attachments and it is not that we do not feel pain when they go, it just fades quickly. Knowing that it's *all illusion*, to buy into it as real is a shortcut to unnecessary suffering. Buddhism is not proposing that we become impersonal machines devoid of emotion. It is saying that by recognizing the empty nature of the *play of illusion*, we do not get caught up in suffering from the loss of something that, in reality, was just one of the more beautiful Aspects of our own minds.

I still feel sadness when my cat goes missing and do what I can to find her again. I don't spend hours wringing my hands or tearing my hair out in despair though. I don't torture myself with terrifying visions of what might have happened to her, or go around blaming others or myself for the situation. I spend the appropriate time looking for her, but at some stage I relax into the perfection of everything, knowing that to be the Natural State. So by my own credo, suffering in a perfect scenario would be pure indulgence, and an error of View. Few people realise just how much they indulge.

I have never been good on patience but drug smuggling had forced it upon me, especially when you have to wait for half stoned, disorganized muppets with no sense of punctuality. Eventually you let go of the irritation at having to wait, and just relax into it. Every single event in ones life has a purpose and it is part of the lessons to be conquered and risen above, as even the most tedious event can school you in valuable lessons.

146

Once you see the perfection and intricate beauty in every event, it is hard not to be swept away by the majesty of the whole thing, and surf reality, high on your self-generated supply of neurochemicals. The deeper you get into it, the easier it becomes, as you come to expect it as the default. The initial highs in the beginning are useful to spur you on. They are also worthwhile benchmarks to hold on to when your herd of Holy Cows are being decimated in the process, which is something that inevitably happens to us all.

This is why it is best to engage the things you like first when you hit the Natural State because this builds up a strong positive charge to bolster you when the going gets tough. Once you have engaged the things you like, you are sufficiently buoyed up to engage the things you don't like, and then it is relatively simple to engage the things you are indifferent to. When you engage the things you do not like it is also best to start small. There are a lot of Holy Cows out there which will all be called up for slaughter so it is best to acclimatize slowly. Start with Brussels sprouts before you move on to the big ones like love, loyalty, friendship, and honour. Don't leave it too long either because it might hit you when you least expect it, and it's definitely best to be prepared.

When you play with swords you will get cut, it is inevitable, but if you survive it you learn skills which will benefit you forever. When you have faced your worst fears and survived there is very little that can touch you. Every ugly and painful moment often has to be felt until it no longer hurts. Pain just becomes a memory which fades and eventually disappears, and then slowly you put yourself back together, pick up your battered sword, and continue on down The Path.

The saying that *"you never get more than you can handle"* has to be taken in conjunction with *"the more you can handle, the more you get"* and sometimes this means large amounts of pain. This is why if you are willing to take it head on, the 'hard and fast' methodology is the safest. The slower we do it the more time the demons have to reform, and then they have to be fought all over again. If you can kill their generals, Doubt and Despair, Fear and Betrayal, all at once, you can sufficiently weaken and disorganize their army.

Once that's done, the rest of them are relatively easy to pick off at your leisure, and can often be sniped from a distance.

It is not that you do not feel emotion, it is just that you do not get dragged down and consumed by it. Of course I cried when my mother was dying, it was horrible that someone so full of life should be vanishing, yet on liberating her I knew I had done all a good son could do. This is the only thing that really means anything at the end of the day, at least in my book, and that is the only book I have after all. She gave me my positive view on women, presenting a healthy, active archetype of a fully functional woman on which to base my Dakini View. For this alone, and for loving me in spite of all my seemingly mad actions and bizarre choices, I wash her feet with my tears of joy.

What is dying when someone we love is dying is the attachment to them and the deeper this goes the deeper the pain. But pain passes and life goes on and the best testament you can give to them is to live your life to the full, in whatever direction you see fit, what more really could they want for you?

The *"Great Perfection"* was considered a secret Teaching passed on only from master to student until the invasion of Tibet, when it was decided that it should be spread to the West. So few people knew about it that it was in danger of being lost forever. Namkhai Norbu definitely has a large part to play in this, and gets endless rains of flowers for spreading the Teachings to the West.

Padmasambhava predicted in the 10th century AD that the people of the Red Star would come in chariots breathing fire. Tibet would be torn apart and the Teachings would spread to the West. This is exactly what happened and it has allowed the Teachings to get into hands they would have previously never found their way into, namely non-Tibetans. Dzogchen has only been out from under the lineage covers for about twenty years, and it actually suits the Western mindset of fast and furious without changing a thing – no need to shave your head or give up any worldly pleasures.

This is why I do not rail too strongly against the invasion of Tibet, as even that was fore-ordained and designed to springboard the Teachings to the rest of world. One thing can't be perfect and another imperfect. It is either all perfect or none of it is, so if you can see the perfection of one event then you are obliged to accept the perfection of everything.

The very state of chaos that is currently ruling the planet is designed to generate suffering, and force people to pursue a path of liberation that will spare them from the ravages of reality. The mood of the Kali Yuga is the mood of Dissolution and if one embraces this, it throws up a range of stimuli that can be used to integrate the Six Realms within ourselves. Flawless, not a molecule or event out of place, pure perfection, as the Dance of Reality plays out its swansong, doing its victory lap. Although the path is often too much for most people, everyone has on open invitation to attend. I bow my head at the feet of the Dzogchen Teachings for preserving such a beautiful and simple teaching on Liberation, that all may engage and free themselves in this very lifetime.

I reached my enlightenment first in Taiwan and then secondly in Johannesburg, both suitably unpleasant places to spur me on. If I had been on the French Riviera without gangsters pursuing me, drug deals going bad, near starvation, and imminent threat to life and limb, I doubt I would have been driven as quickly into the water.

I have faith that Dakini will provide exactly what I need, when I need it. I serve her faithfully, after all she is All of Reality, and that includes me. She is always breaking any binding illusions that hold me into Form, and even though it might rip my heart out at the time, I am ready and do it willingly. If you are willing to give up everything and anything, you often do not have to. You certainly cannot fake this because paying lip service just doesn't cut it...

Sharper, faster, harder, has always been my policy. This is my methodology and it does not suit everyone but it definitely contains less risk in the long-term, if you are up for the truckload of pain that destroying all your attachments at once entails.

I would not have consciously and willingly put myself through such heartbreak, it is horrible, but my commitment to clear all my Holy Cows was so strong that Dakini engineered exactly the situation that would destroy the greatest number all at once. It could not have been any other way, and Samsara turns into Nirvana when you view reality through this lens.

She is a hard taskmaster but fair, and if you offer her your head on bended knee she cuts it off, and sticks it back on for you cleansed.

Even in the depths of despair there is always a poignant beauty in it all – the luminous thread that keeps one going through the shattered nights of the soul.

NINETEEN

Unbinding The **Titans**

*When you start to doubt your visions you are truly
screwed because they exist at your most precious core.
Turning your back on them is like flushing your
dreams – life can only be hell after that.*

The Buddhists say: *"At a certain point in your meditation you will
hear a voice, claiming to be God. Ignore this voice as it is your very Self
speaking. Continue with your meditation."* If one applies this to the
letter, most world religions are in fact the result of meditational
disorders…

The way to distinguish between a religious fanatic and a Liberated Being is the degree of attachment to their visions. Although
they both have mystical or visionary experiences, the Liberated
Being recognizes this at all times to be a part of his own mind, to
be engaged with, but not dwelled upon. Furthermore, the astute
practitioner of Dzogchen will know that one vision always gives way
to another, and another, constantly upgrading itself.

Many times throughout my life the madness of the world has
pushed me to the brink of despair. The only thing that has kept
me going through it all were my visions, which lured me back from
the edge of the abyss, ensuring that I am still here. I honestly don't
know where I would be without it, probably dead.

In the early days most of my visions centred on finding a way out, some exit strategy that would allow me and my friends to be free from the insanity of the world.

One vision I had in plain daylight while walking down a crowded, garbage-scented street, involved a gate through space to another world. The gate was located somewhere in the Great Rift Valley. Unfortunately for me the Great Rift Valley runs for thousands of miles, but it was so real that I went out of my way to convince my cadre to spend everything we had on some four-wheel drives and supplies to get there. Needless to say no one took it very seriously because it was my vision after all, but the sense of urgency I felt at the time was very real, as was my disappointment when no one wanted to come along.

Since then I have envisioned a range of scenarios, from retreating to the desert, to starting up a colony in Kashmir. You name it I have thought of it, seeing it as real-time, detailed, full-colour possibilities. It is hard to argue with visions like that.

I have subsequently crystallized my vision and strategy of what is to come, as I realised over time that I am bound to this planet and to the reseeding of a new age after the dust has settled. I don't need to leave, the field just needs to be cleared a bit so that a new garden can be planted where those that are left can live and create, each one expressing their unit potential without hindrance.

My role as Liberator of the Earth ached in my bones and sang in my blood, and surely one of the reasons I was here was to unbind the titans, to bring back our initial allies, the good guys. Throughout my life I have shunned conventional hierarchies of power, and so have always been driven to free the enchained. For as long as I can remember I have had a powerful affinity for the titans, especially hearing of how they had been bound by the Greek gods in Tartarus, a lake of fire seven days stone drop below the deepest levels of hell.

And so I return to legend and mythology, and the story when pieced together, goes like this. The world dragon *Tiamat* (embodied chaos) formed *Gaia* (the earth) from her blood and scales. From Gaia was formed *Ouranos* (the sky) and from the union of these two was formed everything else. When Ouranos created the gods

(*Zeus* and his brothers), he perceived for some reason that they were misbehaving and so decided to destroy his creations by devouring them. Zeus, being very cunning, managed to chop his way out of the stomach and overwhelm or kill Ouranos - different legends have different versions. Zeus also cut off his testicles which he threw into the ocean from which *Aphrodite* (the foam born) was created. So began the systematic binding of the titans.

The titans would often ally themselves to the humans. There are many accounts of how the titans benefited mankind by introducing us to agriculture, writing, and architecture. The actual stories are less important than the motivation. What it boils down to is that the titans had been punished for basically upgrading our living standard by giving us technology to advance. If so, they must have been the good guys. And by simple logical inference the gods must have been the oppressors, not too hard to figure out.

The story of *Prometheus* is well known. He was punished for stealing fire from the gods and giving it to man, and as a result, forever bound to a rock where vultures would feed on his liver. Being immortal, his liver would grow back every night to be eaten afresh the next day.

When reading the stories of the gods it always involves requests of all manner of offerings and sacrifices from man, everything from bulls to virgins, with very little provided in return. The profile of the gods basically reads as absentee landlords, demanding tribute from us on our own planet, a tribute that is mostly enforced through fear of retribution and annihilation.

A legend I came across was that one of the titans had been bound in a flat mountain on the southernmost tip of the *"Dark Continent"*. This could only be Table Mountain in Cape Town, no rocket science there, and amusingly where a lot of this story takes place. More interestingly, there is also a seperate legend about a titan bound in Table Mountain by the name of *Adamastor*. He is supposedly the one who creates the terrible storms we have in Cape Town, and he does this in anger at being isolated from *Thetis*, his bride, who is in the sea and whom he cannot get to.

I slowly came to realize that since the Forces of Ignorance arrayed against us were of such magnitude, it required the services of Earth itself. The freeing of the titans had always been in my blood and liberating them has always been a strong priority. They would definitely go toe to toe with the gods and in the resulting mayhem they would integrate or destroy each other, leaving mankind free of all their machinations.

If the only way to fix the 'humanoids' as Athena referred to them, was to raise their Kundalini, then it made sense that the only way to fix Earth would be to raise its Kundalini. There was definitely a parallel between the imprisoned and inactive elemental forces and the raising of the Kundalini.

The ancient *"serpent energy"* curled up in the base of the body could be likened to the imprisoned titans, powerful natural forces that are prevented from doing what they're supposed to, forever leaving man powerless to be who he is really meant to be. We continue to be trapped in a world of cold reason and good ideas that never come to fruition because we lack the power to fuel it. Surely what we need to achieve is the union of the two, so it made perfect sense to me that freeing the titans would return the Earth's power back to herself. We would no longer have left warring with right, masculine divided from feminine, and our compassion and skills separated from our power and intuition. Uniting these forces would return us to a state of wholeness, allowing us to claim our true heritage by activating all those gifts and abilities that have so long been dormant.

If I could somehow awaken the base chakra of the world, it would rise up through all the energy channels, clearing and cleaning as it went, until it eventually dissolved into the crown. Then things would operate as they should, war, strife, anger, jealousy, resentment, and dissatisfaction would all be things of the past, and a new Golden Age could be ushered in.

Here we return to legend again. In a comic-book version of Norse mythology it was told that *Yggdrasil* (the Norse world tree) was where *Jörgmungandr* (the world serpent) had been bound by Thor, because it attempted to destroy the world - typical of man to fear his own destruction by uncontrollable powerful forces. It made sense therefore that the unbinding of the World Serpent would result in the same effect as the Kundalini rising. The key, as with the Kundalini, lay at the base. If you place Cape Town as the base chakra of the world, which is not an unreasonable assumption to make because it literally is at the bottom of the world, well then I was right where it was at. It became crystal clear what I had to do and in order to free the titans I needed help, which is where Athena came in.

I took Athena to a particularly powerful forest and the place where, what I consider to be Yggdrasil, grows. It is a massive pine tree with three branches curving upwards, exactly how Yggdrasil is traditionally described, and it towers over the rest of the forest. When we returned to Athena's house I started to feel a weird, heavy, yet excited sensation in my cells, like being slow boiled in a pressure cooker. I realized then that it was another Dakini State coming on, although this time I was the centre of it. Athena was receiving a secondary blast of it which was spinning her out a bit. I reassured her that one generally just had to crawl around if one wanted to move and wait until Dakini had delivered her teaching or information into our bodies.

At the same time one of Athena's archetypal forms, The Sword, came into her mind space and we both saw the bound titan. She was somewhat apprehensive at first, fearing that the titan at the base might be Loki, the Norse god of mischief. I argued that even if it was Loki, why should he be bound? I pointed out to her that it was time for everything to be freed from its state of bondage regardless. Having no doubt about the fact that she had this Sword of Gabriel inside her, and that it was meant to slice through the shackles of oppression, I eventually convinced her to cut the chains with me.

What came out of it after that was a massive gift of love from Gaia to her, and she overflowed with tears of joy. The core elemental force was unbound and global reintegration could begin. I of course couldn't have been happier. To return the world to its unaltered state was key to the grand plan, and having pulled the plug out of the dam I sat down and waited for the end of the world to begin. Not quite knowing what to expect, but knowing that it would be better than

I could ever imagine, I got comfortable and lit a cigarette... Like most affairs of such epic scale these things take time, as the natural forces realign themselves and return to their desired positions.

For people who have never experienced visions it is often hard to accept, let alone appreciate, other people's visions but I would argue that everyone has them at least once in their life, and if not, I believe everyone has the potential to. However, most people experience this when they are young, and as they grow old and battered by the harshness of reality they convince themselves that it was just wishful thinking, and bury their dreams in the back of their minds where it eventually turns to dust.

Then there is also the fear of ridicule or even insanity as people shove their dreams aside because it does not somehow fit into the realm of what the rest of the world thinks of as 'normal' or 'possible'. Horror stories of mental hospitals full of people who get stuck in a particular vision abound, and this further feeds the fear, so we lock the windows in our minds as we scramble to hold up an idea of just another ordinary life.

To be yourself completely is quite a challenge and it will ruffle a few feathers, but on the whole people love you for it, and you can't make everyone happy anyway. If *all is self and self an illusion* there is nothing to lose really and the world to gain. The ego is that little voice of doubt that tries to reason you out of things that you feel good about. It knows that each step you make along the path is a step towards freedom from its clutches, and will throw everything in your way to stop you from achieving liberation.

An earlier vision I had of the titans was of them being bound in Tartarus surrounded by the noble gasses which are inert, thereby keeping them in a state of static slumber. My fusing of the different Realms and the different bands enchaining the titans was one way in which I hoped to break down the chemical cage imposed upon them by the gods, in this way facilitating their awakening.

Sometimes your original visions don't come into form in the way or timeframe that you envisioned but that shouldn't make you waver, quite the opposite. It should inspire you to keep dreaming by engaging situations, things, or people that allow you the space to feed your imagination and nurture your heart. As your Awareness increases the format of your visions will change, and as you learn to refine your mind it will reflect in the quality of your visions, as you continue to get closer to actually bringing them into form. There is always a place and a purpose for visions. The challenge is to make sense of them as they arise and develop, but even more so, to always trust the perfection of it, including when they change.

The indignation I originally felt at the imprisonment of the titans was perfect because it fuelled my own process of Liberation. The first lack of trust and the resulting power struggle by one group over another, echoes the dualistic concepts of 'self' and 'other' and the eternal battle for control. This pattern of domination has been perpetuating itself throughout human history. By setting the titans free I had also inadvertently ensured that I left no possibility in myself to mirror the abuse of power, either of forces within me, or toward other people. As within so without, as above so below, the process of liberating forces 'out there' was a replication of my own processes, just on a larger scale.

When I was in Kashmir, I was exploring my mind space and found a locked door. Athena, the self-appointed Guardian of Hell, had grown tired of the job and had given me the key while I was still in South Africa, so I decided to open it up.

Inside was a sea of demons stretching as far as the eye could see, all lined up and waiting for orders. Their mood was kind of, *"what reality do you want us to harass boss?"* and yet at the same time quite impersonal and almost benign. Make no mistake, they resonated power – they were demons after all. I felt like a kid having opened a candy store feeling just a tad overwhelmed by the implications of so much sugar. I quickly locked them away for future use, knowing that the time to unleash them upon the world had not yet come, and that I would know when to reopen the door.

As I beheld the sea of demons I knew them to be an *aspect of myself* and not to be feared. When one can see the Hell Realm as a pure state it turns into its raw form, undiluted clarity, which becomes the diamond knife that slices through the illusions of reality. With all this said and done, there is still nothing quite like looking at a sea of demons awaiting orders from you.

In Tibetan there is a word *"god-demon"*, seeing them both essentially as interfering forces, that frankly, mankind would be better off without. As far as I am concerned any god version of history is suspect, and subject to doubt. The same way one should brush off the Illuminati and world governments as being a controlling force in ones life, one should see gods and demons as internal forces one should integrate, and make peace with. They then become a part of your adornment, your fine colours that make you, you. If there is no one to pray to or fear, then one is truly free to carve ones own destiny as one sees fit, which is what everyone deserves as their birthright.

This is where Dzogchen once again saves the day. If you can understand the True Nature of the Mind, you can happily allow your visions to play out in form, informing and inspiring you without the danger of getting trapped.

This is when you have to keep in mind that it is concocted for you and by you, in the most entertaining way possible, and in my experience life is pretty meaningless without it – if you can't enjoy your own mind, what else can you truly enjoy?

TWENTY

Taking Up Arms

You know who you are.
There is always room for more, if you can
make the grade.

I have always favoured the 'we all ride to glory together' paradigm but finding people of equal awareness has been more than a bit of a struggle. The roster got shuffled many times as various false claimants were stricken off due to misbehaviour, and the filtering process still continues. Each Rider I find though enriches the picture a thousandfold and makes it worth every moment of seeking.

When I returned after my first taste of Enlightenment in Taiwan I had tears of joy every day, along with visions and revelations and was running on raw enthusiasm and the desire to heal the ailments of all mankind. You name it I was in it, the state of ecstasy, clarity, and awareness fused together – no greater joy could be imagined.

I hadn't yet been introduced to Dzogchen though, so I allowed myself to return to mediocrity for lack of company at the time. The sheer joy and exuberance at being alive, where I could literally call up energy from the earth to fuel me, soon disappeared – I was enlightened but I was all alone. Eventually after about two months of trying to get people to my state of mind I succumbed to the dreary world of Samsara, and I fell from grace. I went into a state near dead for a number of years, going through the motions of life, but not really feeling that total connection with everything that I had felt before.

It can get very lonely out there if you are the only one speaking a language, and having good company you can share your jewels with, is in itself a jewel without price. This is the value of Sangha as you are speaking the same language and their stories inspire you to further heights, and vice versa. What is important is that you are sharing a journey and an experience which is indescribably beautiful, and it is this beauty that binds people together. If you are the only two speakers of Swahili left in the world the other speaker will instantly be a friend. The *"roots that feed, not the chains that bind"* is a phrase I picked up from a mad Rat I lived with once, and it just stuck.

My original plan for enlightening all sentient beings was to wake up individuals who I believed would then take up the banner and begin to wake up other people. This was the idea, it would spread virally – one would infect two, two would infect four, and soon a Plague of Enlightenment would sweep the planet.

I have watched a lot of the folk who are going to make it come to me, each carrying distinct cultures and lineages of whole civilizations in their genes. Some of them realize this and some do not, but they still carry these threads which are beautiful in themselves, and therefore worth preserving.

The viral model failed because it requires a lot of commitment and very few people took up the banner and ran with it, due to lack of confidence, skills, or personal power. After this I came to the view that it would be more effective to create a central core of people of suitably high awareness which would create a dynamo effect. Acting as a centrifuge it would spin out and raise the general consciousness on contact. If I could raise the energy of the core high enough, the whole movie would go nova, and all sentient beings would be enlightened in a spiralling wave.

This failed too as the centre did not hold, it kept fragmenting due to people's smallness of spirit. The lack of true Awareness acted to short-circuit the dynamo, so we never really got to be of one mind. Instead of doing the real work of truly unifying the core, which was required for this particular model to work, I would end up doing damage control as people kept antagonising each other.

There is a ritual in Buddhism called *Ganacakra* (gathering circle), which is basically an enlightenment feast to celebrate important events and give offerings for just about anything. Another part of its function is to repair errors between practitioners. If rapport is broken between practitioners everything starts to fragment as trust is essential when cruising through the backwaters of the mind. Those who disrespected the mood where soon expelled from the party – either everyone plays or no one plays.

Where everyone is on their journey is not that important, and can create unnecessary competition, the 'who is more enlightened' drama. *"Respect the mood"* is the ethos for the Buddha Brats, because anyone who spoils the party ends up destroying the mood. The party must go on after all. It is one of the main and best reasons for being here in the first place... and to benefit sentient beings, of course.

Never turn your back on your friends, human, or otherwise that helped you on The Path in the first place, because to dishonour them is to dishonour yourself. If you do this you are not much better than a spineless slug, always give credit when it is due, it just enriches your reality. Proceed with largesse, head above shoulders, open to the world and what it is bringing you.

This is why the Compassionate View is so important because if one treats reality as one treats oneself, one can only benefit from the experience. I remember Asher once flinging energy around with great force and his daughter showing him that if he did it gently he would get more reward. Nothing likes to be brutalized. *"From the mouths of babes"* so to speak, if only he had listened...

"Discursive elements naturally recede." This applies to things or people that cause you to deviate from your mission, or throw obstacles in your path. This happened with James who tried to get on my good side by bad-mouthing Asher to me over the internet. At the time I was still one of Asher's most ardent supporters, especially

since he was the comrade in arms on my enlightenment holiday in India. So I just cut James out and never spoke to him again. If truth be told, I had always found him rather sleazy anyway, the suit who wanted to hijack the process for his own ends. Then there was Eddie who, although good company, could not resist the urge to fiddle with things and throw spanners in the works, insisting on running his own version of reality.

Once people trash the mood they somehow just seem to leave the picture, suddenly getting called away to another city or leaving the country. They are no longer required because there is quite simply no time for tourists or middlemen in my movie, and once they start to besmirch it they become a hindrance on The Path. It took a lot from me to throw out old friends but when they just wanted to hang out and talk shit they no longer became a positive force for transformation, and as a result got cut from the script.

My commitment is to Awareness, first, and last, and always. It is this very commitment that keeps me warm at night and ensures that no matter how awry things go, it always ends up benefiting my dance towards the Body of the Light. I have kept to this credo and it has never stood me in bad stead. At the time it is hard losing your best friend or lover but it is exactly what is meant to happen and is required for your own process of development.

I hit the Natural State for the first time on my speed binge in Taiwan. Then many years later, when Asher introduced me to Dzogchen, I recognised the State when I returned to it once again. In this instance the saying *"beware of Greeks bearing gifts"* turned out to be too true.

He still gets credit for bringing the Teachings to me, but he shouldn't have tried to control me. What I would have given him out of love I would not give him out of fear. When he thought he was losing control of me, he started destroying my confidence. I gave the world to Asher but he turned around to suck another pint of blood out of me, at which point I had to cast him off. I would have willingly given him the pint, but to try and force me meant that he wrote himself out of the movie. It was one of the hardest things I have ever had to do.

162

The Teachings are too precious and beautiful to be tarnished by using it as ones own little power trip, and I had to abandon the Teachings for a year to rid them of the stench of Asher's abuses. What this did for me though was to take up the mantle of the Teachings with a strong commitment to maintaining their purity.

"It is beneficial to be correct" says the I Ching.
"Why impeccability? Just because" says Don Juan.

It should be tattooed on people's foreheads at birth it is that important, and I stick strongly to this. Any other course of action is unthinkable, and any time I have strayed off the path I have returned quickly, feeling dirty for even having thought those things in the first place.

No one is immune from temptation but the higher up the Awareness ladder one rises, the more drastic the consequences become for straying from the path. In Dzogchen though there is *no path to tread or any levels to rise through* so a more appropriate description would be that of 'deepening into' The State. For someone to abuse the Teachings once they are already very deep into their own awareness would create a very sticky web from which to extricate themselves. While still bound by concepts, the potential for abusing reality exists. It is definitely beneficial to be correct and thus minimize generating karma for oneself.

Any aberration by people I take not as a fault of the Teachings but as their own indulgence. I have met some unscrupulous folk who basically use Dzogchen to convince women that since *all is Self,* they shouldn't let moral rules or even other relationships prevent them from having sex. A clear abuse of the Teachings and these people rarely prosper, the Dakinis protect the Teachings and do not take kindly to people abusing them at all.

Ekajati, the Prime Guardian of Dzogchen is drawn with her foot on the bloodied corpse of a perverter of the Teachings. This should serve as a clear warning to those who would use the Teachings to their own advantage. Reality will punish the miscreants far worse than I ever would, but the righteous injustice at people abusing such a beautiful system still raises up the destroying angel in me. This was why Dzogchen was kept secret for so long, because the potential for being misunderstood by people of a lesser view is always there.

Fortunately Dzogchen is basically a *"no error"* across the board view in all aspects of reality. The potential benefits far outweigh the potential abuses so if even one person makes it through from incorrect exposure to them, it has been worth revealing. If one thing is perfect then everything must be perfect. It just takes a brave, crazy, or desperate mind to take the leap and begin seeing it this way.

If you can solicit assistance along the way it is always useful, just make sure that those you put your faith in have already been down that road themselves. It will be well worth your time to make sure their advice rings true, gauge their motives, and ascertain whether they walk their talk, otherwise they are completely useless to you and potentially dangerous.

There is a special hell populated by double-dicked elephant bulls on Viagra designed for perverters of the Teachings and those who prey on the goodwill of others, exploiting them for their own benefit.

I do not worry about any abuses that people put the Teachings to anymore, having understood that their degree of Non-Duality will determine their degree of advancement through the stages, and this cannot be faked. Nothing is kept secret anymore, all the cookies are out of the jar but they are self-secret, requiring you to understand them as the key to their use. The Natural State prevents abuses of power by not allowing Liberation until you have fused Emptiness and Compassion.

You could no more abuse the power generated by this liberation than you could eat your own head. Anyone who gets trapped in the mires of power, self-importance, fear, or intellect will quite simply not make it, and this is appropriate because we do not want any megalomaniacs on the other side. Nice and neat, self-protected, flawless, happy days, five star super-deluxe special – it could in fact be no other way.

The experience of Enlightenment is glorious, there is no other way to describe it, but afterwards reality still continues. It is forever altered in essence but somehow also largely similar to how it was before, you still go out and party, you still go to work, you still keep up with your friends. The way you do all of these may change radically though, as may your mix of friends. I have had to cut off various friends because they literally cannot get where I am coming from ,and the daily recounting of their mundane existences just bores me after a while. There is only so much casual daily chit-chat you can handle before you return to the meat of Awareness, which is ones natural swimming ground.

I always give more than I take, that is my credo, and being the only one with the homoeopathic dispensary I have a lot to give. I give it willingly if people just play nicely. Once one is willing to sacrifice anything in ones own process, the removal of any useless aspect of your life becomes easy.

There will always be someone to fill the gap in reality and someone after that. No one is indispensable to the process. All of these minor betrayals were just stalking my own need to engage Ruthlessness, and the ability to cut off a diseased limb when it starts rotting on me. Take the best and leave the rest, skim the cream off reality and ditch the leaves and dirt, especially when they start fouling the milk. To the cats go the cream and if you start to demand cream, that is often what will be presented to you.

This is the world I live in and it is no wonder that my group is not large – how many people can even begin to conceive of this reality, let alone believe it. I have no choice, it is me, the visions I have had of it are so strong that they seem at times more real than daily events. Every molecule in me resonates to this function and sings in harmony when I follow it.

Like it or not, some of us just stumbled on the secrets through raw force of will and get to call our own destiny, but the door is open for latecomers and I am always up for pleasant surprises.

You know who you are, and there is always room for more if you can make the grade.

TWENTY-ONE

The **Rebirth** Of **Shambhala**

*The only thing ever stopping you
is your own limited vision, so
dream, and dream big.*

When you step into the inconceivable it steps into you, and then all bets are off.

There is a prediction made by Padmasambhava in the 10th century AD that at a certain point the legendary city of Shambhala would be rediscovered, and that the Forces of Light would issue forth against the Forces of Darkness and Ignorance, and a new Golden Age would be born.

This Charge of the Light Brigade would be led by Gesar of Ling, the enlightened king, who liberated people with his sword on the battlefield. There are tales of Padmasambhava doing the same thing when he found people whose consciousness was too degraded to absorb the Teachings. It was better for these people to die by the hands of a Realised Being, than carry on with their lives continuing to incur bad karma.

Not your average version of happy, rice eating, Buddhist monks but then both Gesar and Padmasambhava were fully Liberated and thus *beyond rebuke*. They say that the actions of Buddha's are inconceivable because they are running on a different frequency to ordinary people, and are thus beyond normal conceptual and behavioural structures and values.

This sounded like a fine legend to build something around, so I began assembling my Army of Light to combat Ignorance of the Nature of the Mind. Wasn't this just the funky combat version of the bodhisattva vow of liberating all sentient beings? The word bodhisattva means *"enlightenment warrior"* and what better to war against than Ignorance of the Nature of the Mind. Warriors go to war, at least in every fantasy novel I had ever read. I styled myself as General Max Zerbu, my personal homage to the Tibetan practice of *nailing down all the things you like, don't like and are indifferent to* on the journey to the Body of Light.

The time had come for the resurrection of the old legends, breathing life into it, making them our own in the most heroic cross-pollination of mythology ever seen. It is the Kali Yuga after all, and everything comes out to play. If *everything is Self* then so too are all the legends, there to be reinvented, transformed, and played with mercilessly.

Nothing less could be expected from the Buddha Brats. Line up the army, organize supplies, get everyone in line, kick back, and wait for the final curtain call. Where it led was truly inconceivable yet pure Crazy Wisdom at its most deranged. Those who could see and feel it were the ones who were going to be there at the end, and those who could not, would not suffer. Everybody wins but the lucky get to keep their personalities and be part of the crew which remakes reality in their own image. Would we have it any other way? I think not.

One of the first Riders that showed up for duty was a Kama. Jerry, a neurotic Dragon, was sufficiently infused with the joys of my skill that he once paid for Kama to come see me. Kama is the name of a Hindu god of love but at the time I thought it was Karma. To be able to sit across from someone and call her Karma amused me endlessly – I would have treated her for free with a name like that. We became fast friends and it wasn't long before it was clear that she was a Buddha Brat.

I soon entrusted her with a range of my remedies to experiment with on the bunch of hapless hippies she lived with. It just felt right to give her a full armoury to experiment with on reality at large. And play she did, dosing the tea of every poor bastard who came through her door. I explained the 'free will' clause to her but she chose to interpret it that since they were arising in her reality she had carte blanche to dose them as she saw fit. It was her decision and one does not question the actions of Dakini beyond a certain point. She earned her badge anyway by always being willing to perpetually push herself into the deep dark holes of her mind, getting stung by the scorpions in her psyche, and then coming out with the gems.

In order to understand Kama you have to understand her remedies which are Swan, Praying Mantis, Sun Spider, a few of the snakes, and Turquoise. Swan has the ugly duckling feel to it and it cured that feeling. This contrasted with the Sun Spider which has no venom but can run 40km/h and literally tears its victims apart with its large crablike claws. The Mantis devours its mate and the Turquoise prevents injury and deals with feelings of injustice from the world. When you throw all these together you get an idea of what a strange creature she was – very active, tearing reality and often people apart with her mental pincers yet with a good and very playful heart underneath. Kama was also part of the planning committee for the water supply job so she always has a special place in my heart.

Kama and Anri are both Metal Monkeys and I have always had great trust in the Crazy Wisdom skills of Monkeys. Maybe it is narcissism, or maybe it is as they say – that Monkeys are the geniuses of the group. They were both fiercely loyal and with sufficient awareness to command and gather more troops, so Kama was my captain and Anri was appointed as my personal aide and in charge of Special Forces. Thor was the sergeant at arms while Ming and Fenrir were lieutenants with their own troops. Luc was running his own show and Athena couldn't easily be cast in any role, except as an equal, and she was also running her own show with her own cadre.

The thing that unites the Buddha Brats, beyond a shared vision, is our willfulness and unwillingness to be told what to do. We are the original group of anarchists resenting any intrusion in our reality from much of anyone.

It is precisely this characteristic that allows us to throw off 'the chains that bind', making us so determined not to become slaves to Conditioning. Not to say that we aren't proud or, in Buddhist speak, full of Vajra Pride. I had often been accused of arrogance, but when you know you know and need no excuses to justify your existence.

We all just play our parts and one of mine was to ensure that the Army of Light was in top psychological condition. I determinedly dosed those around me, bringing them to full flower so that everyone would be fighting fit for the trials that were to come. Perfect from the start and it was my pleasure, if the truth be told, nothing could bring me greater satisfaction. That was part of my function after all, saving the day, swooping in to do some combat homoeopathic surgery on my Vajra brothers and sisters, the finest individuals in creation.

When your reality exceeds your fantasy by a scale of millions, you have truly arrived. If you are going to play it, play it in the mode of Epic Reality with no time to come up for air. We even spent time designing our wardrobe for the final event, nothing would be left to chance or lack of style – the suave police are always on duty. Of course one cannot live in this space permanently, but it is the juice that feeds the soul and makes life worth living, slowly transforming reality into living mythology. What then is not possible?

Girding myself in the armour of the Dharmakaya (Great Ocean of Awareness), strapping on my diamond sword, I would sally forth and let the chips fall where they may. Things can never be the same when the stuff of childhood fantasy becomes daily life, and all you can do is just follow your instinct and let things play out as they will. I had gone so far beyond my dreams that I was in truly uncharted territory. This is not to say that I was never assailed by Doubt. Living the magical mystery tour and interfacing with reality can get a bit schizoid at the best of times but I had my toolbox of 'reality tweakers' in nicely labelled bottles, which helped to keep mine, and everyone else's, show on the road.

In the beginning I bent my head well out of shape trying to figure out the logistical details of numbers and allegiances, trying to figure out who was on the final roster. Then it started becoming a strain and an effort so I just let it go. I gave up trying to figure out where it went or who I was becoming, all I knew was that it felt so incredibly right that I was compelled to follow it.

Like with many things when you let go it forms up again, perfectly and effortlessly. Dakini would work out the details, the fine-tuning, the colour coding, and the timeline. All I had to do was front up to my own movie and play it to the max, in the mood of dementertainment. I stopped worrying about which road to turn down, jumped into the back of the car, and enjoyed the view whilst being driven through reality. Full nuclear-powered holiday till D day – the movie had changed forever from suffering in Samsara to kicking back in the Pure Lands, waiting for the final trumpet to sound.

Then Gesar arrived.... The spearhead I was waiting for. To galvanize everyone into action he started up a café called SHAMBHALA - *"The Restaurant at the End of the Universe"* and I simply could not resist. Playing out the legend in real time, I gave him my full support and some personal training in my particular brand of energy weaponry. In return he fed me Iboga, and I got to see the Vajra Chains, the matrix of reality from which everything is constructed. The Dzogchen Teachings say *"stare into the form of the Vajra Chains and all will be revealed".* I saw long lines of snakelike runes weaving reality into form, possibly the most beautiful thing I had ever seen.

Iboga is a substance made from the bark of the root of the Iboga tree. It is considered to be the most powerful hallucinogen in the world, with a trip that lasts up to 48 hours. It is used as a rite of passage by Gabonese youths, because it aids in revealing ones purpose. It clears cellular memory, and enhances and repairs the relationship within ones Ancestral Lineage.

I put in the intent for the 64 Million Dakini Tantras, hoping to get a few if I was lucky. What occurred surprised even me. Millions of little packets, like library cards, started downloading onto my body. Not wanting to lose these precious Tantras I ripped the meat off my skeleton and a giant spray gun appeared with which I proceeded to burn the Tantras onto my bones in a shade of metallic orange paint. With the information secured on my skeleton, I proceeded to play. Each time I took out one of these library cards a butterfly would appear, and as I blew gold dust over it, it would bring into form a rock, or a tree, or quite simply any organic thing in creation. What to do with this kind of power, literally the power of world creation by breathing things into life?

The next vision was from inside a planetary core where I was sitting and constructing a new world, while people looked on applauding – heady stuff. This was followed by a vision of some backwater planet where a farmer, his wife, and two daughters came up to me, proceeding to request designer specifications for their own little planet, naturally I obliged. Definitely no precedents for this, but then I remembered that I had put a request in for the 64 million Dakini Tantras when I raised my Kundalini eight years before. Some wishes just take longer to come into form.

Gesar and I were like left hand and right hand. Where he was peaceful I was wrathful, and where I was peaceful he was wrathful, and between the two of us few sentients could escape. His thing was re-establishing the grids, complementing my newfound skills of world creation. One of his main goals was to get everyone to pay attention to the detail and the beauty available to us, those fractions in a moment which can quite literally transform any instant into a magical display. He would make altars of everything, everywhere he went, it was his nature, and it showed people the right way to live. A life existing in delirious reverence for all of existence, a flawless expression of One Taste meets Discriminating Wisdom. He came from a more shamanic base than I did but the fusion of our skills spawned some truly astounding new materializations.

I created a new remedy from tears of joy, mine and Lisa's (Gesar's principle student). The tears of joy I cried were a pure expression of the exuberant artistry inherent in each moment and the treasure of having a fellow warrior along for the ride – something which all too often had been a rather solo affair, especially from a male side.

I also made a remedy of the blood of the World Tree from the forest where I unbound the titans. I mixed my own blood with some of its sap and spent two hours in spasms, my body realigning into the necessary energetic format for all my wishes to take form.

Deeper and deeper into the void I travelled, way out on a limb, cruising through my own mindspace with no reference points, what more could one do than continue deeper down the spiral. As my one friend used to say *"Klim in!"* or *"Klim uit daar!"* to indicate when and whether one should in fact climb in or out of the rabbit holes appearing in ones psyche. Of course, any rabbit hole is worth exploring, but then some realities are more beautiful than others.

Gesar certainly encouraged my Crazy Wisdom as I encouraged his, egging each other on to greater heights, consuming anything and everything we could get our hands on, with no thought to the consequences. Existing without reference points certainly has its advantages if one can hold onto ones sanity while scouring the void. If the mindspace could crack then it needed to be cracked and so we tested ourselves and came out of the abyss stronger than when we went in.

Gesar's arrival hailed the recreation and activation of Shambhala. He then proceeded to demolish it and moved on. Restricting Shambhala to a single location would have been the same as getting stuck in one form, and the whole point is to be free from all binding concepts, including the dualities of 'space' and 'time'. The *play of form* which is the Dance of Dakini, can and must be engaged, but always with the knowledge that it is just dancing light.

If you're not living your dreams right now, what the hell are you doing? It is not going to get better in the future if it is not good right now. We make our futures through how we are living This Moment, and if you are waiting for it to get better you might wait a long time, if not forever. It will always be This Moment, and even when the future arrives it is still the present.

It is after all your reality and will you make your own movie a soap opera or a heroic fantasy? The Teachings need to be recast in a modern setting, shaped in your own image, because a lot of what was written was for then and there, and although the core remains the same, they need to be fashioned in a form accessible and suited to the modern mind.

Multiple sleeper agents are waiting to take up the reins and it often just takes a spark, the right key as it were, to unlock their dormant potential. Things only come into being when they are actually needed and before that we play the game of reality masquerading as doctors, photographers, performance artists, writers, strippers, or businessmen. Hiding in plain sight, protected by the sheer inconceivability of the whole thing, we were seeded throughout reality waiting for the final call, announcing the final destruction of Ignorance of the Nature of the Mind.

The truth regarding the legend of Shambhala is that it resides eternally in the hearts and minds of the Army of Light. It has always been up to me to train and gather the troops, and I have come to trust that the 'who, what, when, and where' of it will all be revealed as the moment dictates.

For my part, I am just playing out the role I was born to, and those Buddha Brats who choose to join me on this adventure are as precious to me as my own, rather battered heart.

TWENTY-TWO

Seeds Of Madness And Redemption

*Tweaking the head
often leads you deeper into sanity,
and not the other way round.*

I have fiddled in some very powerful and strange ponds but my sincere desire to delve into the Fabric of Illusion has always somehow protected me from harm.

It has also brought me gifts and insights that are so far beyond ordinary experience that it is quite literally staggering. The perfection of the manifestation makes me weep tears of joy in praise of the inconceivable intricacy and beauty of the whole tapestry.

I once plotted to grind up about a ton of *Datura Stramonium*, commonly known in South Africa as *"Malpitte"* (mad seeds), a particularly strong and nasty hallucinogen, and dump it into the water supply at my university which was situated in a small town. The next day, whilst having their morning cups of coffee or brushing their teeth, they would be well and truly on their way towards a mass hallucination. Everyone would be tripping heavily, seeing things that weren't there, and basically become completely unable to interface with reality.

Of course I would not touch the water, and with my band of

merry men would swoop down from on high, raid the museum for swords, the bank for money, the police station for weaponry, and the supermarket for food. Stealing a truck we would gather supplies and explosives and retreat to Hogsback, a beautiful mountain hamlet, where we would basically take over, planting mines in the road to stop people from entering. We would rely on the dense forestry to keep us hidden, and the general confusion of a town gone mad overnight would hopefully conceal our crime and retreat. I never ended up doing this but it would have worked, and it was the somewhat more malevolent prototype for the dosing of the water supply which I later put into action.

Malpitte is like acid on crack, very unpleasant. It contains high levels of Atropine, a substance used in eye operations to dilate the pupils. Interestingly enough, when humans are in an acute state of fear their pupils naturally dilate. When under the influence of Malpitte one sees a completely different world. Creatures come out of the walls, the garden is at war with itself, and people appear who look absolutely real but end up not being so, yet all of it as solid as your own body.

I took it a few times, in fact Hassle and I became affectionately known in our university town as the 'malpit brothers'.

It has never been made illegal because it is simply too nasty to be considered for large-scale recreational consumption, and on the rare occasions that people do take it, it is either out of stupidity or madness. Technically it is classed as a central nervous system toxin, so there is no more legislation against it than there would be for mercury, snake venom or arsenic.

Full of the youthful sorcerous abandon that I was famous for, I gave it to Misha, Gunther, and Paul around lunch time one day. I was amazed by what I had seen and was therefore sure they would be too. Paul made it back to art school, collapsed and had to be taken home. Gunther spent the night talking to his family who weren't there, but the coup de grace was Misha.

Misha was on the small side and I had given him a smaller dose than the rest but he still tripped out the worst. He went home to his commune and proceeded to cook up an entire meal that wasn't there, in a pan that wasn't there. He then sat down at the table and started to eat his invisible bacon and eggs as if it was just another ordinary day. His housemates were thoroughly disturbed by his irrational behaviour and decided to take him to the hospital.

There at his bedside he experienced a full-on satanic ritual, complete with goats' heads and chanting hooded figures coming to take him away. Of course it was all in his mind but it felt completely real to him. Misha had more than a few bad ideas running around in his head and they literally came to life to torment him. He survived it but only just with his sanity intact, and some of his friends wanted to beat me up afterwards.

Despite being able to clearly see it through my open doorway, I once spent almost twenty minutes trying to walk and then crawl to my bed, but even at a leopard crawl I kept banging my head against some invisible wall.

Basically Malpitte so distorts the visual matrix that what you are seeing is not what is actually there. This effect, although interesting, can be downright scary and potentially dangerous, so it is definitely best to stay at home if you take it. I would not recommend it to anyone though because it is just simply too strong and uncontrollable and definitely not for the fainthearted. You do not do it, like Kundalini, it does you and only if you're lucky might you get to see something worthwhile.

As a homoeopathic remedy it has the feeling of being *"alone at night in a forest, surrounded by wild animals"* so even as a medicine it's not very user friendly. Ironically the first patient I saw in a homoeopathic clinic as a student, needed Stramonium. To escape the horrors of abuse against her by some strange cult that she belonged to, she retreated into the not too wonderful world of Stramonium. I was able to recognise the state immediately since it was so familiar to me, and after convincing my supervisor of the need to give her the remedy she improved dramatically.

From a neurotic paranoid individual who could scarcely leave the house without feelings of terror, she went on to become a successful vet. After this I was completely sold on Homoeopathy and its miraculous curative potential, and also saw the wisdom of taking

176

the raw substance at university.

One night while Hassle and I were tripping at home we heard a knock at the door. We opened the door to be greeted by one very tall woman and another woman in a wheelchair. Ever the generous hosts we invited them in and proceeded to make them some tea. By the time the tea was ready we found the one in Hassle's room, hanging from a beam, and the lady in the wheelchair sitting in the corner of my room with a bag over her head.

By this stage we were fairly familiar with the substance and just waited out the weird bits when they occurred. Some things are just too strange to process and remain sane, so one has no choice but to simply endure it until it's over.

In the Carlos Castaneda books, Don Juan feeds it to him and he ends up 50km away, naked in the desert. It is rumoured that the zombie phenomenon that originated in Haiti is connected to the dosing of victims with Stramonium, after which they would lie as if dead and then be buried for a while. Once they had been dug up from the grave, they are so thoroughly traumatised that they can be brainwashed into slavery, their former personalities completely dead to them. The witches used to make an unguent from it which they rubbed on their brooms, and using the vaginal mucus membranes as an entry point, used it to fly, or so the legends go.

I did not fly but what I saw changed me forever. One of the times that I took it by myself I was walking down the street and had a conversation with Hassle, who wasn't there. At the time I remember getting quite irritated with him because he kept disappearing while we walked down the road. He was asleep on a bus 800km away and he kept winking in and out of existence as he probably woke up on the bus and then went back to sleep.

These instances of self-inflicted dosing unequivocally showed me that there was more to reality than met the eye. This fireproofed me against taking anything too literally afterwards, which was exactly what I was looking for. I also learned that certain things were not for certain people.

Strangely enough my early initiation into Datura ended up being a powerful omen heralding the arrival of my principal student.

The Teachings say that only certain people are drawn to and can understand Dzogchen. There are many instances throughout history of students and teachers having bonds that stretch across various lifetimes and places. These stories often talk about special gifts or visions that would guide the student until they eventually find the teacher again, to continue their learning.

Anri was a Metal Monkey and Metal is originally the Realm of the Gods. Traditional texts say that anyone in the God Realm will eventually have to go to the Hell Realm as part of their process. Her story is an example of conscious incarnation and proof that we choose our own time, place, and exact circumstances of birth.

Anri was the illegitimate child of unmarried parents. Her mother was a divorcée with a nine-year old daughter and had gotten pregnant but the man refused to marry her because he was not willing to take care of the other daughter. The oldest daughter's father threatened to take his daughter away as well, so neither father was prepared to help her in any way. To make matters worse she was working for the South African Army in the 80's and her situation was considered a moral perversion, so they punished her by taking away her subsidised housing and decreased her salary.

Feeling abandoned and literally 'alone in the wilderness' with a very real threat to her safety and that of her children, she was in a classic Stramonium space. One morning in the office of an attorney, collecting the last of her pension, the man noticed the distress of the highly pregnant woman, and upon enquiring she burst into tears. She told of how welfare agencies were hunting her like a pack of wolves, trying to get their hands on the baby. It so happened that his long-time secretary's daughter was looking to adopt, so they immediately consulted the young couple and the adoption process was initiated.

Anri exhibited an acute sensitivity to the injustices of humanity during childhood and as an avid history student would feel the cruelties of various regimes as if experienced in person. Once she finished school she left her culture and country behind, hoping to find answers to the burning questions regarding the role of entrenched belief systems, both its origins and effect on human behaviour. She spent the next four years travelling in a constant Stramonium state so she would literally see and feel the hellish side of life. This fuelled her intense need to help humanity and in her spare time she would study politics and come up with ways to create a better world.

It was at an outdoor Trance party, close to the border of Lesotho, that she met two interesting strangers who took her into the mountains on a neighbouring farm to show her a secret and ancient cave. This apparently was Sangoma Valley, a place where African medicine men, known as *"Sangomas"*, had come for centuries to initiate students or share information amongst their various branches. Ironically enough Stramonium is a substance regularly used by the Sangomas in Africa, sometimes for good, but sometimes to induce states of terror in superstitious folk.

At a small waterfall behind the cave she put her head under the water and suddenly everything around her started swirling while Baroch the Israeli seemed to be chanting to her in a strange language. That moment marked some kind of baptism for her into mystical awareness, precipitating her Kundalini rising as well. Feeling disconcertingly high yet somehow familiar, she returned with them to one of the houses on the hill nearby, and on a blanket outside she proceeded to writhe and spasm for a good four hours. Without realising it she was also experiencing what Cat and I had initially dubbed our Dakini States.

The party entirely forgotten she stayed on with them for a few more days and she was given some Hawaiian Woodrose Seed, a hallucinogenic plant containing lysergic acid. As Cheval spoke to her about activating her genetic memory Anri saw herself as a spark of energy flying across space. She saw various light tunnels in the clouds and spotting a rainbow vortex she descended. Suddenly remembering the moment just before conception she was overwhelmed with joy, realising that the pain surrounding her birth circumstances were a conscious choice to ensure that she pursue a path of enlightenment.

She moved in with her new friends in the Transkei, getting teachings from both of them on various levels and subjects. She describes what Baroch taught her as a type of magical transfer, mind to mind, receiving insights on prophecies and the history and meaning of God. Cheval mostly awakened her genetic memory of her tribal past, an intuitive knowledge of antiquated cultures through the use of ancient musical instruments. During these musical sessions she would enter trance states, hearing voices of ancestors speaking in long forgotten archaic tongues.

It was Cheval who first introduced her to Dzogchen, little knowing that the few words he said were like a key that would lead to a psychosis so vicious that she barely came out of it alive.

All he said to her was: *"There is a tribe in Tibet called Dzogchen, and they believe that everything is perfect as it is"*. Of course the mistake is that it's not a tribe it is a Teaching, but it was enough to send her over the edge. Catapulted into visionary space and unable to make sense of it or turn away from it for more than six months, the strain of forcefully and constantly perceiving the range of visions from the most beatific to the utterly demonic pushed her mind far beyond ordinary limits.

Overwhelmed by the attempt to reconcile the suffering on the planet with the idea of perfection, without further teachings or instructions on the Non-Dual Nature of the Mind she went mad. The magnitude of absorbing so many terrible visions appalled her to such an extent that she eventually stopped eating and drinking and in her agitated state couldn't sleep either, until her body started to reabsorb itself. So far into the abyss that all contact with the outside world was lost, she finally became catatonic.

A typical feeling of Stramonium is that of being *"half-buried"* or *"half alive, and half dead"* and has been used to cure cases of Autism in children.

At the time she was sharing a house with a recovered junky and the only place he could think of taking her was the man who cured him, a shaman living in the forests of Knysna. After several attempts at getting her to eat, the shaman was forced to book her into the local hospital where they put her on strong anti-psychotics and a drip. The doctors considered her lost to the world and informed her parents that she would have to be institutionalised.

As fate would have it a young doctor at the hospital took pity on her, unable to fathom why such a pretty girl with her family background would be in this state. He broke protocol by taking her off the anti-psychotics and within a few days she was completely lucid and coherent.

The shaman agreed to let her stay with him to get back on her feet but soon came to the conclusion that she was there for an apprenticeship. Each seemingly random event conspired perfectly to lead her right to his doorstep to acquire certain techniques from him to prepare for the next part of her journey. After three months he pronounced her ready to face the world and she came to Cape Town.

She came to me a few years ago at the spontaneous invitation of Thor. She had heard about me from Kama and was interested in doing Homoeopathy to find better ways to deal with her intense sensitivity and continuous horrific visions. When she finally told me the details surrounding her adoption I immediately realised that she was a classic Stramonium case.

What had happened was that the terror that her mother felt during the pregnancy infused the child. Stramonium was part of Anri's core programming, as deeply entrenched as the very fibres from which her body was woven. She describes what happened to her once she took it as a miracle, feeling like the universe inside her was slowly turning. She couldn't do anything strenuous for a few days, just resting and letting things take their natural course, and life has never been the same for her since.

Fearlessly allowing the Stramonium blueprint to fuel her visionary capacity as it was originally intended, she is now uniquely able to travel those mind spaces where others fear to tread. I fondly refer to her as my 'Stram Poster Child'.

She mentioned Dzogchen one day and I nearly fell off my chair. Usually I am the one who introduces people to the Teachings and to hear someone say it of their own volition was unbelievable, so of course we became friends.

It became clear that she chose to incarnate how and when she did, putting herself in a situation where she would literally be in the Hell Realm, pre-empting the fall from grace of the God Realm. Putting herself through such torment ensured that she found the Teachings to show her the way out of suffering.

She said that more than anything, her Stramonium programming forced her to seek and recognise teachings that actually work, because true terror simply cannot be ignored, no matter how much chanting, happy thoughts, guided meditations, or group hugs one gets.

She dived into Dzogchen as if into water, immediately recognising it as her original Teaching and as much a part of her as her blood. She also dissolved her Kundalini and we have an unbreakable bond that transcends definition.

Coincidentally it turned out not only was she bound to me by the bond of Datura and Dzogchen, she had also been having dreams of the Apocalypse for most of her life. Her fearless attitude is perfectly suited to my particular brand of Buddhism and we consider ourselves the Anarchist Lineage. This very book is part of our Karma Mudra and we weave this grand spell together.

An interesting story is that of Padmasambhava feeding Yeshe Tsogyel various plant poisons as part of her training to test her Clarity. The plant poisons in Homoeopathy are a particularly nasty group of substances and seem to be the most radically deranging to the mindset. For some reason many of the extreme plant poison remedies have done Anri good and so the Padmasambhava-Yeshe blueprint seems an appropriate format for our interaction.

Over time it has also become clear that another one of her archetypal forms is *Nataraj*, the aspect of Shiva (consort of Kali) dancing what is known as the Dance of Destruction. It is often depicted as an image of a dancing Shiva surrounded by Datura flowers, signalling the wisdom of Divine Intoxication as symbolised in particular by the Datura plant. In my aspect as Kali it is only appropriate that Nataraj shows up so we can dance the dance that unbinds the world...

TWENTY-THREE

Apocalypse Herald

*Since everything is mind driven
our perception of it will make it either joy or horror –
your choice, your life.*

My father once asked me what I wanted to do with my life, to which I responded that I wanted to be a prophet. I watched as his mind clicked over, and typical of the old school, he suggested that I needed to then go to a monastery to learn the craft. Prophecy is something one is born to and for however, and can no more be taught than musical genius.

At the moment my father and I have a 'mutual non understanding truce'. In spite of this I have threatened to read him the Tibetan BOOK OF THE DEAD on his death bed, because it is the least I could do for him.

He is a hard nut to crack being an Earth Tiger, the Tiger's motto being *"I win"*, which he usually does one way or another, and often at any cost. Sometimes peace is worth more than being right, but then that is his lesson. One day he will truly see me and will be immensely proud, and so for the moment we stay on our respective sides of the fence.

My epic visions, having realized the Nature of Reality, have since become a bit more deranged and ambitious than my original dream to become a prophet. I have seen myself riding The Storm and helping to dissolve and reseed a new world from the shards of the best of this world. For me, waking up was not even an option. I have always been driven to it and nothing, including myself, has gotten in the way. I want a life with everything I like in it and the only way to achieve this was to enlighten myself. The children are greater than the parents and this is what all parents want at the end of the day – to see you take all that is good from them and run with it to the ends of the earth.

Everything I have done has been to arrive at just this point and hold it. Even when I was not completely conscious of my actions, I was still being unconsciously driven to this point by everything in reality. It is just the way I am hardwired, and it could be no other way, the bird does not debate flying south in winter.

I style myself as an avenging angel off-duty, waiting for the time when I will be called upon to play my part in the Final Dissolution and subsequent reconstruction of the world. If I had my way, I would have done it yesterday, years ago, but I am not in charge of the timeline. I am just ushering in the New Age playing my part as an Apocalypse herald, gathering the Riders, and ensuring that everything runs smoothly.

Of course I sing the swansong of Non-Duality, it is my allegiance first and last and always, and something I take very seriously, but with a smile. As I said before the Apocalypse is a glorious and joyful event, all your birthdays, happiest times, best love affairs and most tender moments rolled into one. This is what I feel in every cell of my body, I just have to follow this mood and it will bring me everything I ever wanted, and a whole lot more I can only begin to imagine.

I am not a particularly dark character at all, and this allegiance to the Apocalypse is more of an elemental affiliation with the Forces of Reality. The *final dissolution of all form* is definitely going to be the end of the world as we know it. I would bet everything I had on it and more, and I would win. The feeling in my body does not lie because I am aligned to this process and a part of it. Without it I would not have been me, and this story would never have been written.

The Buddhists say that the Wrathful Deities are the most compassionate because they break the Illusion hard and fast, accompanied by more pain, but the result is much quicker. The Peaceful Deities, on the other hand, are considered to be the most relentless because they will let you cross the line again and again, hammering you with the consequences of your actions until you finally learn. There are of course actually no deities or gods, they are all Aspects of Self which one embodies to accelerate ones own process.

At first we are irrevocably drawn to those Aspects that are more in keeping with our own natures yet they are all there to be integrated. In my wrathful aspect I primarily embody Kali and in my peaceful aspect *Chenrezig*, the bodhisattva of compassion. Kali is ultimately compassionate as well though, because she frees us from the *illusion of duality* by destroying it around us.

I see all events within the context of the Kali Yuga and Dzogchen, so any ongoing destruction is just symptomatic of the process of Dissolution which is perfect as it is – perfect from the start, flawless in its process. This is not to say that I just sit on the fence and observe, I see perfect order in everything, and feel no need to change an iota of it. It could after all be no other way, and is thus fulfilling the Grand Plan to perfection. To attempt to fiddle with the process or to campaign for world peace in an effort to stop this process is futile.

If it is your nature to do this then do it, but ultimately realize that it is just the reflection of your own internal process that you are running, and that every tidal wave that occurs was meant to occur. If you can see everything in this context you can continue to learn and suggest changes, which can better equip humanity after the Dissolution, applying your experience in a particular field. Until then, relax into the flow of things, make the most of it, and stay ahead of the game by dissolving your own attachments.

If you are holding the view that you want to bring into this reality the perfect world without a radical shift in your consciousness, you are heading down the road to cancer. The irony in this is that Dzogchen, the *"Great Perfection"*, is the cure for cancer because there is no need to strive to make everything perfect if it is already so. I have cancer strongly in my family but with Dzogchen I have engaged the wisdom energy of *perfection at every moment* without needing to strive for it, so I could no more get it than an elephant could fly.

Just about everything I have done has been to facilitate a seamless and relatively painless transition to a better world. What this means is a space where everyone instantly feels the effect of their actions on others, not being separate from each other. As such, cruelty and brutality would be impossible. This has not been an easy process by any means because I have always styled myself more as a covert operative, plotting the end of the world and the subsequent rebuilding of the Golden Age – taking the best and leaving the rest.

It always surprises me when people react to the destruction of the old world so vehemently. Destruction is an inherent part of nature, things dying to make fertile compost from which new things grow, and it is in this light that the Kali Yuga should be viewed. Nature will redress the balance in the speediest and most compassionate way. People will not suffer unnecessarily because it is frankly quite an impersonal process, as only nature can be – the earth takes its nourishment indiscriminately from the decaying corpses of all people regardless of age, race, or culture, saints and criminals alike...

The old Six Realms Incarnation Model is that when you die you are drawn into the Realm most suited to you through unrequited attachment to anger, lust, jealousy or ignorance. You then play out all your attachments until you reach the State of Equanimity as you no longer have any more attachments to these things. The idea is that you move throughout your various lifetimes, through the Realms until eventually you have learnt your lesson and then finally have a shot at freedom from the Wheel of Reincarnation.

I consider it to be an outdated paradigm because only 1 in 10 million get out, if that, more like 1 in 100 million – not good odds for anyone. As a result the planet just backs up with more and more frustrated souls, caught up in the Webs of Desire and Aversion. It is designed on the premise that the suffering will be enough to push you to a point that you would rather die than continue to suffer. Combined with this are the dire warnings of the 'enlightenment dealers' who go to great pains to let you know how difficult the whole process is. This makes it only a possibility for the really desperate or the slightly mad.

The Six Realms Reincarnation Model clearly does not work and so will be deleted. It was definitely a nice idea and beautifully conceived but when something doesn't work or it only works for a tiny handful then surely it is time to begin afresh. This is the essence of the Kali Yuga, scrapping dysfunctional systems which no longer serve. How people fail to see the compassion and beauty of this process is unfathomable to me.

As Master of Homoeopathy for the Earth Church I take my role as protector of the planet very seriously. This is a fine planet and not something that should ever get so messed up. The way we behave is actually an atrocity and blight upon our consciences which everyone has to cure in themselves. I am not talking about the whales here, fuck the whales, they are just symptomatic of the way we treat things and each other in general. Until that changes there will never be peace on Earth.

This was why I originally dosed the water supply in an attempt to bring everything back into balance, to remove the binding patterns that condition people into fear-based behaviour and keep them small. It did not work the way I anticipated, since the lesson was for me and hence totally personal, but it showed me the way to unbind myself and gave me a taste of it which is a gift that has no price.

After the Dissolution we will keep the planet, it is a great planet, and most people will return to their original constituents which is Dancing Light. Those who are aware enough to handle the Breaking of Form get to surf on through to re-establish a new blueprint where the cruelties and brutalities of this world can never manifest again. I reckon that maybe one in a million people will make it, if we're lucky. Dzogchen guarantees Enlightenment after all, in this life time and if not, at the point of death – a bold claim that no other system I have seen so far can match, and this is why I write this book.

Just as I am called upon by Reality itself to play my part, so too are others called upon to play theirs. We are irrevocably and inevitably drawn to each other whether we like it or not. Take the cream of reality, those individuals who carry different threads of lineages or civilizations in their DNA, in order to reseed the New World on the other side.

It is the Age of Unbinding and it is going down whether people like it or not. As the frequency raises it will become harder and harder for people to maintain their false Identities, until they basically vibrate at such a frequency that they cease to be and become one with everything. The only thing that will save people is if they do the work on themselves and suitably distance themselves from their own binding obscuration of being a separate and concrete entity.

Athena, Anri and I are the most gung-ho on the Apocalypse. This said, Athena had children so wanted to delay it a bit to bring them up properly. Thor is down with it and fully for it, but in typical Dragon fashion is hedging his bets. Luc is a bit of a fence-sitter and although he does not really believe it, will come over quickly when the time comes. Rats are expert at jumping ship when it starts sinking.

Anri had visions of it for most of her childhood which resonated with mine, always a promising characteristic in an Apocalypse Rider and most of our plans tie in together closely, so we will probably be in the same place at that time. In all honesty I am the most gung-ho on the Apocalypse – Kali cannot after all but totally support her own creation. One should see the Apocalypse as an analogy for the deconstruction process in oneself. My own process definitely runs alongside the destruction of Reality and hence is a good indicator for me. But mainly I am wedded to it, it is in my blood, under my skin in the tiny muscles of my heart, in a sense it is my heart and it is bliss.

The rest will come on board when the winds change because no one wants to be left behind when the crystal ship sails, especially if they have an invitation. One vision I had was of a net that I could scoop up some stragglers with to drag along, and I presume the other Riders will be able to do this as well. This is still in the prototype phase but anything that can be seen can been done, and it is all a question of your own degree of Realization which will determine the numbers you can drag through. This will not be an easy technique because it will require that you stabilize the other people's panicking minds while you deal with your own. If you do not have sufficient personal power or you still have a hoard of your own Personal Demons to fight, I would not recommend it. It will definitely put a strain on you and possibly cause you to stumble and fall at a crucial moment.

I am more than willing to go with the Mayan 2012 date for the beginning of a New Age but I also had a dream where I met Amma the Indian saint who hugs people for a living, and is presumably an emanation of Kali. In the dream she reckoned 8-10 years but either way it is coming, and I am resigned to enjoy myself and harvest the fruits of my labour in the meantime. Many things are as yet unfolding but without worry or effort. It will all be fine across the board as those who have earned their places will have them and those who are suffering will cease to suffer. Could it really be any other way after all?

The Natural State will guide me flawlessly through and how can it be wrong if my natural state is in fact me? If it was not meant to be or I was going against my own nature it would just not happen, full stop – self-protected perception, perfect from the start.

One thing I did modify is that I hardwired my doubt reflex shut, knowing that I would be called upon to make some fairly heavy decisions, and that doubt in that instance would literally tear me apart. So I made a pact with Dakini that I did not necessarily need to know the exact where, when, and how of what I was doing, but that my commitment to the Teachings would transform me into a diamond sword which she would wield as she saw fit. To be free of the Demon of Self-Doubt forever was a small trade-off for a bit of freewill but an exchange I would make any and every day, if it came around again. To become the blade carving through the aberrations of dualism without the thought of moral implications holding me back, was a strategic modification that I never regret making. If one senses a potential pitfall in the future it is good to make your magical adjustment then and there, to avoid later catastrophe.

The 'how to do it' part is hard to explain as the particular details will be unique to each person, but the basic tech involves that you just intend whatever it is and then seal it shut with your mind – done. It is best done at times of heightened awareness when your senses are highly charged, then it tends to stick and does not need to be done again later.

I would argue that everyone will have one of these junctures, a point sometime in the future where ones application of and commitment to the Teachings are tested in a decisive conflict with ones greatest fears. It is in preparation for this event that one will have to make a small trade-off for the benefit of all sentient beings. What that trade-off is for you is inconceivable, and only you will know and once you know only you can act, but the implications of not doing it are simply too disastrous to even begin thinking about. It is beneficial to be prepared and you just have to trust implicitly in yourself, knowing that you will make the right decision at that moment. More than that cannot be readily expressed as it will be too personal and individual.

I have carved out a path for myself which is truly unique and I stand by every word I say. I have always felt an overwhelming love of the Apocalypse as a blissful state of Ultimate Dissolution in order to bring out all the new forms I am capable of and just waiting to embody. This is the Dance of Life and the only thing that has really meant anything to me and kept me going through the dark times, of which there have been many.

It still comes down to the fact that everyone has to run their own ship, clear out the bilges, and make sure they are sea ready when The Wave hits. If it is your nature, there is really nothing you can do but abide in it, and by abiding you gain everything you ever wanted and a whole lot more, just the way you like it.

A Zen koan goes *"things are not as they seem nor are they otherwise"*. This is a curly way of saying give up any preconceptions of what things are and where they are going, just enjoy the show.

Feel deep inside yourself for the thread that connects you to the Dissolution. Feel the accelerating vibration in your cells – this is the call of the Apocalypse, the call to the final battle with yourself.

TWENTY-FOUR

Dissolving The **World**

This is the mood for the end times – whatever occurs,
just keep laughing, because if you are laughing
and singing you can hardly be screaming
and crying after all.

No one is going to be there with you when you are dying, and if you have not perceived the truth of the *illusory nature of self and reality* by then, it will probably be too late...

Some people have been doing work on themselves quite diligently for a while, but like with most things it is a part-time activity, as people dip their toes into the waters of awareness. It needs to be a fulltime process, which is what is required to quite literally haul your ass out of the fire.

The important thing to remember here is that it is the Age of Unbinding and things will get worse before they get better. It is just mirroring ones own ongoing *process of dissolution* except now it is happening anyway, with or without your volition. You definitely want to have done a lot of this work already when The Energetic Wave hits because then it will be done for you all at once, an experience which will tear most people apart.

This process is what normally occurs at the time of your death, but then one goes through it over the period of a few days as one begins to die. As one dies this process continues, and this is why the Tibetans read THE BOOK OF THE DEAD to the corpse for up to forty days. This is traditionally done in order to prevent people from falling back into one of the Realms and incarnating again as a human, animal, or demon, whatever your particular Poison was in life. The difference now is that there will be no other Realms to incarnate into – the Six Realms are closing down and so you either have the potential to be preserved as a fully Realised human, or become part of the cosmic soup.

It is the final curtain call and everything is up for grabs. If you can ride the whirlwind of your own desires and aversions, it is a very exciting time indeed. As the Six Realms arise and melt into each other, all your personal Demons, Hungry Ghosts, Animal Aspects, Jealous Gods, and Gods will come up to do battle with you. This process is echoed by the dissolving of the Kundalini into the crown chakra in an individual, therefore anyone who has done it will definitely be eligible for passage on the crystal ship which will ride high on the Wave of Dissolution.

This Age of Unbinding represents a great chance for Liberation because everything literally starts vibrating faster. This vibration favours dissolution because the faster we vibrate, the more memories that lock us into form become liberated. The actual point of Dissolution will not be pleasant for everyone. Imagine all your attached memories being dislodged all at once – every fear you have ever had, every craving, every aversion, all hatred, and even every hope, flushing into the mind in the space of a few hours.

Having to deal with all of this at once in the course of an hour, and remain undisturbed, is not an easy task by any means, yet this is what will be required. If at this point you can see all these fears, hatreds and anxieties as just the *impersonal play of the mind* then you get to ride the whirlwind and take your personality with you, since you are suitably unattached to it.

If we see this as a good thing it can be experienced as pleasure but if we see this as a bad thing and try to hold onto Form, it becomes pain and suffering. It is the same vibration but since everything is mind driven our perception of it will make it either joy or horror – your choice, your life.

Anyone who is still bound by these concepts will literally be torn apart as they try to hold on to a perceived solid form while the whole thing starts shearing at the seams. Those who don't make it will return to the constituents from whence they all came, to become the new matrix – the building blocks from which the rest of us will create a world anew. Not so bad but then it depends where you feel you fit in, building block or builder.

This is the Whirlwind I am talking about and people are either going to ride it out, or be destroyed. You would not believe how much memory is stored in your body, each moment of prolonged unhappiness is engraved into you as in a book, and it all needs to be erased before you can legitimately claim to be *free from suffering*. Certain things like raising your Kundalini can get you to a point where it moves into automatic erase and it becomes increasingly difficult to write new states onto the body.

One of the upsides to this point in time is that we are compelled to discover better ways of doing things in response to the negative processes going on around us – thus, from the fetid bog of decomposed humanity is born the lotus of our dreams.

It is strange that it is conceptual structures that bind us, mere ideas, and yet they are stronger than diamond rope, and the amusing thing is that we are often the ones who bind ourselves with it. Where then to point the finger? It is easy to point at government, countries, global warming, capitalism, big business, and crime, but it is much harder to take the same finger and point it back at yourself. This is not a guilt trip, it is about viewing the actual culprit and targeting that.

This book is not about apportioning blame, it is about freeing yourself from the chains of your own mind. This is never a comfortable situation and there is a lot of squirming involved as you see yourself simultaneously as jailor and prisoner. The problem is that most people like their little conceptual jails and are very attached to them. Having said this, it is fixable, and if you set some belief system or fear in stone initially then it must be true that you can blow it up with the dynamite of Awareness, and reconstruct it thereafter.

Hope springs eternal but the sooner one starts this process the better, there is much to be done and many things to be unravelled before it all comes apart.

The gauntlet has been thrown down but whether you choose to pick it up and put it on is another thing entirely. It is a decision that everyone has to make sooner or later – now, at the point of death, or during the Great Unveiling. Most people are feeling the increase in frequency at the moment and everyone is welcome but whether they have the guts to use this to accelerate their own process of personal dissolution and systematically destroy their own illusions, remains to be seen.

No one is going to, or can, do it for you, and what is there really to lose at the end of the day? That little voice that keeps you small should be shot on sight, no questions asked. How dare it invade and despoil your dreams. There should not be any voices in your head, who is talking about what anyway?

If there are, you should exterminate them as they imply the Duality of a 'self', talking about itself. This assumes the Demon of an Identity which is always a painful thing to have to deal with. The sooner you destroy it the better because if not, it builds and has the potential to become something much larger and nastier which will eventually tell you what to do. Either this, or it will so paralyze you with doubt that fearless action become impossible.

Either of these alternatives are things to be avoided at all costs. Club the crocodile before it eats you and your dog. Ask no questions even if it looks cute and harmless at first. So much can be prevented by heeding early warning signs, stopping the leak in the roof before it becomes a flood and soaks your bed.

The final conflict is basically you against your own Assumed Identity. Round 1, bell rings, the fight begins, who is going to win, who has the most to lose? It is a tough fight but once won you become unstoppable and a beacon of hope and inspiration to those around you. You figuratively need to kill yourself in order to live. Your current Conditioning is the second skin that is stuck to you like sea-serpent slime, and it requires every trick in your book and a whole lot more to defeat it.

Far better if you have already integrated these forces before it all melts down because then you might even enjoy it - I certainly intend to. If you set the intent for the integration and dissolution of everything that holds you into form now, there is still a chance. With wicked scythes and sharp axes Mara is already in the field where your Holy Cows graze, and the slaughter is about to begin. The only thing that will protect you from the horror of the bloodshed is the concrete understanding that it is all an Illusion.

If you can hold the View that not one shred of the movie has any more meaning than any other, as they are equally Empty, it will save you - it is after all just *a dance of coloured lights*.

One Taste saves the day again and again and is the only real rock you can cling to. I loved the concept of One Taste from the first, dived into it like a fish to water, and it has definitely saved my ass on many occasions. I strongly recommend it for anyone who has the guts to engage it. It is a hard taskmaster and ultimately spares nothing, but the freedom one gains on the other side is incalculable and worth every moment – all you have to do is endure it until you start to like it.

Fearlessly we step into the void – become the Diamond Sword that slices the *fabric of reality* and reweave the universe in the image you see fit. Why people would not jump at the conceptual liberation presented by Dzogchen always amazed me, but then sometimes they are not ready, and sometimes it is just a case of pearls before swine. Dzogchen asks a lot from you in terms of accepting a completely new conceptual framework, but it brings you the earth in return.

As it nears the end, more and more of your attachments will start to come up in order to be challenged and get brought under the banner of One Taste. How you handle this will determine the state of mind you will be in at the end. Just let go, surrender to the process. It is irrevocable anyway and the prize at the end is Total Freedom from Suffering Forever – surely that is worth more than anything.

There are perils everywhere but every pitfall is a potential point of Liberation if it is seen from the view of the *empty play of form*.

Unfortunately though, there are not many who choose to use these techniques to liberate themselves. It is up to everyone to ensure that when the earth's Kundalini completely raises that they are sufficiently unbound by concepts and attachment to 'self'. If you do this process properly you get to ride the storm and come through with your personality intact.

Fear is definitely a strong demon and one well worth killing as soon as possible, and Chod is one of the best techniques I have ever found to destroy the concept of ones own frailty. You are ahead of the game if you do far worse to yourself in your mind than reality could ever do to you. When you watch demons sucking out your eyeballs, dogs gnawing on your spleen, and vultures plucking out your brains, what then is there truly to fear from reality?

All hail Machig Labdron, the founder of Chod. Without this particular tool to break the *identification with form* and kill the Demon of the Illusion of 'self', we would be in a very tight corner against the ropes, bleeding heavily.

Truth be told, I am not expecting a lot of people to make it but then it is about the quality of the lineage strands carried across, more than quantity. Everyone has a shot at it though if they want it, and no one will be excluded if they make the grade. The arena is wide open and everyone is invited but it is far beyond easy, but then fortune favours the brave and the slightly mad.

The energy of the Kali Yuga is actually ecstasy and bliss but you have to discard your concepts of holding on to form in order to feel this. You have to relax into the chaos around you, and when you make it through the maelstrom to the other side everything will be cleansed and new. See the fires of suffering blazing around you, remember that it is empty, and step into the terrifying void, you will experience for yourself the alchemical purification and come out transformed on the other side. Watch it all become one integrated *play of awareness* with the overriding taste of bliss as its base note.

This time is one of the most wonderful times to be alive on the planet if you can remember how beautiful this place can be if you hold onto your dreams. The Kali Yuga is a rite of passage basically forcing you to fuse your consciousness with your dreams, step up and be counted.

Can you create reality from your visions without attachment, conditioning, and ignorance? If the answer is yes, then Vajra warrior, let go into the moment and the mood, and let the Wave of Dissolution carry you to the shore of your very own promised land.

This is the only exit strategy left to you, I will not lie.
I intend to be on stage, singing the final song on my 50ft speakers as it all comes apart.

TWENTY-FIVE

The **Hero Tantra**

*Beyond rebuke
one ventures forth into the world
living ones dreams, fearing nothing,
and loving everything.*

The Hero does not always start out as the hero, he forges himself into one. The forge is made from doubt, despair, and fear that we lack worthiness, and one has to hammer the metal till it holds a sharp point.

This hammering is going to hurt like hell, so best be willing to bite the bullet or chew through your own arm if you want your dreams to come true. After that moment, pain is just a memory that never happened anyway. It is a moment in time with some reference sense data, irrevocably deleted by the Eternal Moment that we find ourselves in if we consciously and constantly live in the present.

The Hero always gets wounded along the way and has his moments where all seems dark and without hope, but he always comes back fighting with freshly garnered resolve, and saves the day for all within his power. This is the Hero Tantra, the wandering mercenary who overcomes his own internal greed and saves the village from the bandits, and in so doing saves himself from his own selfishness.

Who does not want to be the one kicking back in the palace,

married to the princess as reward for ones selfless actions at the end of the day? Hans Solo in the first STAR WARS is a perfect example of this, just waiting to be one of the good guys that comes back to save the day from the forces of evil, thus also overcoming his own instincts for self-preservation.

To learn the Hero Tantra you basically just have to watch enough James Bond movies to get the idea. The hero always wins and gets the girl. It's not rocket science, and all it takes to embody this is to move into that '007' mindset to activate your reality into manifesting that way. Interestingly enough the numbers on the Periodic Table they chose were antimatter and nitrogen, 'emptiness and enjoyment' in a nutshell. If one can take on the hero aspects in this mood, the forces of darkness can never assail you. James is indestructible and you know he is going to come out on top in the end. The Heroine Tantra would be slightly different for women but I will let them tell their own story.

Play with archetypes relentlessly, they are all Personal Aspects for you to become. All the archetypes are there to be downloaded, in full Technicolor often, and if one just pretends it so for long enough, one sees it to be so – then, miraculously you are the hero and the kingdom opens up before you.

The only thing ever stopping you is your own limited vision, so dream, and dream big – everyone loves to swoop in and save the day. It is fear of things like injury, failure, loneliness, or ridicule that we have to stalk first, which is all part of the manifestation of the neurotic ego. If we did not doubt at times we would not be human, but it is the overcoming of this doubt that makes us truly superhuman, able to forge a destiny that is out of this world. Put a gun to the Demon of Doubt's head, pull the trigger, and thank yourself for it later.

Even the Buddhists are waiting for the *Maitreya*, (the Buddha to come), but if *all is self* then surely the Maitreya is you? From my perspective it is definitely me, but then I have no issues around stepping into my mantle as a Chakravatin, a *"Universal Monarch"*. You are reading this though, and therefore technically I am just a manifestation of your own mind, and you are the Buddha to come. Reality is just waiting for you to step up to the plate and take your rightful position in Reality.

From your perspective there is actually no one else out there, it is all the sound of your own voice returning to you, and this book should be seen in that context, it is the only truly valid context. Would you have it any other way? Taking up your mantle and taking back your power is the name of the game, no one else can do it for you. Although some people can point you in the right direction, it is still your Self pointing out to you the correct pathway to take for maximum enjoyment and liberation.

Of course it helps some people to hold the view that there is someone looking out for you, ready to help when it is crunch time. This is a hollow crutch however and will support you as much as a pillar of air when reality starts to deteriorate around you, Reality being Empty and all...

There are clearly powerful forces at work in our lives, no doubt, but it is ourselves, *"boundless, perfect from the beginning, source of all manifestation"* and only perceived as 'other' because we choose to remain shackled by the bonds of Ignorance, Doubt, and Duality. The reality is that you are much larger than you think – you are the centre of the cosmic Mandala (pattern) and all the potential in the universe is just waiting for you to wake up to it. When you do, the sky will literally shower you with flowers and blessings, eagerly revealing its innermost treasures, just for you.

If you are waiting for Jesus or the Antichrist to return, since they are all *manifestations of your own mind*, then you quite possibly will manifest them so you can continue in your lackey status and worship at someone else's feet. The truth of the matter is far more radical and exotic – you are Jesus, God, and the Antichrist all at once, and they just represent different Aspects of your Self playing out in the mind.

Given this, what role would you have yourself cast into? Do you really want to be trying to kiss the hem of Jesus' robe or fleeing from the whip of the Antichrist? It sounds rather like the plot of some mediocre melodrama to me.

Will the days of ones life be suffering in Samsara or kicking back in Nirvana? Your choice, you are the director, cast, and producer. The question remains whether you have the guts to make a heroic fantasy from your reality. Are you trying to squeeze in a 30 minute episode of some soap opera where everyone just tries to screw each other over, gets old, and dies, or are you brave enough to tell a story of gripping action, heroic battles, and extraordinary victories?

If you are waiting for a Messiah to take you by the hand and drag you up to heaven you might be waiting for a while – salvation is personal and not something that anyone else can accomplish for you. This said there are definitely those that can lead you in the right direction having been there themselves. You should grab onto these folk as they represent your Skillful Means to run your own processes. Technically they are all you anyway so there is no need to postulate an external saviour because it is literally your very Self talking back to you. Brad Pitt's character in the movie FIGHT CLUB represents this – the Tibetan concept of Daka, masculine of Dakini and an embodiment of your own wisdom energy, which you project outwards in order to guide you through the mazes of reality and the byways of your psyche.

I have nothing against religions – I just feel that they do not present people with the required techniques to help them forge their own Liberation. I consider this a grave crime against humanity. The game is only ever about Liberation from the *captivity of self-image* and anything that helps is your friend, and anything that hinders is your mortal enemy. It is really just a question of people getting their priorities right, seeing what is truly important to them, and throwing the rest away. The time of complicated lineages, initiations, and hierarchies are past, and the game is wide open to be seized, if you dare. All the elements you need are on hand waiting to be grabbed, internalized, and then expressed.

This is why the Chinese invaded Tibet so that the Teachings would spread to the West and an outbreak of enlightenment would occur, spreading across the world like wildfire. It just takes one spark to ignite the whole thing and it is only you that can do it, it is your fire within that needs to be ignited not mine. If you take up the challenge, be sure not to stop half way, as stopping is potentially more dangerous than not starting at all. Tasting the nectar of immortality and then returning to Samsara will make everything else taste like baked beans on dry toast, and you will never be satisfied with the paltry offerings of this illusory reality again.

If you have the chance to reclaim your position in Shambhala, the legendary city, and join the Forces of Light issuing forth against the Armies of Ignorance, why not take it up? Even if you are sitting in a trailer park transcendence beckons, but whether you take it and transform your reality is ultimately up to you. Everyone suffers until they decide to stop, and it is often only the desperate that are truly willing to take the necessary measures to complete the process of Dissolution.

If you can dissolve yourself into light then you have clearly made the grade, paid for your multi-pass out of here with the only coin that is accepted, the 'self'. When you finally realize that there is no concrete 'self', and that you represent a Dance of Form with a million potential faces which are all you, it is one of the most liberating events of your life. It was for me, and should be for you too. Those that fear losing their personalities are clearly deluded. You cannot lose what you never had in the first place, and the fact that we represent a pool of pure potential for any and every form should send you into raptures.

This is why I religiously chop myself to pieces and offer up the bits to whomever wants a piece of me, since *it is all self* after all. The more one chops the less easy it becomes to hold onto the belief that you are a separate discrete entity, and that there is actually anyone else out there at all.

Dzogchen is not a religion it is a View on reality and is considered in Buddhist circles to be the highest View. It has a lot in common with Zen although in my opinion it is a more complete Teaching. Therefore you could quite happily be a Christian dzogchempa but God as a separate entity would have to go sooner rather than later. It would just end up holding you back and hamper your progress through the maze of the mind.

So from the Dzogchen View, where are these Illuminati that think they are running the world? Sounds more like residual god-syntax to me. Anyone who reads the papers just has to look at the ambient chaos to see that no one is really running the show, except perhaps Kali. Even Kali is an Aspect of Self, that aspect of destruction which it is wise to enlist in the obliteration of the Ego and any other states that hold you in a fixed form.

Maybe there are those who genuinely want to be sheep and wait for a shepherd to come and herd them out of the paddock. In that case the shepherd will manifest and they will happily be herded to fresh grazing. For the Hare Krishnas it is to sit at the feet of Krishna and worship him as he plays with the milkmaids. If that was my movie I would definitely be Krishna playing with the milkmaids, sending the worshipers off to make some cheese and wine, at least let them feel useful.

Whatever your mythology or religious view, just take it on completely as personal teaching, dissolve the dualities of 'self' and 'other' and fly off into the sky matrix. You've got to love it – the beauty and quite exquisite, deranged perfection of the whole thing. Not an atom out of place, not a speck of reality not doing exactly what it is meant to be doing, flawless like space, yet aware and manifesting ceaselessly.

They say that the Buddha chose to die so that his followers would not deify him, and instead focus on their own enlightenment. Being a good Earth Monkey and having spread the Teachings, he probably got tired of chastising aberrant monks for rubbing themselves up against trees, and was more than ready to go anyway.

They also say that the Teachings begin to degrade the longer they are around and strange interpretations start creeping in. This is why, as the original context gets lost, it is so important that we keep them alive by making them truly our own. The more you do something the more automatic it becomes, until it becomes the default, and all of a sudden it is the normal face you put on every morning.

I have the Hero Aspect when it comes to dealing with sentient beings, I know I can't fail and I never do. When I am in this Aspect I am relentless and unstoppable, as long as they play along of course. If they choose to drop the ball and retreat there is nothing I can do, it has to be a two-way street. Conversely, if they put their faith in me to do the job I always see it through, using everything and anything in my arsenal to propel the process.

I talk about the Teachings because it is my Nature and it could not be any other way, a Dzogchen machine just waiting to be unleashed. In the old days I would talk non-stop for three days and nights on speed, until the person in front of me had to flee from being so saturated with Teachings, but that is often what it took. You keep reminding the mind of its Original Nature, giving it a taste of itself enough times so that it stays there. The best method for doing this is total assault on the corrupt matrix of delusional patterning. Anything less would simply not suffice to get past the hi-tech defensive screens and allow access for the Dzogchen-Deluxe Anti-virus software to decontaminate the infected drives. If you leave the job half done the computer soon reboots, still crippled by the toxic trespassers in its hardwiring. Enlightenment for me was always an all or nothing package, half measures just frustrates me.

Luc even came up with a name for these strategic Dzogchen transmissions that I bombarded people with – 'ennas', concentrated thought forms sequentially downloaded into the person's mind to give it the right program and enough support structure to allow them to maintain it. These ennas are the Teachings and I have honed them to a razor's edge, stripping away all the unnecessary 'Buddhist-speak' and sexifying the hell out of them. Concentrated into pure essence, with the precision of a surgeon and the stealth of a sleeper-agent I plant little time bombs, which once detonated bursts into radiant flowers of Awareness. It is a priceless gift and the only thing I ask in return is respect and commitment, a small price to pay, all things considered.

The Buddhist archetype of compassion Chenrezig, also known as *Avalokiteshvara*, had so much compassion for sentient beings that he split himself into a thousand arms and thousand faces in order to benefit more beings. Chenrezig is one of my core personal archetypes. It is probably the most commonly used archetype in the Buddhist pantheon and is often used to engender compassion for others in people, precisely because of his commitment to alleviating the suffering of humanity.

A lot of Buddhists mistake him for an actual being, rather than a Personal Aspect to inspire them to greater heights of beneficial acts for others. This is a wrong view because there are no gods in Buddhism. It is all personal and indulging in externalist dualistic views makes one a theist, and therefore no better than a Jehovah's Witness.

So many things are misunderstood and when viewed from the correct stance one literally dissolves in the gloriousness of every morsel of reality doing exactly what it is supposed to be doing. No error across the board, beyond rebuke, a full nuclear-powered holiday till D day. We were all insane enough to choose the Kali Yuga as a time to manifest in order to dance our final Dance of Perfection, dissolve into light, and have a whale of a time doing it.

Since it is all the *empty dance of our own awareness* anything basically goes, as long as it is following your Intrinsic Nature which is felt as inspiration, delight, and joy at being alive. If you are in this State you can be doing nothing wrong, this is what Reality really tastes like and if you are not in this State then do anything and everything to get into it. It is quite simply magnificent and often too beautiful to even describe in words.

To be pumping full of the joy of existence, running your own movie at full tilt, volume turned up to 12 – who could be happier? Every moment should be a flood of exultation and if not, I definitely want to know why. I am the first to go hunting for aberrant bits of syntax in my own head and relentless in destroying them, their nature is Suffering and the only compassionate thing to do is to kill them.

"Nothing to do, nowhere to go, just to be yourself completely" is the challenge that is held up to every man, woman, and child, and it is definitely within everyone's grasp if they choose to engage it.

This is my story and I am sticking to it. Where it goes is largely inconceivable and actually irrelevant, as long as the movie continues to manifest in interesting and entertaining ways, I will continue to play. If everyone decided to pick up their respective torches and run with them, what a story we would have and though not everyone is cut out to be a rock star it does not mean that we cannot derive some pleasure from singing.

Give up any preconceptions of what things are and where they are going, just enjoy the show. Jump in the back of your own car and be driven through the movie, stopping from time to time to enjoy the scenery, what else are we going to be doing? Head above shoulders, the 'Shambhala Warrior Ethos', so we enter the abyss of our own minds, realizing at the core that we are indestructible and paying no attention to the various beasties that assail us along the way.

Take the Teachings deep inside, distil them in the vat of your clear-cutting intellect and when ready, spread them to the world. The world is waiting for just one Buddha and that is you.

TWENTY-SIX

Beyond Rebuke

*The plan for my grand exit strategy is
to go out with a bang that the whole
universe can hear.*

They say it takes a Buddha to recognize another Buddha as *"awareness knows itself"* and can never be faked. The way someone conceives
and speaks of their reality is something that can never be mistaken.

Brigitte, a neuroscientist who had given it all up to become a na-
turopath and then a witchdoctor, was basically dreaming her way
through reality using sound as her medium. A mother of three and
in the process of discarding all her *binding obscurations*, she was
always singing, you had to love it.

Even the labels of 'mother' and 'wife' were being shed and
watching the way she lovingly dealt with her kids and ex-husband
during this process was truly inspiring. He was not that happy
about it, but then a few eggs always need to cracked especially if
they are binding you into a particular role. He would appreciate the
perfection of it in time, it happens to be one of the jobs of Dakini
to break attachments in men.

Technically she did not need to change anything, according to
the Dzogchen tenet of *don't change a thing*, but this was her movie

and I was just watching. She had many visions of Shiva and at one stage had snakes coming out of everywhere, even the toilet. It seemed appropriate that during this process that she would embody Shiva, the Destroyer. In true Buddha Brat style people often embody archetypes that are different sexes, woman embodying masculine Aspects and men embodying females Aspects. It made perfect sense to me that all the archetypes would be concealed in those one least expected. It helps scramble a lot of our preconceptions about these archetypes which might prevent us from understanding their true meaning.

Brigitte had various visions of things coming into existence in the future and this for me always represented a person who is part of the final picture. She reminded me of the Atlantean technology where generating a sound fine enough could literally cut through metal, slice the fabric of space itself, and reform a new reality.

This was the way our world would be created anew, it would be sung into existence and another vision was born – it would involve 50ft speakers, the Apocalypse as glorious backdrop, and a writhing crowd of people, all reaching enlightenment en-masse to the greatest rock band ever, mine. Fully automatic Dzogchen for the people – spread it far and wide as the only real lifeline people have. Anri agreed to be my bassist and I have had visions of the other members of the band. I will recognise them when they show up.

Dzogchen for me is all about sex, drugs, and rock 'n roll, and using these forces to liberate oneself from the matrix. To pluck the lotus from the water without getting wet is the name of the game, and it is played in the mood of Effortless Elegance.

Part of my mission is to sexify the hell out of Buddhism, dazzle them with the beauty of the Teachings and my special take on the syntax. To weave such an exquisite tapestry that people have to succumb to the sheer beauty of it. The old image of miserable, shaven-headed monks dragging their heels around the monastery with the lighting of butter lamps as the high point in their day, is gone. The more traditional Buddhist approaches of extended meditations and dark retreats where one stays in a dark room for up to three years seem unnecessarily harsh to me. My take on it though is that whatever does the job is good and whatever doesn't, should be discarded like an old rag.

The real power in Dzogchen lies at it starting from a Non-Dual space. No 'self' no 'other', no 'god', no 'demons', nothing but the impersonal and beautiful *play of the mind* as it entertains itself. Why is it like this? To which I respond *"does one question a bowl of ice cream as to its goodness or truth?"* No, one just consumes it. If there is honey on the tongue does it matter where it comes from?

I spent a long time pondering the question of behaviour of Enlightened Beings, reading different accounts of their behaviour, dress and conduct throughout the ages. I soon came to the conclusion that as long as you were firstly, Enlightened and secondly, *"benefiting beings"* it did not really matter how you conducted yourself. I definitely favour leather pants and jackets, my bike Tiamat and Marilyn Manson over robes, sandals, and deep-throat liturgies.

The 6th Dalai Lama made nightly forays into town to different young ladies' houses and when accosted by the monks on his behaviour he nonchalantly unzipped his pants and urinated over the edge of the palace wall. As the stream was about to reach the bottom he drew it back up and into himself. He stated that in all the nights he spent making love he had never lost a single drop of semen and that his love of women was just the expression of his own Natural State. No doubt the local girls must have been delighted to be sleeping with the secular and spiritual leader of Tibet, but that is another story.

No specific commitments to keep, no particular conduct to maintain unless you want to. To abide completely in your own Nature and treat the reflection the way you like to be treated, is the Path and the Goal. Sounds pretty good to me, and having found previous precedents of unusual behaviour I came to realize that it actually did not matter in the least what I did. The passions and the poisons once overcome can be worn as adornment, ones fine colours that make you uniquely you. Accepting your own Nature, its hugeness and emptiness, is the means to accomplish this.

Everything and nothing, and at the same time total freedom.

If it is all Empty anyway does it really matter what happens in the next moment? Given this, one might as well have the reality one wants, whatever that might be. Everyone has a different take on it, but this is the prize that is on offer if you care to claim it.

I used to take great pleasure in India asking Hindus to bring me God as I wanted to eat him, watching the shock and horror as I ploughed through a whole field of their Holy Cows with a battleaxe. What I was really doing beyond being a brat, was to destroy their dualistic concepts of 'self' and 'God' as separate entities, and I like to humour myself that it had some effect, if only just to dent the servile attitude they approach divinity with.

I have always favoured the 'monkey see, monkey do' mode of learning and whether it was Asher telling me how he stared at the sun on Acid, or Garab Dorje sending the whole of Oddiyana into Body of Light, if it has been done, ever, by anyone, then it is doable, and I love sinking my teeth into a good challenge. The Sun Gazing I have since integrated as one of my practises and the global liberation of all sentient beings is something I am still working on as it is a taller order of reality.

Everything is done for the benefit of all sentient beings of course, and also for ones entertainment, lest we forget. If by *abiding in your nature*, a central tenet of Dzogchen means you are at your best around friends having a great time, then as the I Ching says, *"No error"*. If my entertainment directly benefits all sentient beings, well I guess I will just have to remain entertained for the benefit of all sentient beings, something I certainly have no objections to. Are there any limits as regards to conduct and behaviour at all? I think not, the actions of Buddha's are inconceivable after all, especially to the un-enlightened – sounds like an invitation to the most monumental party in the universe to me.

One of my mottos is *"I will not even allow myself to get in the way of me having a good time"* and I try to stick to this at all times. Taking the view of a Chakravatin, we launch forth into the world engaging whatever arises for the benefit of all sentient beings. I even have a T- shirt that Luc made which says *"Beyond Rebuke"* in STAR WARS font – a statement of my intent towards reality.

When you wake up to your Natural Condition there is literally nothing that is beyond your scope and ability to manifest. Certain things take longer than others to come into form, but then what is time other than a mere mental concept anyway?

Beyond rebuke one ventures forth into the world living ones dreams, fearing nothing, and loving everything. The truth will out eventually anyway so you might as well play it wide open with no guilty secrets needing to be hidden to trip you up later. People will think whatever they want anyway and not everyone will love you, but if you love yourself others will automatically love you and to hell with the heel biters, those too small of spirit to do anything else other than take pot shots at you. I am doing the work of the angels so fuck them all anyway let them point, ten fingers inevitably end up being pointed back at them, and who asked for their opinion anyway?

I still intend to be fabulously wealthy. Why because it really makes no difference and why on earth not? When it happens it will of course be for the benefit of all sentient beings as it would otherwise not happen, and I will share the wealth with my Vajra brothers and sisters who are as much a part of me as my blood. They make the whole thing worth doing in the first place. It is totally in keeping with the Buddha Brat ethos and since I am not attached in the least to being rich or poor, I might as well be rich, stupidly, and insanely rich. Of course it is rather meaningless either way as one cannot take any of it with you but while one is here, one might as well play.

Thereafter, well to quote Louis XVI, *"After me the storm"*.

The fetid bog is as pure as the crystal palace, it is just our minds that leap into judgement proclaiming the one bad and the other good. This is the hard lesson of One Taste and it is definitely a bitter pill to swallow in the beginning. As one proceeds along the *"path without a goal"* one sees this more and more. Slowly one frees oneself from judgement of any kind and then the fetid bog is the crystal palace, and vice versa.

It is said that when you have reached the peak of this View that everything turns to gold as it is the view that binds or liberates you in any moment. Once one has truly engaged it one can live in the crystal palace or the bog with equal pleasure. Why not then live in the palace if you have a choice, since it is all the same and makes no difference anyway?

All we can really do is hold up shining examples of what is possible – to act as blueprints for people to follow if they so choose. In doing this we are transmitting and continuing the lineage of whatever is worth keeping as people follow what they like, and turn away from what they don't.

This allows you to take your rightful position as a World Ruler in your own world, with no apologies or need to appeal to higher powers. Where are those aliens anyway, a lot of talk and hysteria but has anyone actually ever seen one? If you believe they are there then they will appear to you because the mind will bring them into existence as surely as it will bring a new car into your reality. This does not make them real, it makes them a *play of the mind* which has the infinite potential to bring into form exactly what you want to see. I believe that certain people need the concept of aliens to spice up their rather boring lives, and it is no coincidence that they tend to appear to rednecks out in the Styx. If you were an advanced civilization capable of interstellar travelling, would you bother anal probing white trash in trailer parks? I think not.

The warrior's true and only purpose is to fight the war within and destroy the illusion that is 'self'. Once accomplished he goes out and liberates himself from all concepts that bind, allowing him eventually to transcend his human form and embrace his birthright of *all forms, yet no form*. Then the Demons of Suffering and Despair become like thieves entering an empty house, there is quite simply nothing left for them to take.

The Dzogchen Teachings and the tales of the Buddha Brats are so beautiful they simply have to be shared because they represent the potential of Realisation for everyone. This surely is the most compassionate thing that I could do with my time regardless of how long the whole show continues to run for.

My mind has been my grand work, systematically eradicating any neuroses that bind me into Suffering and I take great pride in my achievement. I will happily go toe to toe with anyone on this. I have Homoeopathy which, when used properly, is definitely a priceless tool for propelling you through the mires of your own mind and towards enlightenment.

When this is combined with *the Great Perfection* of Dzogchen and is fuelled by the forces of Kundalini, well quite simply you become unstoppable. Two snakes untwining in the air, spontaneously liberating any residual tweaks left in your psyche. Take back all your goodies stashed in the secret spaces of the mind, if you can get them then they are yours to do with what you like.

The Dakini Teachings say that nothing proceeds without Dakini blessing and never a truer word has been spoken in my experience. Many years ago I even wheedled a promise of eternal blessing from Claire, her being a woman and therefore representative of all of Dakini. I figured that a guarantee like that would safeguard me against any mishaps.

I don't need safeguards any more though, I just start something and if it is supported unconditionally I know it is right. I just play my part and can only play it if it is meant to be, if it is not, I will have no more success than elephants can fly.

None of my grandiose schemes from bombing the water supply to the unbinding of the titans and discovering of Terma with Cat would have occurred unless they were meant to be. The results of these actions were always completely different to what I had envisaged at the time, yet all were perfect in their manifestation. The surprise outcomes only add to the grandiose derangement of the scheme, and if we play our parts with a smile then all the blessings of the universe come flooding to our door, drenching us in a lake of ambrosia.

I have been aided many times and at each juncture Dakini has been there winking at me through my ecstasies and agonies, encouraging me on to further heights. Even at the most painful I have kept faith in The View and this has ensured that I am still here playing the game, and not succumbing to my various self-destructive impulses when the going gets tough.

A strong part of me at times really did not want to be here, but another stronger part of me has always pulled me back from the brink of despair or existential angst, reminding me of the point of the whole thing in the first place – the Liberation of Mankind.

The covert ops time is done and it is time to assume the Unwavering Confidence in knowing that everything I have ever done had in fact been perfect and could have been no other way. Whatever your position in reality is at the moment, the time is around the corner when it is no longer necessary to hold up the illusion - shed your cloaks and assume your full Aspect as Rider of the Apocalypse.

The saying that the actions of Buddha's are inconceivable I basically take as a license to do whatever I like without doubt. Doubt being one of the main mind killers and to be shot on sight.

'Hide in plain sight' is part of the Buddha Brat ethos, make the whole thing seem so deranged that no one believes you anyway. This gives us the perfect cover to bring about the final touches to the stage we call Reality, before the final curtain falls. Coming soon to a reality near you...

TWENTY-SEVEN

Dancing On The Wire

*What would be the point of Enlightenment
if you did not get to do anything and everything
you ever wanted to?*

We do not stand on ceremony we dance upon it and this is the attitude that needs to be taken in order to allow the fullness of our expression to manifest. Holy Cows, what Holy Cows? If they were that holy they will be resurrected anyway so let them all out, butcher them, and then watch them come back to life purified.

If you can do it, reality will support it if it is right, and if not there is no real potential for damage anyway. A lot of the secrets are self-secret and can only be used and applied if you come with the right intention anyway. So any potential for abuse is nullified but if you are going to throw people to the lions at least give them a sword, it only seems fair.

This whole book is a collection of swords to use in slicing off the binding illusions that are stuck to you. It also goes into some teachings on basic and advanced swordplay, but who will take it to heart is up for grabs. It is the End Times and everything is coming out of the woodwork, literally anything and everything can be used as Means to Enlightenment.

If you apply this with wisdom and insight, my fervent hope is that I see more, rather than less of you, on the other side. Whoever makes the grade will be there.

I would argue that by the very act of playfully and sometimes mischievously engaging reality we are accelerating our process immeasurably and that it is actually our responsibility to ourselves to do just that. VIP Passes to all corners of reality, *"open all night"*, XXX road show, super-deluxe five stars special – bring it on. Once you have the keys to Reality there is no turning back or shirking your responsibility, there is so much to do and so much that can be done, especially when everything you do turns into Enlightening Buddha Activity and flushes the mind in the process.

The last of the Dakini Cards is called The Last Laugh, and this is the mood for the end times – whatever occurs, just keep laughing. If you are laughing and singing you can hardly be screaming and crying after all. Keep it light, upbeat, and fun, respect the mood of the moment, and you can't be doing too much wrong.

Always with a smile, one never loses ones sense of humour and this saves you from the Demon of Seriousness which in its own way is as ferocious as the Demon of Despair. The playful attitude towards reality is essential since the very Nature of Reality is also light and playful, ceaselessly toying with us and prodding us ever onwards.

What would be the point of Enlightenment if you did not get to do anything and everything you wanted to? What we like to do is often our Means to Enlightenment, a very interesting little fact. Follow your nose it works for cats and dogs. The trusting of instinct should never be underrated and as long it is in conjunction with your heart, there can really be no error.

Where we go and what we do in this world is largely irrelevant since it is all the *empty dance of dakini* and has no more meaning than a mirage, but it is in the pleasure of the shifting forms that we carve out our Liberation. So in this sense it is important and in fact crucial that we enjoy our movie, because by enjoying it we are dancing our way clear of the Six Realms and any future incarnations.

If *the path is the goal and goal is the path*, then every step we take on it should be treated as the only moment there is and to be valued and cherished as such. Even the idea of the Body of Light is just a beacon to spur us onwards, the juicy bone to be gnawed at the end of a long and glorious life.

If you do not carve and live your dreams then no one is going to do it for you because in fact, there is nothing else actually out there but the *manifestations of your own mind*. We are perpetually called on to step up to the plate and bring into being the reality we want to live in. One need never suffer either, it is only the mind and its attachment to outcomes which causes us to suffer, but since everything is perfect anyway and could be no other way, there is no need to ever suffer the pangs of frustrated fortune.

Another main tenet of Dzogchen is that of Spontaneous Accomplishment, the notion that all things being born from a single essence, exist beyond time and space. This means that any thing or action is never separate from the Now, and therefore technically comes to fruition in and of itself, without the need to strain to bring it into form. It is only our mistaken dualistic view that makes the illusion of something needing to be accomplished, seem real.

If all time exists in this moment it is all already done anyway, so there is truly nothing to worry about. The Demon of Time can happily be taken out the back and bludgeoned to death with a half brick. If one can see the future, which one can upon occasion, then surely the future has already occurred as part of the Eternal Present which represents all time. Time's only function is to synchronise consensus reality but is subjective at the end of the day and putting numbers on moments which are experienced as sound, light, and sensation has always seemed rather ridiculous to me. Nirvana and Samsara are the same thing and you can be in either one in a second. It is the state of mind in the present that matters, and it is either the embodiment of bliss and joy or suffering and despair.

Luc had written an extensive tome on 'Chronomics - the Theory of Time' but for me it was all represented right here and right now in this very moment. Either be happy in This Moment or suffer like a pig and die, waiting for the moment when you will finally be happy.

Certain things are not worth thinking about as it gives them

218

power and one has to be very deliberate about what one puts into ones Wish Fulfilling Gem – it will bring fears into existence as surely as dreams. What stops us from manifesting exactly what we want are residual fears of not being good enough or not deserving to have certain things. Once we delete these patterns there is little that can stop us from turning Samsara into Nirvana in a single thought.

Everyone has their own Wish Fulfilling Gem. The workings of the *gem that is your own mind* are simple – wish in, reality out. Nothing is cast in stone, it is all up for grabs and this is why you write a hundred wishes after you hit the Natural State. Quite simply to give the Wish Fulfilling Gem something to manifest to keep your movie playing.

As you conceive it or dream it so it comes into form, as long as the workings are not distorted by fears or feelings of lack. If you address the gem with *"please Wish Fulfilling Gem, if you have time, maybe, could you, if it's not a bother give me a new car?"* it is going to take a long time to manifest. Each negative syntax structure is slowing down the whole thing immeasurably. If, on the contrary, you address it with *"I want this now"* and even better *"it is already done"*, it frees up the manifestation to come into form remarkably quickly.

Try it out, take up your position as a World Ruler and *"the Buddha to come"* and literally command your reality. If you have doubts about your own impeccability you can always add at the end of the wish *"for the benefit of all sentient beings"* to keep it clean and tight.

When the wish actually comes into form of course depends on the viability of it coming into being, and whether you are heeding the signs that are leading to the fulfillment of your wish. If you are wishing for 100 billion dollars it might take a while to come into being, it might not drop through your fireplace one merry Christmas morning, but instead you might be offered a business opportunity which becomes the conduit for your financial success and you might instead make ten million instead of a hundred billion.

On the other hand if you wish for a car and you get a Beetle and not a Porsche, you should be equally grateful as it complies with the wish specification, which was very broad. If you reject its offerings as being sub-standard you are more likely to slow down its potential for manifestation, as negative reinforcement hardly ever works. It is your own fault for not specifying your wish properly or being too attached to the form of the wish.

The more grateful and thankful you are for the Gems' offerings the more it tends to shower down upon you. The best thing about the Wish Fulfilling Gem is that you can have infinite amounts of wishes, so enjoy the ones that come true and perfect your skills for even greater and more precise wishes.

If you want a girlfriend and wish for Cindy Crawford you might not get her, but rather someone more in keeping with your own nature, which you will end up enjoying more. The better you know yourself, and the more in tune with your Nature your wishes are, the better they will manifest. Fantasies often don't stand up in the light of day, yet reality is such an epic fantasy anyway when you open your eyes and admit to the staggering beauty of the whole thing. Then, when one is so stunned by the majesty of it all, it rewards you further by continuing to manifest whatever you want.

It would be nice to do a sequel to the movie THE SECRET, called REVENGE OF THE SECRET where the techniques they talk about are unleashed in the hands of a seven-year old child - mountains of candy start appearing in the middle of the city, everything turns purple and the rivers change into chocolate milk. The old adage *"be careful what you wish for"* is only half true. One should wish strangely and exotically, watching as the Wish Fulfilling Gem joins the dots. The less you wish for the less you will get, and what is even truer is that you get what you think you are entitled to, because this is what you allow yourself to manifest.

If by some strange chance you do not know what it is that you want, work it out from what you do not like and do not want because people often have a clearer idea of this. By this process of exclusion you will then arrive at what it is that will really make you happy.

I wished for someone of equal awareness, pretty, younger than me so she could keep up, and in a separate wish for knowledge of Chinese medicine, and Cat popped out of the woodwork. I of course forgot to add *"someone who would love me forever and suit my nature"* and this is what caused the rub at the end of the day. She was studying Chinese medicine at the time and she loved Homoeopathy but our dance was not destined to last, although amazing things did come out of it.

The Wish Fulfilling Gem will manifest what you ask for to the letter of the word but it is not inherently intelligent, it is just a tool and it does exactly what you ask of it. This can be a problem as you always tend to leave out the little things which end up flipping the chessboard over mid-game, but so it is that we learn. If we did not learn to use it there would be no joy in the refining of it. This is part of the pleasure of the ongoing *dance of reality* and something we would surely not want to do without.

My wish for a new motorbike had manifested in the form of an out-of-the-box Yamaha XT 660, a sleek black metal beast that propelled me at high speeds through reality. Even when I dropped it in the rain on my leg it forced me to remain housebound, and finish this book. Hobbling around the house with a torn ligament would have been the perfect excuse to suffer had I indulged it, but seeing the perfection of having to miss out on my trek to the Fish river canyon in order to finish a great work seemed a small price to pay for inheriting the Earth.

Sitting in a sea of old Camel Filter packets, scattered teacups, peach and grapefruit juice containers, I wished the future into being. To the strains of Juliette Lewis, Muse, Marilyn, Nine Inch Nails and Gogol Bordello I plotted and schemed and dredged the residues of my mind for storyline. The very act of writing was proving to be one of the greatest *hide nothing in your house* methodologies I had ever come across – it is one thing telling your friends about ones wild past but it is another completely telling the world. Everything I had kept secret and under wraps for so long was surfacing, and entailed ditching the covert feeling of secrets needing to be hidden.

It was all already done anyway, reality just needed to catch up. How or why would I ever create anything that would harm me in any way, and how could it not be everything I ever wanted? The covert ops time was done, and it was time to assume the Indestructible

Confidence in knowing that everything I had ever done had in fact been perfect, and could have been no other way.

The huge relief of letting go of all of this, let them think what they want, there was no longer any time or need for secrecy. Everything was in place, and Reality would dance its final dance with me. I had done my work and so was lining up for my rewards although now I would do it right out in the open, in everyone's faces, and they would love me for it.

It is time now to get published and fly around the world on book tours and healing forays. Why not appear on some American talk show, just for the hell of it? I already agreed to give the movie rights to Anri and the proceeds of all these projects would go into making a band that would literally rock the cornerstones of reality, the only way I could think of getting my 50ft speakers. One might as well be singing the final swansong of reality as it all comes crashing down, and I could think of nothing better to do with my remaining time.

Lead by example, show them the joys and the liberation of the Natural State, of the mind functioning flawlessly and bringing everything I ever wanted into existence. To be free from the Demon of Public Ridicule is a big one, especially when you are on show, but if you can slay this demon you will rise through the ranks of the superstars and take your position on the throne. If I can do it so can you and part of this book is to show you that you just have to take on the mantle of everything you ever wanted and bring it into existence.

The rock star thing had always been one of my dreams and all dreams need to come true lest one falls prey to the Demon of Dissatisfaction. Unsatisfied desire only leads to the grasping of the Hungry Ghost or Jealous God Realms and if it goes far enough, to the hatred of the Hell Realm. I would do it for the benefit of all sentient beings although I doubt that I would mind the groupies and the adoration, especially if it was for a good cause.

Whatever one does when one hits the Natural State benefits sentient beings anyway, so had I chosen to sleep under my bed for the next five years it would have been *enlightening buddha activity*. I am of a more proactive nature though and love missions, something

I can really sink my teeth into, a *cause celebre*, a *raison d'etre* as it were, to shine in use as we are all meant to.

To be the diamond sword that slices through the Fabric of Reality ceaselessly benefiting sentient beings whilst being in a rock band sounds like a job description that suits me just fine. All it takes is passion and guts and when it comes to liberating sentient beings I am relentless. Pouring out the Teachings to masses of people, giving them a taste of the Natural State, and showing them the techniques of staying in the State whilst having a fabulous time, seems to me like the best thing I could be doing.

No need for excuses or justifications, your actions become quite simply *beyond rebuke.* No one could point a finger at me - the actions of Buddha's are inconceivable after all. If they choose to point fingers, which people like doing, it is often out of jealousy and it's their stuff not mine. I had been well trained in resisting insults by my father, one of the best teachers I could have in this particular discipline. If the Forces of Reality were on my side and allowed me to proceed, how could I fail? The only thing that ever really gets in my way is myself, and I am generally faster on that than I can spit.

When you have dissected and chopped yourself up and served yourself as hamburgers to whole parties, no petty arrows can take you down. I play for and serve Dakini at the same time. She, who is me and the whole of Reality, would never allow her favourite child to be harmed as long as I played her game, which is something I do with pleasure. All I have to do as Daka, her masculine aspect, is flower and show off my fine tungsten petals to all of reality, for her and my own pleasure. No man was ever born that was not born of woman and for the gift of life I would pour out my soul happily in thanks to Her.

The line in the Monkey poem goes *"we are put together for our own entertainment"* and as the final curtain called, one last song needed to be sung which would unbind and then reconstruct Reality. To live your own dream, clad in black leather pants, silk shirts, and sporting bone jewellery, people just lining up for your attention seeking the Gems that would Liberate them from their own suffering – what a beautiful dream, and it is my dream, and I would live it as surely as the sun rises every morning.

I was born in Boston and I fully intend to return to my people if they will have me – the prodigal son returns. What other country would accept me after all, and love me for my wild ways? Everything returns home to roost at the end of the day and if there is one thing you have to give the Americans credit for, it is that they celebrate those that dare to dream huge. Any country that could produce and celebrate Marilyn Manson, Jim Morrison, Hunter S. Thompson and Madonna could not fail to love me. What my patients who know me as the good doctor in South Africa will make of this I shudder to think.

Those that throw caution to the wind reap and ride the Whirlwind and it is definitely time to come out from under the covers and play the movie to the max. Since it is all One Taste you might as well make it your own taste, and forever destroy the smallness of spirit in you that pushes people to end up as chip fryers or clerks in department stores.

From a Dzogchen perspective there is *no need to change or renounce anything* in ones life *as it is all perfect*. Drawing lines in water we do only for fun. One takes the view that one is automatically in the perfect feng shui position at all times, it is all perfect and if it feels wrong it probably is. Only you can change the script of your movie from a tragedy to an epic reality.

From the ashes of the atomic fires we recast ourselves in indestructible form, giving birth to the Diamond Age.

EPILOGUE

Lighting The Fire

This is the dream...

One thing I will tell you for free is that the 144 000 places booked by the Jehovah's Witnesses will be empty. That number strikes me as far too high anyway. From my view, if there are even 10 000 left after the energetic wave hits it will be a lot. Just knowing that whoever gets through will be impeccable though, is enough to keep me warm at night. There will of course be surprises in who gets through but the only acceptable token of Transcendence is sufficient dissolution of *the concept of form* in oneself. Since anyone who gets through will be carrying multiple lineage strands, we do not actually need that many physical bodies but the door is open if you can make it through, and diversity is definitely the spice of life.

I am not saying that the forces arrayed against one are not manifold but it is doable, and it can be done. Then and only then do you get the universal multi-pass, your ticket to the Pure Lands, or to any reality you want to inhabit, your choice. For most though it is a case of too little too late. Deprogramming yourself from the ground up takes time or pain, whichever coin you are willing to pay, and time is running out.

This is just a description of an indescribable event. It will be epic though, the most epic thing ever to happen in fact, because it is the destruction and rebirth of an entire culture and civilization, which is truly the most dramatic event to have ever occurred.

The way I see it is that it was a glorious organic experiment on the process of bringing Conscious Thought into Material Form. We created this entire thing ourselves to extract information on the nature of Reality and the Mind.

The process could not have been interfered with as this would have invalidated the results. The whole thing had to be left untouched, and even evil and hatred had to be given free reign. We wanted to see whether we can carve out our own Freedom from the raw substance of chaos. This is the only way we could be sure of the authenticity of the Teachings and our abilities as creators. Some of the most unspeakable events during our human epoch have lead to inconceivable acts of beauty and compassion by some of our species' finest individuals.

The time has come now for the experiment to come to an end. Having learnt the lessons from history and taking the best from each age we will spawn a New Era that we actually want to live in and bring children into. The planet will be largely unchanged, it is a beautiful planet and we like it.

Most people will be returned to their original constituents, basically happy soup, and those that have ridden their own Personal Apocalypse will get to remake the new world as they see fit.

We will build communities where everyone looks after everyone else, and will no more be able to hurt each other than they are capable of chopping off their own foot. The pain they generate in others will immediately be felt in themselves.

I will personally teach Dzogchen and Chod to the kids to prevent them falling prey to Dualistic Fixations. They will be capable of seeing everything as purely the *play of their minds*, and never something to be taken too seriously. It is after all bound to pass in a moment, giving way to a new moment which will in turn inevitably give way to another.

A lot of the visions people have had are visions which apply to after the Grand Dissolution and they often struggle to bring them into form now, because their time is yet to come – like it or not the whole thing is going down, and no number of good ideas are going to change the system as it is.

If you see this as happening in your own life it is just a question of becoming Zen with the idea of *dissolution* and riding the Whirlwind to the Promised Land.

The other Buddha Brats all have their specific wishes post-Apocalypse and for the moment are all waiting in the wings. Wanda has been trying to bring into form the ideal community and suffering for it because it will only be set up after The Wave. This has all been part of her learning to accept Effortlessness as her lord and saviour.

Ming probably wants a small country to run and is poised like a viper waiting to strike, just dying for a mission, gobbling up whatever Dzogchen texts and deranged remedy combinations I send her way. In the meantime she is perfecting the art of fusing Yoga, Shiatsu, Chinese Medicine, Tai Chi, and Acupuncture, so that we can keep the Buddha Brats at peak performance levels when the time comes.

Luc wants to go off journeying around the universe and for now has been helping me engage little bits of the things I was indifferent to by luring me with *pate de fois gras* so I will watch rugby with him – the last bits of One Taste that need to be sampled before the plate is completely clean.

Gesar has been dosing all and sundry with Iboga in an attempt to accelerate the process for people. Brigitte is singing her way through it all, which seems like a pretty good idea because when the chips are coming down you can't be screaming if you are singing. Hassle wants to build, it is his first love. Swamiji is a Rajneesh-following chaos magician and fabulous company, and has gone back to Johannesburg to make his millions.

Athena wants a long rest in the Pure Lands followed by retractable scales and wings. For now she is still living for free at an ex-mental hospital which was turned into a community, although it is more like a charnel ground than a community. I have infinite faith in her ability to dance the matrix but for the moment we are not speaking.

Jona and Cat are probably still around and we will make peace post-Apocalypse. I have a lot of faith in both of them because they were part of the original crew. Sometimes it is definitely best to let sleeping dogs lie, mine and theirs, because no matter how much water there is under the bridge certain roads are not worth crossing until the time is absolutely right. Cat originally wanted to be the chief re-creator of species so she could fiddle endlessly with genetics, ever the artist. Asher will have to make his peace with the Guardians of the Teachings and is no longer my concern.

Besides wanting fresh flowers sprouting from her head every morning Anri also commands her Scorpion Legions from the Underworld, whose sole purpose is to guard the Teachings and wipe out corruption. She wants to restore and renovate all ancient holy sites and temples, while in her spare time rewriting the cosmology. Who knows what Kama wants, probably a lot.

Thor has since been struck by lightning in the mountains of India. As is typical of his legacy he raised the bar for going out in style, heralding the Dawn of the New Age and daring all of humanity to live true to their natures and leave with a bang. He was cremated in a traditional Buddhist ceremony, as befitting a Buddha Brat. I never got to eat him unfortunately but am planning to make a remedy from some of his remains to honour our pact, thereby immortalising a part of his essence for all eternity – what could be more appropriate for such an archetype. Strangely enough less than a few months after his death the film THOR was released. Sometimes one cannot but marvel at the synchronicity.

And me, well I want a bit of everything – a bit of organizing, a bit of teaching, a bit of healing, bit of exploring, a bit of redesign and quite simply whatever takes my fancy. I definitely want polychromatic fur for those cold nights, and a tail and wings could be useful for a range of things, all retractable of course. Having broken the Illusion of Matter we will be able to reform our bodies with reality shifting at a thought. I will also personally go around destroying the dams with my plutonium-tipped arrows, allowing the natural forces to return to their original state. The unbinding of the Elementals who inhabit the waterways has always been a strong urge in me, as has the protection of the Forests.

Implementing a new paradigm is going to require many hands on deck and we shine in use so are happy to be busy. Everyone in short will do exactly what they love and want to do, and hence what they do best. There will of course be a whole lot that I do not know yet, fellow Riders still to be met. There will be some mystics, some high tantrikas, some Zen monks, Sufis, other Dzogchen practitioners, and an assortment of those lucky or crazy enough to ride the Wave of Dissolution.

Everyone is waiting, some more proactively than others, but still in readiness for the call to arms before the Army of Light issues forth from Shambhala Reborn to sweep the Forces of Darkness and Ignorance from the planet. For my part I have gathered the troops, done my level best to push up the timeline on the Apocalypse, and have come to the point where I am just doing some final touch ups on the Buddha Brats.

The plan for my grand exit strategy is to go out with a bang that the whole universe can hear. To be myself completely for the benefit of all sentient beings requires me to become a rock star to gather any stragglers who are just waiting for the honey of the Teachings to alight upon their tongues.

This is the dream and I am busy forging it as I write this. Nothing to do, nowhere to go - just expressing ones truth in the most beautiful and dramatic form possible. As they say in Dzogchen *"it is all already done"*, we are just waiting for reality to catch up. Nothing is given, everything is possible. This is my story and everything in it is true...

> *"When vision is an obstacle, you need a friend.*
> *When vision becomes a friend, light a great fire."*

The Beginning of The End.

Glossary

A

Afrikaans
A language spoken in South Africa, my second language.
It is classified as an Indo-European language due to its blend of Dutch and Malaysian but it also contains some ancient San words (from the original inhabitants of Southern Africa). Originally the language of the slaves in the Cape of Storms later adopted by European immigrants and is officially the youngest language in the world.

Allopathic
Opposite to Homoeopathic, it is governed by the principle that one applies something opposite ("Allo") to the disease state in order to cure it. Modern western medicine falls into this category.
See Homoeopathy

Amanita Muscaria
A hallucinogenic mushroom used primarily by Shamans in Siberia.

Apocalypse Riders
Unlike the four riders of the Apocalypse from the Christian tradition, these are not harbingers of death and destruction. Instead we see an Apocalypse Rider as someone who is able to ride through the coming storm without turning into cosmic soup. That is, someone whose sense of 'self' is diffuse enough that when faced with their own shifting forms are able to see them for what they are - dancing light, sound and sensation, thereby remaining fluid enough to dance with and in it.

A somewhat equivalent experience might be demonstrated in traditional Christianity as 'coming face to face with God' or in Judaism as 'entering the holiest of holies' except we see it as coming face to face with a wave or frequency of vast and infinite knowledge. Those who are able to deal with it will not shear apart, those who don't, will turn into light by being liberated from their bodies and those part of their personalities that cause them suffering. We believe that someone who is established enough in their practices will be able to pull through a certain amount of stragglers by stabilising their loved ones' minds during the process. This however will not be an easy feat.

Raising and dissolving ones Kundalini, regular Chod and any other practices from other traditions that focus on becoming familiar with the radiant nature of the mind as it projects external reality outward according to our moods, will be highly advantageous.

It is important to understand that no external agency determines who makes it and who doesn't, as the shift is ultimately an impersonal force taking place as a personal experience.
Compare to Cosmic Soup.
Also see Bodhisattva, Apocalypse, Buddha, Kundalini, Chod and Non-Dual View

Arhat
Literally translates as *"worthy one"*.
It is an enlightened being who has realised the goal of Nirvana, but doesn't necessarily include the fate of all other beings with his own.
Compare to Bodhisattva.

Armies of Mara
Those faces of Mara that appear terrifying or can cause one to doubt oneself or feel intense despair. Some examples would be – loneliness, anger, fear. An example on the path to liberation would be if one made a decision that feels right but then fear of failure sets in, making one too afraid to go through with it.
Compare Mara, Daughters of Mara and Holy Cows.
Also see Six Realms, One Taste and Zerbu.

Ascetism
Renunciation of worldly things, including food, comfort and most pleasures in an attempt to come closer to the true nature of things.

Aspects
From a specifically Buddha Brat perspective it refers to two things. Firstly it acknowledges and includes any and all personality traits, emotions as archetypes and faces that span the infinite range of human expression as our natural heritage. Secondly it indicates the skillful use of these faces or traits in the service of ones own enlightenment.
Compare to Yidam.
Also see Six Realms.

Ayahuasca
A South American hallucinogen made from the bark of the *Banesteriopsis Caapi* vine, mixed together with leaves from the *Chakruna* bush. It contains high levels of the psychoactive substance DMT.

B

Baby Buddha
It indicates someone who has newly arrived at the Natural State but is still a bit shaky and not particularly confident in being able to maintain it due to the newness and strangeness of the whole thing. Or it is someone who wrongly presumes that by hitting the Natural State that they have arrived and do not deem it necessary to maintain it ongoingly.
Compare to Chakravatin.
Also see Lion's Roar and Vajra Pride.

Bardo
Translates as *"Intermediate state"*.
Commonly refers to the state of consciousness and lapse of time between death and the next rebirth, but can also indicate other transitory phases such as before and after meditation, dreaming or even the gap between two moments or thoughts.

Bodhisattva
Translates as *"Enlightenment Warrior"*.
One who reaches enlightenment and then vows to not 'leave' until all sentient beings have been released from suffering.

From a strictly Non-Dual View this process is inevitable anyway since 'all is self', so ones own process of Liberation will be echoed by the liberation of all of existence, including 'other' beings.
Compare to Arhat, Apocalypse Riders, Buddha Brat and Chakravatin.
See Non-Dual View and Thogal.

Body of Light
The pinnacle of Dzogchen where one dissolves all remaining dualities holding one in form and turns into light.

In the Tibetan tradition the hair and nails are considered to be impurities and therefore left behind. When the transformation into light is achieved while the person is alive, it is referred to as the Great Transfer and no hair or nails is left behind.

According to the Buddha Brats the Body of Light or Great Transfer is not in fact a transcending of the physical form as such, as if the 'physical' is some gross thing that needs to be discarded, but rather, a state wherein the physical matter itself is liberated from our own incorrect mental constructs which obstructs the 'physical' from being what it REALLY is - moving, dancing

Light, Sound and Sensation. It is believed that ones personality survives this process and thus one can express ones unique understanding whilst not being bound into any particular form. It is also believed that once this happens one can take on any form at any time, able to be and do whatever one wants. Compare to Cosmic Soup.
Also see Thogal and Thigle.

Book of the Dead
The Tibetan account of the various visions and the corresponding sensations experienced on and after dying. Read to the corpse for up to 40 days, guiding the soul through the various stages of Bardo to maximize awareness and avoidance of rebirth in undesired.
Also see Bardo and Six Realms.

Buddha
Translated as *"awake"* or *"awakened one"*.
Traditionally it is used to refer to Siddhartha Gautama (or Sakyamuni) as the founder of Buddhism - a system to free people from suffering and ignorance.

According to Dzogchen all beings have always had 'Buddha nature' and that this truth has never changed and never will. It proposes that suffering is caused by the wrong perception that Buddhahood is something outside or separate from ourselves that needs to be attained. According to Dzogchen all that is necessary is to be shown this inherent Buddha in oneself directly, at which point one recognises it to be ones Natural State. What is left then is to remain constantly aware of this state during all activities both day and night whilst removing all mental constructs that obstruct this ultimate truth.

To understand the Dzogchen perspective better it is necessary to familiarize yourself with some of the aspects that set Dzogchen lineages apart from other Buddhist lineages. The key aspect in all of this is the meaning of the word Buddha.

Although all of the different schools that has preserved Dzogchen as a teaching acknowledges the historical Sakyamuni as a human Buddha, some of these do not view him as the only Buddha but rather as an incarnate emanation of the primordial Buddha Samantabhadra, which resides within all beings as the potential for Buddha-hood.
By viewing it in this way each successive Buddha can all be seen as different versions of this same Primordial Buddha, each arriving at unique places and times in order to expound further on the same body of Teachings. In fact, it is believed that each incarnate Buddha appears at specific times and places to teach methods appropriate to the capacities of the people at that time.

According to the Nyingma classification of the nine paths Buddha Sakyamuni taught what is known predominantly as Hinnaya (the lesser vechicle) and Mahayana (the greater vehicle) according to the capacities of the people at that time. It is called *"lesser"* and *"greater"* because of the different aspirations of the pracitioner.

In Hinnayana the aspiration is purely for the liberation of the individual, to the exclusion of others. In Mahayana the aspiration is for the pracitioner to become a bodhisattva, someone who vows to work for the enlightenement of all sentient beings. These teachings are collectively known as the Sutra system, or Teaching Lineage and comprises the path of renunciation and the path of purification respectively.

The Tantras of the Vajrayana (diamond vehicle) also known as the Practice Lineage, comprises of the paths of transformation and are said to have been revealed by Vajrasattva, a trans-historical visionary aspect of Buddhahood. This means, not a human Buddha but an aspect of primordial Samanthabdra perceived by certain enlightened beings in mind space. That is how it was possible for the great Mahasiddhas to receive transmission of these teachings directly from various emanations and visions by their own pure perception. The Dzogchen tantras or path of self-liberation on the other hand are said to have been revealed directly by the primordial Buddha Samantabhadra. With each of these paths one can glimpse the successive stages of revelation of related teachings over time. It is therefore believed that later incarnate Buddhas like Garab Dorje (who taught Dzogchen as an independent system) and Padmasambhava (who taught Dzogchen in the context of Anuyoga Tantra) manifested because the time was ripe for people to receive, quite literally, 'the next installment'.

In truth, all of these incarnate Buddhas are seen (or should be seen) as the multifarious display of the primordial Buddha Samanthabdra and in this way really part of a singular but limitless being of pure and total consciousness. This 'being' is not an entity although he can be depicted as a blue buddha without ornaments but this is merely a symbolic way to represent consciousness itself.

The word Buddha literally means *"awake"* and rather than denoting any specific person it rather points to the quality of *awakeness* itself which is why Sakhamuni pronounced himself to be "Buddha" when someone asked his name. He was saying that he was indeed, Awake.

Naturally, incarnate beings who display this aspect of *awakeness* to a particular degree has been historically referred to as Buddha. This ultimately means that anyone, past, present and future, buddhist or not may be called a Buddha if he or she has brought this aspect of his/her inherent awakeness to fruition.

Most importantly, and this is a key precept of Dzogchen, it is understood that each and every person is in fact already Buddha, even more so, that every speck of dust in the universe is Buddha - Awake. We simply need to recognise

it by discarding the conditioned patterning of our ignorance, allowing what is already there to naturally shine through.
Compare with Natural State, Wheel of Conditioned Existence, Ego and Mara. Also see Padmasambhava.

Buddha Brat
It is an enlightened person who takes their particular set of teachings to heart and expresses them playfully as part of their realization.
One not unduly concerned with maintaining tradition once understanding has arisen.
Someone not necessarily enlightened yet, but has enough imagination or gall to stand a good chance at making it through the Apocalypse in tact.

Often Buddha Brats are typified by their interest in many different systems and their ability to reinvent, adapt or bring to full fruition any one system or a combination of many, as part of their journey to self-liberation. Buddha Brats are generally individuals with a unique outlook on life. Most of them seem to be naturally rebellious and prefer to jump in the deep end instead of following the safety of well-tread paths. They are usually anti-establishment and often fanatically committed to their own process.
More than a few have naturally developed healing, oracular, psychic or artistic abilities.
Compare Buddha, Bodhisattva and Apocalypse Riders.
Also see Enlightenment and Cosmic Soup.

C

Carlos Castaneda
Born in 1925, he was an anthropologist and famous for his supposedly auto-biographical novels about his experiences with a South American shaman by the name of Don Juan. Novels include *The Teachings of Don Juan, A Separate Reality, Journey to Ixtlan, The Art of Dreaming* and more.
See Don Juan.

Chakra
Translated as *"wheel"* it is used to describe the junction of subtle energy channels in the body.

Chakravatin
Can be literally translated as *"for whom the wheels are turning without obstruction"*. It is used in the context of a 'universal monarch' or 'world ruler' and

in particular one who rules righteously. It can be used to indicate the secular parallel to a Buddha (which represents the spiritual).

According to Buddha Brats it means the mantle of power that a realized being steps into, taking full responsibility for his/her own reality. To be a Chakravatin means to be fully aware, able and deserving to 'rule one's own reality'. This is not to the exclusion of others and the ideal according to the Buddha Brat vision of the future is where all beings are Chakravatins in their own right. The confidence in being able to take on the mantle is not in any way due to egotistical clinging or purely intellectual understanding but the realization that one IS the Buddha.

Compare to Buddha and Bodhisattva.

Also see Lion's Roar and Vajra Pride.

Charnel ground

The Tibetan equivalent of a graveyard.

Due to the hardness of the earth, burial is prevented so corpses are chopped up and left above the ground to be eaten by vultures, jackals and other wild animals. It is a favoured place for wandering holy men and in particular Chod practitioners to meditate.

See Chod.

Chod

Translated from Tibetan it means *"to cut"* or *"to sever"*.

In Buddha Brats it specifically denotes the *Chod of Machig Labdron*, a particular system of teachings that focus on *'subduing the demons that are obstructions to Awareness'*. It entails visual destruction of the physical body, aimed at breaking ones attachment to the *"Illusion of the Self as a separate and concrete entity"*. The author strongly recommends it as an invaluable tool to progress on the path of Non-Duality.

Compare Dakini, Mara, Five Lights and Demons.

Also see Machig Labdron.

Clarity

The aspect of mind associated with the ability to recognize and engage all external appearances and internal feelings and thoughts as arising from Emptiness. This is when one correctly perceives things for what they are, just the temporary movement of light, sound and sensation.

Compare Rigpa.

Also see Emptiness and Dzogchen.

Cosmic Soup

The primordial constituents of matter namely Sound, Light and Sensation. This is what most people will return to during the final stages of the Apocalypse.

When The Wave of Awareness hits the planet at once people will either be able to ride it out or not. Those who ride it out will be able to carry their current personalities over. Those who don't make it will sheer apart and dissolve into light. This light will then make up the substance from which a new world is made.

According to the Buddha Brat understanding, most of people's suffering is due to the human form they find themselves in. For most sentient beings their physical existence is the very thing that causes them to suffer and so, when they turn into soup, all of their previous neurosis, psychosis, addictions and fears will simply disappear along with their bodies and neurotic egos.

The Buddha Brats believe that this 'soup' WILL have sentient Awareness. These particles of awareness will get to be wind, water, fire and all the myriad of elements on this planet. The Cosmic Soup will be happy, relaxed and free from the traps of Form that previously bound them, and will also have the option of incarnating in human bodies again, when they are ready later on. In this way, the 'soup' is really a therapeutic experience and is truly the most compassionate thing that can happen to sentient beings. In many ways, the Cosmic Soup is like the Body of Light experience en masse, the only difference being that the enlightened soup will have the opportunity to enjoy being free from ego-clinging until it is ready to take on a body with a personality, without falling into suffering ever again. The Buddha Brats believe that in some cases parts of this Cosmic Soup might prefer to manifest later on as titans, ethereal beings, conscious creatures or whatever else takes their fancy, choosing not to become humans at all.

People whose current idea of Enlightenment involves a state of blissful union where they perceive there to be no individual mind or body and no activities, just *"nothing"* are according to the Buddha Brats really expressing an inherent longing to be part of the Cosmic Soup.
Compare to Apocalypse Rider and Body of Light.
Also see Dakini and Thigle.

Crazy Wisdom
A Buddhist path and form of conduct which includes, what is perceived by ordinary people to be, seemingly irrational actions but are in fact part of the enlightened being's methodology toward his/her own Liberation.
Compare to Chakravatin, Vajra Pride and Lion's Roar.

Crowley, Alistair
A spiritualist, teacher and magician of the 19th century responsible for revealing all sorts of hidden magical secrets, a part of the *Order of the Golden Dawn.*

D

Daka

Translates from Tibetan as *"Sky flower"* and is the masculine form of Dakini. According to the Buddha Brats ethos it denotes that part of Dakini that takes on an individual form at a particular moment in time and space. Both the masculine and feminine are inherent in all things and all people.
Compare to Dakini and Thigle.

Dakini

Translates as *"Sky dancer"*.
This is not to be confused with the Indian Hindu tradition of witches or lesser deities as it plays a very different role in Tibetan Buddhism.

Used to denote firstly that feminine principle prevalent in all things and from which everything is formed. In particular it symbolises the infinite potential of the *fabric of reality* to be anything at any moment. In truth, Dakini is that which gives birth to our mental projections, bringing it into what is perceived to be physical form. It is important to remember that it is always a projection of our own minds and never anything more than sound, light and sensation. In the Buddha Brats book it is often referred to as Reality, the Dance of Reality or *the play of the mind*.

Traditionally the word can also be used to refer to specific human individuals who embody this principle to a high degree, and can technically be both men and women.
Compare to Thigle, Five Lights, Wish Fulfilling Gem and Mara.

Dakini Cards

A deck of cards called *The Secret Dakini Oracle* by Nik Douglas and Penny Slinger.
It is based on the 64 dakini temples in Orissa, India representing 64 aspects of the feminine surrounding the masculine.
See Dakini.

Datura

It is a plant belonging to the *Solanaceae* (same as belladonna and potatoes). It belongs to a group of plants known as the 'witch's weeds' along with mandrake, henbane and deadly nightshade, due to its toxic hallucinogenic qualities. All datura plants contain the alkaloids of atropine, scopolamine and hyoscymine the effects of which when ingested, include delirium, intense fear, photophobia and amnesia.

In the depiction of Nataraj he may be seen to be surrounded by either flames or datura flowers, signaling the *'dance of destruction'* or the *'dance of divine intoxication'*.
Compare to Holy Cows.
Also see Mara, Armies of Mara and Wish Fulfilling Gem.

Daughters of Mara

Those attractive faces of Mara that lures one into suffering by the fact that one becomes attached to them. These can include friends, loved ones, success in ones career and more. An example on the path to liberation would be when one falls in love and forgets to remain Aware, and then losing the person and suffering as a result.
Compare to Holy Cows.
Also see Mara, Armies of Mara and Wish Fulfilling Gem.

Demons

Literally means *"obstacles to awareness"*.
There are two types of *demons* discussed in this book. These demons are not at all external beings in any way, and in fact there never are external demons with any inherent existence, but only ever Aspects of ones own Mind. The first describes the 'demon Aspect of Self' which hails from the Hell Realm, one of the Six Realms depicted on the Wheel of Conditioned Existence. This is discussed under Six Realms.
See Six Realms and Wheel of Conditioned Existence.

The second type is described for example as the Demon of Doubt, Demon of Despair etc. The word demon really means *"obstacle to Awareness"* and can indicate both pleasant and unpleasant sense experiences, emotions and thoughts that obscure ones ability to perceive the truth. Machig Labdron, the founder of Tibetan Chod explicitly states that demons can come in the guise of 'gods' to describe for example the Demon of Exaltation, a particular stumbling block for practitioners who like to congratulate themselves for achieving a certain state of mind. This experience is in fact an obstacle to true Awareness, because from a Non-Dual perspective, *pride in practice* reinforces the idea that there is anything at all to achieve, which is a direct violation of Dzogchen.

The way to deal with both types, the Demon of Anger/Hatred from the Hell Realm and the *demon obstacles of awareness* is of course Knowledge of the Nature of the Mind. However there are three specific secondary practices used by the Buddha Brats to ensure overcoming these.
First of all in the case of the demons of the Hell Realm which represents Anger and Hatred is to reintegrate these Aspects of oneself into oneself.

240

The second method is Tibetan Chod, cutting delusion at the root by destroying the Demon of the Illusion of 'self'.
See Chod.
The third method particularly useful to kill Doubt and Despair, is to quite simply *"shoot it on sight"* or *"bludgeon it to death with a half-brick"* whenever it rears its ugly head. These Demons of Guilt, Doubt, Despair and even Seriousness are never useful in any way, and to be automatically destroyed.
Compare to Mara and Ego.
Also see Wish Fulfilling Gem.

Dharmakaya

Translates as *"Dimension of the Essence"* or *"great ocean of awareness"*.
It is the place from which everything originates and ultimately returns and is associated with Emptiness that is Aware.

According to the view of Dzogchen all things arise from this 'place' and yet even though things may appear to arise and return to the Dharmakaya, they are actually never separated from the Dharmakaya and therefore have never left it in order to return to it. The goal of Buddhahood is to be aware of this Dimension of Being and remain present in it at all times.
Compare to Non-Dual View, Clarity, Rigpa and Natural State.
See One Taste, Thigle, Wish Fulfilling Gem and Dakini.

Discriminating Wisdom

The ability to decide which option has the most inherent value and acting accordingly. Usually follows the practice of One Taste, having conquered it and then choosing between different options free from attachment to the outcome. One can only truly claim to be applying Discriminating Wisdom once One Taste has been conquered.
See One Taste, Chakravatin and Vajra Pride.

Don Juan

The central shamanic character in the series of books by Carlos Castaneda, dealing largely with focusing the attention, cultivating fluid assemblage points and being open to formerly unknown realities.
See Carlos Castaneda.

Dzogchen

Translated as *"the peak of the mountain from which all other peaks are visible"*, and also known as *"The Great Perfection"* or *"Great Relaxation"* (Ati Yoga in Sanskrit).

Dzogchen is considered the highest Buddhist view and culmination of all other (including non-Buddhist) paths of self-liberation precisely because it represents the completion of the journey - the Enlightened State itself.

Due to the advanced and radical nature of these teachings, over centuries it was only passed on directly from master to student, 'mouth to ear' as it were. Transmission often took place in charnel grounds under the cloak of night, not only to prevent abuse by the undeserving but also at times when the prevailing authorities sought to suppress it - hence its reputation as *"the whispered teachings"*.

Emphasizing strongly the inherent perfection of everything, it is epitomized by central credos such as *"give up the disease of effort"*, and *"perfect just as it is, don't change a thing"*. Its primary practice is that of Rigpa (present awareness) yet any and all other practices may be used to bring the practitioner back to, or help the practitioner remain in 'the state of Rigpa'.

The basic premise that it is based on, is the view that all things are inherently empty (yet filled with infinite potentiality) and primordially pure, and that by truly understanding this, one gives up any grasping or rejecting and instead of struggling to alter things, one just relaxes into the Natural State. By doing this, all thought forms, emotional experiences and external things are allowed to appear and disappear of their own accord. Through this process one perceives the truth of ones own true Buddha nature and Liberates oneself as a result.

Conduct is typified by the fact that there are no specific vows to keep and no particular behavior to adhere to.

Because Dzogchen is the enlightened state, it cannot be explained or passed on conceptually, one can only experience it. In order for the teachings to have any real effect, the practitioner has to have had a taste of their own Natural State - this is called 'Direct Introduction'. For this reason most of the methods help to point out this innate understanding of ones own Mind. The Teachings therefore simply helps one to recognize, understand it once seen, and then to remain in that state at all times.

See Buddha, Rigpa and Natural State.

E

Effortlessness

The core ethos of Dzogchen based on the view that effort is the disease that keeps us from realizing our Natural State as ALREADY Enlightened beings.

This does not mean that one simply does nothing, unless that is what one wants to do, and even that will eventually change because we are naturally dynamic beings.

What is meant by Effortlessness is the Awareness when something doesn't feel right and then choosing not to force oneself to do it out of guilt, obligation or any other type of poisonous emotion. When one applies this it is often amazing to see how quickly things change. Often one just needs to let something go for a while, until the desire naturally arises to do it, at which point the action itself is entirely effortless and as a result, significantly more effective.

Effortlessness as it relates to Dzogchen can be described in the following way:
- **Nothing to do** This moment which is part of everything is never separate from the source of all creation. By striving to modify it in any way in fact prevents us from truly experiencing it by failing to see what is always, has always and will always be right here, right now. Therefore on the contrary, by relaxing we actually experience the Natural State as it is.

- **No meditation** By altering the Natural State through attempted meditation, we are creating a superficial experience that takes us OUT OF the Natural State, which is always present. Hence Rigpa (present awareness) is not meditation as such, but the authentic and natural experience of awareness in every moment. This is why Dzogchen practitioners meditate with their eyes open, because whatever one experiences with ones eyes closed is subject to personal fantasy which in turn is colored by desires and aversions.

- **No Discipline** By forcing ourselves to maintain certain states of mind or codes of conduct we are immediately moving away from the Natural State, which is relaxed, spontaneous and highly personal. By each person expressing their unique attributes we celebrate the multiplicity inherent in the Non-Dual State.

- **Nothing to Achieve** Because the Enlightened State is immediately accessible at all times, and never removed from us, there is no goal to achieve and no destination to arrive at. Any ideas we have of elevation is merely projection of falsehood because by 'going' somewhere to 'find' this elusive State only leads to failure in seeing the Truth. By looking for enlightenment we fail to see it, because it is not ever something other than 'this'. In this way those who strive to be good or better never find the Enlightened State, because they are chasing the mirage of conceptual constructs.
See Dzogchen, Buddha and Natural State.

Ego
According to the Buddha Brat view, it is used specifically to indicate the perpetual incorrect mental assumption that we are ever anything 'other than Buddha' and the resulting effect on our behavior.
It is that part of ourselves that obscures our true nature and incorrectly perceives itself to be all the myriad things that humans mistakenly think they are.

The ego according to the Buddha Brat ethos is therefore a collection of wrong views we have about ourselves that are continuously enforced by conditioned response patterns. It is anathema to the Natural State.

From a Homoeopathic perspective people often have layers of embedded response patterns which govern their reality and can be removed with judicious dosing.

It is for this reason that Dzogchen and Homoeopathy are such complimentary tools in the removing of 'ego' obstacles.

Compare to Natural State, Buddha and Mara.

Emptiness

It is the true nature of all things, the place from where it comes and the place where it returns. This emptiness is not the same as that which leads to the wrong ideas of nihilism or existentialism and does not stand in direct opposition to 'form'. It is an emptiness that is pregnant with potential and in constant relationship with 'ceaseless manifestation'.

One of the symbolic ways of understanding this is to make the sound 'ah' with your voice. Although the mouth is empty and hollow, it also filled with sound of the 'ah'. Emptiness is also one of the three aspects of the nature of ones mind, along with Clarity and Bliss.

Compare to Dharmakaya.

Also see Vajra Pride and Chakravatin.

Enlightening Buddha Activity

Actions of enlightened beings that, not only enriches the enlightened beings' experience on the path to Liberation, but also has untold and numerous benefits for sentient beings at large.

See Vajra Pride and Chakravatin.

Enlightenment

According to normal conceptions this is seen by most non-religious and religious people as a point in time where a person supposedly progressed to the point where they are 'all-knowing' or 'all-powerful'. At this point they supposedly leave this 'physical' realm to continue their 'good work' as some ethereal being, or they choose to stay and teach, usually performing miraculous feats of sorts. At this point according to various traditions the person is seen as an Avatar, Saint, Ascended Master or Holy Man. Other ways of describing the person includes 'non-physical', 'higher being', 'of higher vibration' and the list goes on.

According to the strictest interpretation of Buddhism as far as Dzogchen goes, Enlightenment would equate to the moment at which point a being realizes his or her Natural State or True Nature. As the very word Buddha itself means *awake* the Buddha Brats believe that Enlightenment literally means to reach the point of understanding the Knowledge of the Nature of the Mind and then expressing it at all times, therefore forever having escaped the clutches of Samsara by no longer being drawn back into Suffering.

According to the Buddha Brats the view that Enlightened Beings are necessarily vastly different in appearance and conduct to ordinary people is a mistaken view and that there are possibly many Enlightened Beings living seemingly ordinary lives. In fact, the fixation on the enlightened state as something that appears to be god-like or inhuman is in fact an obstacle to true Awareness, and can in some cases lead to people grasping at an intellectualized concept which is utterly out of touch with not only human nature but also the Truth. This also means that many accomplished beings fail to realize that they are already enlightened and they continue to strive to become so. This is in fact completely at odds with the non-duality of Dzogchen and which explicitly states that we are *never not enlightened* and that this State is always present. We just don't realize it because our perceptions are obscured by ignorance.

The proof of someone's Enlightenment is and always will be *"the degree to which they are liberated from suffering".* This is an important point, because people may be able to do miracles, but unless they are free from dualistic clinging, they cannot be said to be truly free.

On the other hand, in some practices of Dzogchen they talk about instances where the practitioner starts seeing the various emanations of Buddhas depending on their level of awareness and it has been mentioned before that these 'deities' can only be perceived when ones perception has sufficiently developed. Therefore it is possible that people are literally not able to identify that someone is in fact a Buddha, appearing to them to be just normal people, the reason for this being that their own awareness is simply too degraded to perceive the truth.

Compare Buddha, Knowledge of the Nature of the Mind and Ignorance of the Nature of the Mind.

Also see Samsara, Nirvana and Vajra Pride.

F

Five Lights
The ground substance from which everything is made.
Traditionally it denotes the five emotions that give birth to material form and hence our human experience. When these five emotions become obstacles due

to our attachment or aversion to it, they give birth to thoughts, experiences or things that cause us to suffer.

Then it is referred to as the *five poisons* which lead to entrapment on the Wheel and the Six Realms. When these emotions are simply experienced as pure in themselves, it is referred to as the *five wisdoms* and gives birth to the joyous and blissful experience of all of reality.
Even though in traditional Buddhism there are specific teachings around the Five Lights, according to the Buddha Brat ethos the actual number of lights is not something to be fixated on. The main focus is the principle behind it which states that the emotions and the mind are the root of all existence and yet that the nature of existence itself is nothing more than the *play of light* changing at any moment according to ones mood. It is for this reason that the State of Ease and Effortlessness is so important because if one is constantly relaxed it generates a reality that is relaxing and enjoyable.
Compare to Dakini, Mara and Thigle.
Also see Six Realms and Dzogchen.

G

Garab Dorje
Founder and original teacher of one of the lineages of Dzogchen, he is reported to have lived from 520 BC in Oddiyana. He is most famous for his Three Statements known officially as *"The Three Statements that Strike the Essential Points"*.

These statements are:
- *Directly discover your own natural state.*
- *Remain completely free from doubt.*
- *Achieve confidence in self-liberation.*

The first point clearly indicates that one can only discover ones Natural State, it is always there, one just has to have a personal experience of it, a taste as it were.
The second point clearly states that the overcoming of the Demon of Doubt is essential.
The last point is often overlooked because of the popular notion that so-called enlightened beings are supposed to be meek and mild, always humble and never supremely confident. The Buddha Brats saying that *"when you know, you know"* is the expression of this.
Compare this confidence to Lion's Roar, Vajra Pride and Chakravatin.

Gesar of Ling

The legendary leader of Shambhala, the 'City of Light' who was prophesied to return, heralding the Army of Light to issue forth from Shambhala and vanquish darkness and ignorance forever.

Golden Mean

Is represented by the Greek letter *phi* and is often referred to as 'the divine proportion'. It is a specific mathematical ratio that is found throughout the cosmos, including living things. Its decimal abbreviation is (1.680339887499...) and is directly related to the Fibonacci series of numbers.

Guru

This literally means *"remover of darkness"* and is most often use in the context of a teacher.

According to the Buddhist system a guru can be any teacher who introduces one to the knowledge that "removes darkness from the mind" but the distinction is made between an ordinary guru and a 'root guru'. A 'root guru' is the one teacher who brings one to full realisation and quite often is not necessarily the one with whom the student spent the greatest amount of time.

For those students of the traditional paths, the purpose of Guru Yoga is clearly described by illustrious teachers such as Namkhai Norbu, as their own mind. Despite this and through compassion for sentient beings masters play the role of Guru in order to point the nature of the student's own mind out to him/her. The aim however is always, and has always been, for the student to unite with their own minds as supreme guru at which point they have basically 'arrived' at the Natural State. This is one of the most important aspects of Dzogchen because despite the fact that 'devotion to guru' plays an important role in establishing the type of relationship with the master that is conducive to learning, it is (or should be) understood to ultimately lead to the student realizing their own Natural State as the ultimate Guru. Once this has happened the master only really exists to support the practitioner in the practical application of techniques necessary to remain in the Natural State of Self-Liberated Perfection. According to us, and presumably to all teachers, the greatest gift a practitioner can give their Guru is to become realized.

H

Hinayana

Translates as the *"lesser path"* in Buddhism, focusing on renunciation in order to overcome the passions.

Supposedly takes five lifetimes due to the difficulties in negating natural passions on the path to non attachment. Taught first by the historical Buddha Shakyamuni and is representative of the monastic school of Buddhism.

Holy Cows

Objects and concepts, especially nice ones to which one still attach a high degree of importance. These can include – loyalty, honour, trust and more. Compare to Daughters of Mara, Armies of Mara and Mara.
Also see Samsara and One Taste.

Homoeopathy

Also spelled as Homeopathy by some.
A System of medicine created by Samuel Hahnemann (1755 - 1843) which operates on the principle that *"like cures like"*, and which is made through a process of dilution and succussion
The word 'homo' means 'the same' and this medicinal system is in direct opposition to the Allopathy, the predominant medicinal system in the West.

Remedies are made from a myriad of substances which are diluted beyond the point where any physical traces are left. The result is that one can use substances such radioactive materials, animal urine or blood, and poisons which would normally be unpleasant or harmful in its crude form.
Use of the remedy is strictly based on proving. This is a process whereby the homoeopathic substance is given to a group of healthy individuals. The symptoms they generate as a result are usually the symptoms that the remedy will cure in diseased patients. Once the proving has come to and end, the symptoms disappear shortly after. The beauty of this system is that there are never any permanent side effects and yet disease can be cured permanently because it removes the mental causes of the disease. Homoeopathy can successfully treat mental illness when done properly and is also useful in preventing so-called genetically inherited diseases such as cancer.
See Allopathy and Succusion.

I

I Ching

Also known as *"The Book of Changes"* is an ancient Chinese text and divinatory system.

Ignorance of the Nature of the Mind

According to the Buddha Brat ethos this is the only true evil that exists in

the world. It describes the state of ignorance that is directly responsible for all suffering because we are ignorant of our Natural State. According to Dzogchen all that is really necessary to achieve Liberation is Knowledge of the Nature of the Mind.
Compare to Natural State and Buddha.
Also see Ego, Mara and Samsara.

Island of Jewels
A Visual representation of reaching enlightenment.
Compare Enlightenment and Nirvana.

Intuitive Wisdom
It is the feminine qualities represented by the Kundalini serpent at the base chakra which needs to unite with the masculine qualities of Skillful Means represented by the lotus at the crown chakra.

Intuitive wisdom is the ability to know something implicitly, similar to 'gut instinct' but more refined as it is not so much based on the type of animal instinct for the purposes of survival. Instead it is a deep and abiding knowledge that comes from personal and intimate experience with the nature of things, especially those things that are unseen, unknown, and often inexplicable. Understanding gained through mystical experience, empathy, visions and transmission through symbols and oracles are some of the gifts of Intuitive Wisdom functioning as it should.
Intuitive Wisdom, represented by the 'snake' is also the raw power source that fuels us, the life force as it were. Wherever the Kundalini is situated is where we feel, focus or express an abundance of energy. If it is trapped in a particular place this energy can become overwhelming, aggressive, and erratic.

When the Intuitive Wisdom is not united with Skillful Means, it has the symptoms of uncontrolled emotionality, premonitions and fears about things without knowing how to deal with it, or the lack of objectivity.
See Skillful Means, Kundalini and Chakra.

K

Kali Yuga
The *"Age of Destruction"* in the Vedic system of cosmic cycles.

It is referred to as a time of insecurity, war, famine, disease and the degradation of human values and knowledge. Like the composting of dead matter this age precedes the birth of the *Satya Yuga* (Age of Truth) or Golden Age.

Traditionally this time is feared by many but according to the Buddha Brat view it is a great time of accelerated energy which can be used to speed up ones personal process of dissolution. This is necessary in fact because from a strictly Non-Dual View where 'all is self' ones own process of Liberation will be echoed by the liberation of all of existence simultaneously. This is considered the 'absolute view' in Buddhism.
Compare Thigle and Thogal.
Compare Apocalypse Rider, Non-Dual View and Buddha.

Karma
A Sanskrit word meaning *"action"*.
In Dzogchen it is not seen in terms of good or bad deeds but rather the consequences of the degree to which one is 'holding on' to a particular emotion or action. It is not wrong to get angry, but to still be angry after the moment has passed, affects one adversely. It is also not something that can affect others or be affected by others but one is solely responsible for ones own 'karmic' consequences. Therefore, the degree to which one lives effortlessly is the degree to which one is liberated from karma.
Compare to Wheel of Conditioned Existence and Samsara.
See Six Realms, Natural State and Non-Dual View.

Kundalini
Sanskrit word translated as *"serpent fire"*.
It is the primal life force residing in the base chakra which needs to be brought up to the crown chakra to unite in order to properly unify female and male aspects within a person. While the process of uniting the two is incomplete one is quite literally not functioning at the capacity that one is truly capable of.

The predominance of Kundalini energy in certain chakras (when it has not been united with the crown chakra) will manifest certain symptoms. For example if it is stuck in the base chakra, the emphasis is predominantly on sexuality, or if it is stuck in the throat there is a strong urge to be seen as a spokesman or leader for some cause and can be powerful orators.
See Intuitive Wisdom, Skillful Means and Chakra.

L

Lion's roar
It is the physical process of roaring at the heavens to signal Realization.
A Buddhist practice which is done at a time when the practitioner has arrived

at the Natural State and is secure enough in it to triumphantly announce to the heavens that he/she will never be drawn into suffering again. It parallels the third of Garab Dorje's *"Three Statements"* which states that one should 'achieve confidence in self-liberation'.

Compare to Vajra Pride, Chakravatin and Bodhisattva.

Also see Garab Dorje, Island of Jewels, Enlightenment, Nirvana and Apocalypse Rider.

M

Machig Labdron

The famous 11th century female adept and teacher who founded Tibetan Chod was an emanation of Yeshe Tsogyel among other things.

There are indications that she fused some of her native Bön shamanic practices with the Dzogchen Teachings.

Compare Chod, Buddha and Yeshe Tsogyel.

Mahasiddha

Translated 'Maha' means *"great/supreme"* and 'siddha' means *"practitioner of siddhi"* or *"adept"*.

Traditionally the name usually denotes one of the great Buddhist tantrikas from the time of the first flowering of Buddhist Tantra, in the wake of Padmasambhava. These beings are usually numbered to have been 84. Each Mahasiddha came to be known for certain characteristics and teachings and among them there have been kings, scholars, prostitutes, fisherman, slaves, weavers, hunters and many more.

Besides for the traditional focus on powers attained, the Buddha Brats view Mahasiddha as someone who has realized the *supreme siddhi* which of course is Total Realization itself. Most of these beings also displayed various other powers as a natural expression of their enlightened state, but what typifies them is that they were fully liberated beings.

Compare to Siddhi, Buddha and Knowledge of the Nature of the Mind.

Also see Tantra and Padmasambhava.

Mandala

Translated from Sanskrit means *"circle"*.

Traditionally denotes a specific organization of forms or shapes to portray a Buddhist concept or teaching. In certain practices it can refer to ones body, ones life and the way that it is organized around certain boundaries.

According to the Buddha Brat view it is all of this and more, the entire gamut of human existence which becomes an expression of beauty and perfection once one has realized the Natural State.
See Natural State and Non-Dual View.

Mandarava
She is along with Yeshe Tsogyel one of the two principal consorts of Padmasambhava. She was a princess in the 8th century CE and later became an adept and teacher.

Mara
Traditionally means *"The Lord of Illusion"*.
Sometimes Mara is perceived to be an actual deity but this is incorrect.
According to the Buddha Brats view Mara is identical to Dakini in the sense that both are in essence the impersonal *play of the mind* or *fabric of reality* or Dance of Light. However when one wrongly perceives this *dance of light* to be something other than just that and suffers as a result, it is called Mara. Therefore Mara literally is an illusion that we have been bound by.
Compare to Dakini, Wish Fulfilling Gem, Buddha and Non-Dual View.
Also see Samsara and Wheel of Conditioned Existence.

Miasm
Means *"infecting taint"* and indicates forms of disease either passed on genetically from parents or acquired during the course of life.

N

Natural State
The unpolluted natural state of the mind or 'Buddha' which is our true nature and present at all times. It is often described as unborn, undying, unobstructed, indestructible, undefiled etc.

For most people this truth is obscured by the karmic traces of incorrect mental constructs which leads to confusion and suffering. As the sun is always present, even when obscured by clouds, so the Natural State is always present, even when obscured by wrong views. As these clouds disappear and the sun shines again, that is what is meant by 'waking up' to ones true nature – Buddhahood.
Compare Buddha, Dzogchen and Ignorance of the Nature of the Mind.

Nirvana

Literally means *"having gone beyond suffering"* and denotes the state of mind that is free from grasping or rejecting.

According to Dzogchen even though it may indicate a 'place' or 'state' that one arrives at, in actual fact it simply means manifesting what was inherent right from the beginning without the need to modify anything. Typically in Dzogchen the concept of Nirvana is hardly ever mentioned because it is implied that once one enters the Natural State, one is naturally and immediately Beyond Suffering. In some of the other schools the Natural State is not so prevalent in the teachings and the students are still very much involved in trying to 'get out of' Samsara with Nirvana often a far away ideal rather than something immediate. From the Non-Dual perspective of Dzogchen Samsara and Nirvana are actually the same thing, it is only the way we view it that makes it either suffering or joy.
Compare to Natural State, Buddha and Dzogchen.
Also see Samsara and Wheel of Conditioned.

Non-Dual View
The View that everything originates and remains in the unalterable and undivided primordial state of the mind.
Therefore that all so-called 'internal and external appearances' are but the singular *play of the mind* and that there is no external reality out there that is concrete or permanent in any way. This means that there are no dualities that imply a 'self', an 'other', 'time' and 'space' with any inherent existence at all.

An important aspect of understanding this view is to know how it differs from what in Dzogchen is called the 'Four Philosophical Extremes'. These are nihilism, eternalism, monoism and dualism.
Dzogchen differs from nihilism in the sense that there is not only Emptiness, but that reality is a *constant dance between Emptiness and Form.*
Dzogchen differs from eternalism by the fact that reality is a *constantly changing and dynamic expression of awareness* – everything is bound to change and give way to something else.
Dzogchen differs from monoism in the sense that Non-Duality does *not negate the existence of multiplicity.*
Dzogchen differs from dualism in that *all things are interconnected in the inseparability of the mind.*
Compare Buddha, Natural State, Dzogchen and Effortlessness.
Also see Wish Fulfilling Gem, Wheel of Conditioned Existence, Demons and Samsara.

One Taste

The doctrine that states that since everything comes from and is made of the same ground substance (Dharmakaya) that all things are hence equally perfect. Thereby the need to prefer or reject one state or object over another, which is the cause of suffering, is removed.

An analogy often used to describe it is to imagine that if everything was made of gold, no one thing could be said to be any more or less valuable than any other thing. According to One Taste this should apply to all thoughts, emotions, experiences, moments in time, actions, objects and people.
Compare to Zerbu.
Also see Non-Dual View and Dharmakaya.

Padmasambhava

Translates as the *"Lotus born"*.
In Tibet he is considered to be the second Buddha and the being who had a great influence in spreading the Tantric teachings to Tibet. In Tibet he is more revered as than the Buddha Gautama.
Compare Compare Buddha, Bodhisattva and Chakravatin.
Also see Tantra, Mandarava and Yeshe Tsogel.

Rigpa

The continuous state of Present Awareness which is devoid of ignorance about the Nature of the Mind and thus dualistic fixation.
It is the primary practice of Dzogchen as one should endeavor to remain in this state during all waking and sleeping hours of ones life as well as during and after death. It is said that when one can maintain this state throughout, enlightenment can happen *"even in the space between two breaths"*.
Compare Clarity, Dzogchen, Natural State and Buddha.
Also see Zerbu, One Taste, Discriminating Wisdom and Chod.

S

Sadhana

Translates as *"Means to Enlightenment"*.

Traditionally it refers to specific practices used to further ones awareness on the path to enlightenment.

According to the Buddha Brat view, absolutely anything and everything can and should be used to remain in, or return to the state of Rigpa. It is especially important to adapt and modernise it in this day and age to keep the Teachings relevant and personal.

Compare Dzogchen and Rigpa.

Also see Chod, Homoeopathy, One Taste and Discriminating Wisdom.

Salvia Divinorum

A hallucinogenic plant that is typically smoked in a very hot pipe. It causes extremely intense hallucinations that last for a very short space of time, around ten minutes.

Samsara

The *"state or world of suffering"*.

This is the state of mind that one liberates oneself from. Traditionally it can be viewed by some people as this plane of existence or a plane of existence where there is a lot of suffering.

According to all the Buddhas, suffering is the direct result of attachment and aversion and the only way to overcome suffering is to stop our grasping and rejecting.

From the Dzogchen perspective Samsara and Nirvana are the same thing, it is only our view of it that makes it suffering or joy.

Therefore, the Buddha Brats view the main cause of suffering as Ignorance of the Nature of the Mind.

Compare Wheel of Conditioned Existence, Six Realms and Demons..

Also see Nirvana, Island of Jewels, Enlightenment, Buddha and Dzogchen.

Sangha

Means *"community of enlightened beings"*.

Traditionally this would mean ones fellow practitioners.

From a Buddha Brats perspective we do not only see other Buddhists as part of our Sangha, but rather what we call 'The Riders'. These are people deeply committed to their own processes but not necessarily on a Buddhist path per se. There are as many paths to enlightenment as there are beings to walk them so we consider those we meet on the journey along the way a valid Sangha too.

San Pedro
A mescaline containing cactus originally from South America. It has similar hallucinogenic affects to peyote but grows much faster.

It is considered a medicine plant or 'teaching plant' because of its ability to grant the user deep insights into the nature of things. It is not addictive and cannot cause fatal overdoses.

Self-secret
The concept that powerful information which 'should not be allowed into the hands of the uninitiated' is in fact by its very nature unavailable to those of degraded awareness.

The truth can be blatantly apparent and yet if someone is not ready they will quite simply not understand it, and therefore essentially be unable to do harm with it anyway. This removes the need to keep things veiled in secrecy because there is absolutely no way one can fully understand Dzogchen and then abuse it.

It is for this reason that the Buddha Brats believe that any so-called powerful or enlightened being who abuses his or her power is in fact not enlightened in the true sense of the word and not to be feared at all.

Shambhala
The legendary *"City of Light"* from which the Armies of Light will issue forth to sweep away darkness and ignorance from the world.

It is the intention of the Buddha Brats to fulfill this prophecy, ushering in an age of global enlightened awareness.

Siddhi
Translated from Sanskrit it means *"accomplishment"*.

It is used to describe certain powers acquired on the path to enlightenment and after and is usually associated more with the Tantric paths. Siddhis can include walking through walls, flying, curing the sick, reading minds, being able to understand all languages to list but a few.

It is possible to acquire a siddhi without necessarily being fully enlightened which is why in Dzogchen there is less emphasis on siddhis and more emphasis on Realization. The argument being that once one is realized, siddhis spontaneously develop without having to strive for it. The supreme siddhi is considered by all paths to be Realization itself. For this reason Dzogchen is considered a direct path because it *aims directly at the supreme goal*.

Six Realms
Description of the *"six states of conditioned existence"* according to Buddhism. Pictured on the Wheel of Conditioned Existence it comprises of the Hell

Realm, Hungry Ghost Realm, Animal Realm, Human Realm, Jealous God Realm and God Realm. Each realm is related to an archetypal emotion starting at Hell with anger, greed, ignorance, attachment, jealousy and pride. In some of the traditions these realms are seen as actual places where one is reborn into depending on the prevailing emotion during ones life and/or ones state of mind at the moment of death.

The TIBETAN BOOK OF THE DEAD is a document that focus specifically on how to prepare for death and how to guide a soul onward after their deaths, to avoid them falling prey to an emotional fixation and thus being reborn. The goal is ultimately to free oneself from the cycle of entrapment entirely.

According to the Buddha Brat view these are all inherent emotional states that represent Aspects present within all human beings. The goal is to integrate all these realms in oneself, turning its 'poison' into wisdom. Anger turns into clarity, greed into generosity, ignorance into intuition, attachment into enjoyment, jealousy into productivity and pride into benevolence. In this way one can either be trapped or free in a moment, depending on whether one is unconsciously caught up in a 'poison' or effectively expressing the wisdom energy of a particular realm.

It is for this reason that Tantric adepts are depicted with five or six skulls around their necks, to signify their mastery of the six states - literally turning obstacles into personal adornment.

Compare to Wheel of Conditioned Existence and Five Lights.

Skillful Means

The masculine qualities represented by the 'lotus' at the crown chakra from which one drops nectar to lure the Kundalini upward from the base chakra. In this way feminine is united with masculine.

Skillful Means is the ability to identify and then employ a particular skill or set of skills as appropriate to the situation. More than just analysis based on the intellect, the balanced display of Skillfull Means is the effortless expression of knowing exactly what needs to be done and then doing it effectively. The ability to ascertain what is needed in each moment, then to bring about a certain outcome with detached compassion is some of the characteristics of this quality.

The 'thousand petalled lotus' at the crown also represents the innumerable siddhis or powers available to every human. However it is possible to express one or two siddhis without the lotus being fully activated by the power of the Kundalini but once the two are united, the petals start unfolding naturally and without any effort whatsoever. The 'lotus' by itself can appear as fixed ideas and narrow-mindedness.

A typical symptom of Skillful Means that is not united with the power of the feminine is overemphasis on the intellect and knowledge that is based more on fact or analysis than direct personal experience or understanding. See Intuitive Wisdom, Kundalini and Chakra.

Speed
Common name for crystal methamphetamine and other amphetamines. Crystal methamphetamine is the pinnacle of the amphetamines, its most notable effects being the ability to stay awake for long periods of time and a strong sense of mental clarity.

Spontaneous Accomplishment
It is an important and central Dzogchen tenet that indicates the pure potentiality inherent in emptiness. Form is never separate from emptiness and emptiness never separate from form. Therefore, all things already exist while at the same time being empty. Because of this everything is accomplished without effort in the Natural State of the Mind.
See Dzogchen, Non-Dual View and Dharmakaya.

Succubus
Female demon, normally well proportioned.

Succusion
The homoeopathic means of maintaining and strengthening the essence by agitation.

Sufi
It is a person usually considered to be an Islamic mystic, however some consider Sufism to pre-date Islam itself.

There are many similarities between Sufism and the higher Buddhist paths like Tantra. These include a focus on a direct, personal experience of 'the divine'; the idea that our original state is primordially pure Awareness and that nothing can defile this Natural State and the eventual relinquishing of any Dualities, including that of the 'self'. It also relies on direct transmission from teacher to student and includes a doctrine of 'subtle centers' similar in function to the chakras. Repeatedly chanting the 'names of God' aloud is another practice similar to the use of mantras in Buddhism. More detailed explanations remain elusive to those outside of Islam. There is a rich and beautiful artistic history to Sufism with Rumi being one of the most famous of its poets.
Adamas once bumped into a Sufi somewhere in India and described it as one of the few times where he found himself *"speaking the same language"*

with someone else.
Compare Natural State, Non-Duality, Buddha and One Taste.
Also see Dzogchen, Tantra and Hinnayana.

T

Tantra
Translated means *"weave"* or *"continuity"*.
As a path it focuses on transforming passions from their 'impure' state into a 'pure' state, a faster path than Hinayana but much slower than Dzogchen. The essential difference between the tantric path and Dzogchen is that according to Dzogchen nothing is impure and nothing needs to be transformed. At the same time Dzogchen allows one to practice any other methods, including that of the tantric path, if one so wishes, but these practices are only secondary to the primary practice of Rigpa. Padmasambhava is usually credited for the flowering of Buddhist tantra in Tibet.
From the Buddha Brat perspective when it is mentioned that tantras were *"written into"* someone's body it is specifically referring to tantra as a Body of Knowledge.
Compare Terma.
Also see Dzogchen, Rigpa, Sadhana and Hinnayana.

Terma
"Teaching Treasures" traditionally referring to specific texts or objects hidden on the earth especially in Tibet, principally by Padmasambhava and Yeshe Tsogyel but also by others.
It includes treasures hidden in the *secret space of the mind* that are available to those who can access them.
Compare Non-Dual View and Guru.
Also see Terton, Padmasambhava and Yeshe Tsogyel.

Terton
People who reveal or discover hidden or previously unknown teachings and who may choose to reveal them to the world or conceal them again until a later date.
Compare Terma.
Also see Bodhisattva, Vajra Pride and Arhat.

'Theist-swine' spray
A homoeopathic spray designed to dissolve the mental obscuration of dual-

istic fixation that leads to the belief in an external 'god', separate from the individual.

According to Buddhism there literally is no such thing as an external 'god' so theism, along with dualism, is considered an abhorrent and incorrect view.
Compare to Buddha, Natural State, Non-Dual View and Demons.
Also see Wheel of Conditioned Existence and Six Realms.

Thigle

Literally translates as *"drops"* and is traditionally used to describe spheres of rainbow light which is considered to be the ground substance reality.

In traditional Buddhism it is sometimes understood to be a very specific form or shape. However, from a Buddha Brats perspective it is the actual visual experience of the true nature of the universe seen as particles of light which can appear as spinning or moving dots or wheels, both large and small. It can also sometimes be seen as squiggles or moving shafts of light. More precisely its nature can be described as Dakini (sky dancer) because of the way it constantly moves around. Its form can be described as that of Daka (sky flower) when one sees the specific form that the light particles take. This gives one a direct experience of Dakini and Daka as moving, dancing light.

The practical experience is somewhat similar to that of static visible on a television screen. A good way of becoming aware of it is to look directly at clouds on a humid day. When one looks at it one can see these tiny sparks of light jumping around all over the place. These particles of light can sometimes be seen to be strung together in strands or at other times form part of large spiralling discs. Another example is to look at a dense arrangement of plants just after doing some strenuous exercise. Often at these times one sees the leaves making a kind of spinning circle.

The trick is to realise that this is the true nature of reality, emptiness containing moving bits of energy. Once one experiences this, it is important to remember that everything is made of the same substance, including ones own body. It is also imperative to remember that it is in fact a projection from your heart and exiting through your eyes, playing out 'out there'. This provides one with a direct visceral experience of the Nature of the Mind and the more one integrates it the more one is liberated. Total integration is the final process known as Thogal which results in the Body of Light or Great Transfer.
Compare Dakini, Daka and Five Lights.
Also see Thogal, Vajra Chains and Wish Fulfilling Gem.

Thogal

Translated as *"direct crossing"* or *"leap over"*.
It comprises of the final stage practice in Dzogchen in order to 'attain' the

Body of Light, although in actual fact it is ones true body and one is merely dissolving that which obscures it. Practices include sun and sky gazing, staring into the Vajra chains, various yogic postures and the Six Lamps of Awareness. In short, it mostly involves literally integrating the universe 'out there' with ones consciousness. Realizing that it is all made up of dancing light and that it is in fact your very Self, one eventually (re)turns into light, able to take on any form at any time and go anywhere.

Thogal teachings are often hard to find or so veiled in what is called 'Twilight Language' that one can only access its meaning through direct explanation by a realized master, or through the strength of ones own awareness. Sometimes thogal teachings are hidden amongst ordinary teachings in such a way that one would not recognize it for what it was unless one knew what one was looking for. However, the correct teachings eventually find its way to the fortunate practitioner who is ready to receive them.
Compare Body of Light and Thigle.
Also see Self-Secret and Terma.

V

Vajra
Most commonly refers to a ritual implement used by Buddhist lamas during certain rites. It symbolizes the 'diamond-like' aspects of luminous reflectivity and indestructibility.

Vajra chains
"Indestructible chains of light, reality or awareness".
It is described as strings of connected thigle that make up the various forms of so-called 'external' objects of reality.
According to the Buddha Brats expression of Dzogchen, the exact form and experience of the Vajra Chains may differ from person to person depending on their cultural or personal predilection. For example, Adamas experiences them as a combination of DNA-like structures with some type of runes embedded in them. For Anri it takes on the form of cellular structures similar to that of plants, animals or people. It is uncertain at this point whether the Vajra chains stay the same in appearance to each person, or whether it evolves with time and increased insight. Once again it is imperative to remember that everything seen as 'out there' is merely a projection of the 'self' onto the screen of space so the Vajra chains are in essence a visual experience of ones true Natural State.
Compare to Thigle, Dakini, Thogal and Natural State.
Also see Five Lights and Siddhi.

Vajra Pride

"Indestructible or unwavering confidence".

The state of knowing that one reaches through direct understanding and realization of the Teachings and the confidence that arises from this knowledge. It is only really possible to understand this state of knowing once one has actually reached it.

This state is typified by true impeccability and the fact that one no longer needs to justify anything, fully trusting that one is in absolute synchronicity with Awareness. It is assumed that one already embodies true compassion and there is no need for false humility which can be an obstacle to expressing ones Realization.

Compare Enlightenment, Chakravatin and Lion's Roar

Also see Guru, Discriminating Wisdom and Self-secret.

W

Wheel of Conditioned Existence

The symbolic representation of the Six Realms, which traditionally refers to the process of reincarnation. The Buddha is usually depicted standing next to the Wheel and pointing away from it.

This indicates that the only way to free oneself from the Wheel is to get off it completely.

It is said that being born in the Human Realm is most fortunate because it allows one the greatest chance at achieving Liberation. The reasons cited for this are that in the Hell, Hungry Ghost or Jealous God Realms one expends too much energy to cultivate understanding of the Teachings. In the Animal Realm one is too ignorant to grasp the Teachings. Even from the God Realm it is harder to attain enlightenment because one is too wrapped up in sensual pleasure to have the motivation to get off the Wheel, and the unfortunate and inevitable result is that the God Realm reverts to the Hell Realm eventually.

From a Buddha Brat perspective these Realms don't exist as actual places but rather states of mind and that we as humans have a unique capacity to express each of these Realms. The key is to make peace with and integrate these realms as personal Aspects, thereby freeing oneself from being bound by it due to aversion or attachment to any of these states.

Compare Samsara and Six Realms.

Also see Aspects and Buddha.

Wish Fulfilling Gem

The mind which is *that which accomplishes all wishes*.

Technically everything is a creation of the mind and it unfortunately brings fears as well as wishes equally into form. This is why understanding of the mind is so vital because if one can truly understand it, the mind becomes the gem that has the infinite potential to literally manifest the world of ones dreams.

This is why practices that release one from aversion and attachment are essential because whatever one has a strong emotional response to will manifest. In the case of aversions, it will surely bring into form things that one tries to avoid in order for it to be visited, tasted and dealt with. In the same way those things that we are attached to will either not manifest, so one can learn the lesson of giving up grasping, or it will manifest and then be taken away so one can learn to let go.

Practices that help to cultivate the ideal circumstances for optimal use of the Wish Fulfilling Gem include Chod, Zerbu and One Taste.

Also see Dzogchen, Holy Cows and Dakini.

Y

Yeshe Tsogyel

One of Padmasambhava's two principal consorts along with Mandarava.

She was one of the main disciples of Padmasambhava and a famous adept and Teacher in her own right. She recorded most of Padmasambhava's teachings with her photographic memory and hid many terma in and around Tibet to be discovered when the time is right.

See Padmasambhava, Mandarava and Terma.

Yidam

Usually translated into English as *"meditational deity"*.

Regardless of the many unintentional dualistic misconceptions that at times may creep into tantric practice, the so-called 'deities' depicted in Tibetan thankas (religious paintings) represent various aspects of the practitioner's own mind. Usually the teacher will identify a particular 'deity' for a practitioner to visualize in fine detail with all the accompanying subsidiary deities, ornaments, weapons or instruments with the goal in mind that the practitioner will 'take on' the attributes symbolized by the specific deity. This type of practice is usually considered fairly risky and advanced and is often shrouded in secrecy, precisely to prevent the practitioner falling prey to mistaken dualistic fixation which could lead to the student thinking that the 'deity' is an actual being to whom one must pay obeisance (a clearly mistaken theistic view) which is utterly at odds with the atheistic view of Buddhism.

According to the Buddha Brats, any person, movie star, film or book character and mythological archetype from any and all cultures can be used as yidam. Through the process of realizing that 'all is self', these archetypes can be immediately accessed and embodied without any laborious practices in order to fuel ones experience and expression. The key is to be that archetype in a moment when it is appropriate, and then let go of it and move onto the next as the situation requires, effortlessly adapting and playing out the entire range of human emotions to perfection without getting trapped.

Compare Aspects, Skillful Means and Six Realms.

Also see Sadhana and Non-dual View.

Z

Zerbu

Translated as *"affixing a nail"* or *"nailing it down"*.

This is the practice whereby one engages the things one likes, the things one doesn't like and the things one is indifferent to.

The reality of life is that our minds will manifest situations in which we are forced to deal with these things anyway, so it is wise to consciously engage it because then one is not at the mercy of random events forced down upon one. The goal is to be able to move through reality without any stress caused by having to deal with things that can upset or disturb one. Anything that causes one to deviate from the Natural State leads one into suffering so by practicing Zerbu one chooses to engage all these things on ones own terms.

Compare to One Taste.

Also see Natural State, Holy Cows, Samsara and Wheel of Conditioned Existence.

Suggested Reading

Baker, Ian A

The Dalai Lama's Secret Temple,
Thames & Hudson, 2000

(Detailed pictorial and written account of Tantric and Dzogchen practices culminating in the Body of Light, highly recommended)

Dowman, Keith

Eye of the Storm,
Vajra Publications, 2006

(Translation and commentary on Vairotsana's Five Original Transmissions and a perfect sample of what is known as 'Radical Dzogchen', very highly recommended)

Flight of the Garuda,
Wisdom Publications, 2003

(Songs and poems on liberation specifically from a Dzogchen perspective)

Masters of Enchantment,
Inner Traditions International, 1988

(Short stories of the 64 Mahasiddhas, a good introduction to Tantric teachings for beginners)

Sky Dancer,
Snow Lion Publications, 1996

(Story of Yeshe Tsogyel and Padmasambhava, covers a range of Tantric teachings)

The Divine Madman,
Dawn Horse Press, 1998

(The story of Drukpa Kungley, an introduction to Crazy Wisdom for beginners)

Edou, Jerome
Machig Labdron and the foundations of Chod,
Snow Lion Publications, 1996

(History, practice and core philosophy of Tibetan CHOD)

Harding, Sarah
Machik's Complete Explanation,
Snow Lion Publications, 2003

(In depth explanation of the Tibetan practice of CHOD)

Kunsang, Erik Pema
& Schmidt, Marcia Binder
Quintessential Dzogchen,
Rangjung Yeshe Publications, 2006

(A text covering instructions that fall under what is known as The Fourth Dharma of Lonchempa and Gampopa, *"Confusion Dawns as Wisdom"* and the The Fourth Empowerment of Vajrayana Buddhism intermediate to advanced)

Namdak, Lopon Tenzin
Heart Drops Of Dharmakaya,
Snow Lion Publications, 1993

(Translation and commentary of the original text by Shardza Tashi Gyaltsen containing detailed threkcho, thogal and other advanced practices of the Bon lineage of Dzogchen)

266

Norbu, Namkhai

Dream Yoga,
Snow Lion Publications, 1992

(Simple instructions on the *"Practice of the Night"* including brief introductions to the other components of the Six Yogas - highly recommended for readers of all levels.)

Dzogchen Teachings,
Snow Lion Publications, 2006

(Further details on Dzogchen teachings and practices)

Dzogchen – The Self-Perfected State,
Snow Lion Publications, 1989

(Simple explanation of Dzogchen that is good for intermediate students and a great read for advanced practitioners, highly recommended)

The Crystal and the Way of Light,
Snow Lion Publications, 2000

(Good introduction to the basic principles of Dzogchen)

The Cycles of Day and Night,
Station Hill Press, 1989

(Garab Dorje's core teachings)

The Supreme Source,
Snow Lion Publications, 1999

(Translation of and commentary on the fundamental Tantra of Dzogchen called the 'Kunjed Gyalpo' - meaty but highly recommended)

Reyonolds, J M

The Golden Letters,
Snow Lion Publication, 1996

(Translation and introduction of, and commentaries on Garab Dorje's Famous Three Statements)

Simmer-Brown, Judith

Dakini's Warm Breath,
Shambhala, Boston & London, 2001

(In depth explanation from the Vajrayana view of '*The Feminine Principle in Tibetan Buddhism*' aimed at western scholars - highly recommended.)

Wangyal, Tenzin

Wonders of the Natural Mind,
Snow Lion Publications, 2000

(Detailed introduction and practices of the Bön lineage of Dzogchen)

Made in the USA
Las Vegas, NV
14 August 2023

76076113R00171